MUSIC MAN

BY THE SAME AUTHOR

Jolie – the Al Jolson Story
Salute to Irving Berlin
James Cagney
Fred Astaire
Sophie: The Story of Sophie Tucker
Errol Flynn (in America, *The Two Lives of Errol Flynn*)
Jerome Kern
Gregory Peck
Maurice Chevalier
Peter O'Toole
The Warner Brothers
So Let's Hear The Applause – The Story of the Jewish Entertainer
Dino: The Dean Martin Story
Jack Lemmon
Katharine Hepburn
The Secret Life of Danny Kaye
Shirley MacLaine
The Goldwyn Touch: A Biography of Sam Goldwyn
Leonard Bernstein
Jane Fonda
Liza With A 'Z'
Dustin – A Biography of Dustin Hoffman
Kenneth Williams
André Previn
Sean Connery – A Biography
(With Morecambe and Wise) *There's No Answer To That*
(With Walter Scharf) *Composed and Conducted by Walter Scharf*

This book began as a tribute to an outstanding father. It is dedicated to the blessed memory of my own father, David Freedland, who was also outstanding, loving, caring, amusing and, above all, hugely respected. He also loved to sit in a park, listening to the band. I think of him daily – and always with a smile.

Contents

List of Illustrations

Foreword

When my father married at the age of 31 he was a recognized cornet virtuoso and a widely traveled and experienced musician and conductor. He was recognized in his teens as a musical prodigy, having been made at the age of 14 the conductor of 27 mature musicians, members of a municipal band. He entered marriage as a mature, sensitive man blessed with the attributes, gained primarily from his parents, of high standards of conduct, deep respect for the rights of others, intuitive understanding of those about him, unmatched capacity for giving love and a deep motivation to succeed. Near the end of his life I asked my father during a walk how he had accomplished so much. He responded: 'I was blessed with a little God-given talent and I worked very hard.' I doubt that anyone had a more loving father than we Simon boys.

Many people knew him in many ways – performer, cornet soloist, conductor, composer, teacher, friend, fellow-citizen and neighbor.

It is noteworthy that one who knew him for over 70 years and who played with him as a child has said: 'I have never heard anyone say an unkind word about him.' There are many others scattered over the country who echo this opinion.

I hope this biography reflects not only his many accomplishments as well as a good part of the history of American band music, but, more importantly, Father's essential humanity and his love of freedom and his fellow-men which stands as a model to all.

David L. Simon MD

Acknowledgements

I have often found the Acknowledgements to be the hardest part of a book to write. After all, there are people who need to be thanked and others who think they need to be thanked – and the two are not always the same.

This book is the exception which proves the rule. The thanks come easily. They begin and end – and take up much of the middle – with David Simon, son of Frank, who in another life is an eminent physician (the kind whom patients would wish to have at the end of a consultation line) and who conceived the idea, nurtured it, devoted more of his time to it than many people would have considered reasonable, and who in the course of that time became a close, treasured friend. His wife Jane offered him the kind of support that any husband needs to carry through a project of this kind and, because she did, was able to help me immeasurably. Her friendship and hospitality to me, essential ingredients of that help, were at all times superb.

I also had the great delight of getting to know David's brother, Joe Simon, who with the love of a son for a father coupled with a magnificent dry sense of humor, was a wonderful aid whenever called upon.

One of the delights of a book such as this is the great introduction it proved to be into a world that is one of the least sung – or played or, in this case, blown – in showbusiness. More valuable even than that was the opportunity to meet people from Cincinnati living in a (to me) hitherto-unknown dot on the American map called Middletown, which turned out to play such an immense part in this story.

There are others for whom I developed a similar enthusiasm,

people all over America who are involved in the band movement and for whom Frank Simon was not just a colleague but a mentor, a teacher and a friend – a potent combination.

So to them, my thanks. They include: Paul E. Bierley, Gene Blee, William Caiazza, Maurice Callahan, George Crout, Harry Finkleman, Betty Glover, Rabbi Albert Goldman, Morton Gould, Colonel Dale Harpham, Mark Hindsley, the ever-fascinating Al Hirt, Bridget Hirt, Robert Hornyak (who allowed me to read his own perceptive writings on the subject tackled here), Jack Lee (who not only filled in so much of the chapter dealing with Frank Simon's life in Arizona but almost got me to share his enthusiasm for mariachi singing), Alice Whiteman Lytell, Robert McFadden, Charles Payne, Helen Gerber Ramsdell, Dr William Revelli, Bill Richardson, Emil Schmachtenberg, Frank Simon II, Dr Jack Watson, Dr Al Wright, Gladys Wright and Gene Young.

The assistance given to me by Frank Byrne and the other librarians of the United States Marine Band (the President's Own) in Washington, DC, is also much appreciated. And Lois Hall, Rayetta McDonald, and Susan Pittman, three ladies in Dr Simon's office who had to put up with my encroaching on their time and their desks – to say nothing of their fax machines – also deserve my very grateful thanks. Some useful early research was done by Professor Paul F. Erwin of the University of Cincinnati and I was glad to be able to use in particular his interview with the late Alma Ritter Crowe.

One other thing needs to be said: the fact that this became a feasible project was due in no small way to my own wife, Sara, who over more than 30 years has learned to cope with a great deal from her husband. My frequent absences thousands of miles from home over 18 months of work on this book were not easy for her, but without them, and certainly without her, it would never have happened.

Had it not, I would never have got to know about Frank Simon. And that would not have been just my loss but that of everybody else who is fascinated by the talent, inspiration and sheer drive that it takes to pick up a brass horn and make sweet music.

Michael Freedland
London, 1993

1 · *Introduction*

Frank Simon had been dead for almost a quarter of a century that hot summer night in 1991 when the open-air auditorium at New York's Lincoln Center was crowded with people listening to the Goldman Memorial Band – an evening dedicated to Simon's memory. That a concert should be held in tribute to a man who had last conducted a band so many years before was an incredible tribute in itself. That he should have a name strong enough to help draw a capacity crowd so long after he had died made him almost unique. But it was the tribute of a different kind that Frank Simon himself would have appreciated most. He was a man who respected the opinions of his fellow-musicians more than those of anyone else – and half a century before, there had been no more direct competitor to Simon's own musicians than the then Goldman Band.

But this was proving a point – two points, in fact. It was recognizing that in his field, in his day, Frank Simon, cornet player and bandmaster extraordinary, who looked incredibly like his contemporary Paul Whiteman – a man who led a band of a different kind – had been without peer. More than that, it was reminding a generation more used to hearing on their radio and TV sets, on the corners of every street and in a thousand movies the a-rhythmic beats of rock 'n' roll, that once upon a time, band music had been part of the lifeblood of their country.

Frank Simon was at its heart, because above all else – or almost all else for, as we shall see, he was devoted to his wife, his children and to his friends and his eyes would well with tears at a good sob story – he loved a band. He was in good company. All America had loved bands since the years when the century changed, when suddenly people were discovering that the horse and buggy were not the only means of transport.

That was the era when every town or city worth the name had its own band and every park a gazebo bandstand or a bandshell. An age when America was made that little bit more colorful by the sight of mustachioed bandsmen wearing glorious scarlet tunics and pom-pommed pillbox caps who oompahed their way through 'The Stars and Stripes Forever' or perhaps the first movement of *Scheherazade* – while young couples held hands, little boys and girls ate candies and old men snoozed in their deckchairs.

It was for a very long time an essential part of American life. The Army, the Navy and the Marines, of course, had their own bands and for millions, the face of Christianity had been changed for ever by the lads and lassies of the Salvation Army who, while breathing blood and fire in the taverns of nations on both sides of the Atlantic, proved their founder General Booth's dictum that the devil should not be allowed to have all the best tunes.

But it was also very much a small-town entertainment phenomenon; the band always played and everyone always knew where they did so, because that was *the* place to go. Not that the larger cities did not have their bands – splendid ensembles which marched through Main Streets on the Fourth of July or when victories were declared and conquering heroes came home to the strains of music which confirmed that, bruised and bandaged though they may have been, they really had conquered.

Then there were the industrial bands – bands that showed that paternalistic companies were almost as concerned for the welfare of their employees as they were for their profits. Not quite, but almost. The fact that these men – who, when they were not blowing into bassoons and French horns, were toiling over roaring furnaces, digging coal by hand or pulling at the levers of ear-bursting machinery – were also providing a very good vehicle for advertising was beside the point.

From them all had come the really big bands – not the swing outfits of Glenn Miller and the Dorseys, Benny Goodman and Duke Ellington, but those which were the logical development of the marching ensembles and those industrial organizations; the big star groupings who in the 1930s were prime-time favorites on America's radio networks.

In their day, the bandsmen were what a much later generation of pop singers would be. Towns and hamlets which did not have a vaudeville house, much less a legitimate theatre – some of them not even a nickelodeon in *their* heyday – would have a band. Al Jolson and a host of other performers may have had their professional starts in the minstrel shows, but it was in the bands that paraded through the streets announcing those shows that countless musicians began their own careers and dreamed the American dream – frequently doubling as members of vaudeville theatre pit ensembles and sometimes local symphony orchestras. They learned to walk with long strides to make the bands seem bigger than they really were. When they were not marching it was those bands which provided simple entertainment for the unsophisticated citizenry who came to hear them. Then, as the years went by and tastes became more polished, so did the talents of the musicians. They may have been pop stars but they were also classicists, playing symphonies and tone poems in a style that was all their own but which never belittled the compositions.

But the influences of the bands' own origins would never completely disappear. The minstrel parades and the circus lineups were merely further links in the chain that had begun with the docking of the immigrant ships at Ellis Island. They were in place even before that way-station (always considered to be in America but never part of it) was established close to the Statue of Liberty, built just a year before Simon was born.

After all, people who had come fleeing from the potato famine in Ireland, from the pogroms of Russia and Poland, or simply because they saw promise of a better economic future than they might have had in Germany or Scandinavia were becoming a nation. The melting pot was white hot and its ingredients were doing just that – melting.

They brought with them their particular entertainments as they brought their foods. Irish jigs, Russian kazatzkis and German band music all came to America along with stews, gefilte fish and sauerkraut, and, like the accents of the people who brought them, before long they became rounded off and . . . Americanized.

The influence of the German bands was plain enough in the part of the Middle West where the Simon family settled. As we shall see, it was no coincidence that one of the areas where the young Frank worked was called Over the Rhine.

There had, of course, always been bands in America, right from the colonial days when there was no more an American representation in the military bands than there was in a polling booth. But with independence came bands to cheer the troops along. The pictures of the bloodstained American Revolutionaries playing fifes and drums are not just of legends, they are part of history.

Yet there were also British immigrants who brought their civilian brass music to America, just as they had imported the military tradition of a regiment going into battle, marching to the sound of a band. Ninety years later, the American Civil War not only advanced the industry of mass slaughter by quantum leaps. Just as it took a peripheral trade like photography into a new era, it turned bands on both sides of the Mason-Dixon Line into almost as essential a part of the business of waging battle as installing field kitchens. An army that marched on its stomach had to be made to feel that it did so in as good spirits as possible, even though all around them other men were leaving legs and arms behind. But unlike the food served in the mud of Gettysburg, the men in blue and grey liked to remember the music. They *wanted* to take back home with them the tunes to which they had marched. 'When Johnnie Comes Marching Home' was something to be savored when finally Johnnie did come marching home. Battlefield hash was to be forgotten the moment the dysentery cleared up.

Even then, at this time, band music was not all militaristic, although the tradition brought by the musicians from Germany owed a lot to leaders who had once worn shiny brass helmets, who never walked if they could march and who rarely spoke if they could shout. The Germans who settled in and around Cincinnati brought their own groups, the kind of German bands that Irving Berlin wrote about in one of his first turn-of-the-century song hits. But by the early 1900s the American band had already developed a sound of its own, augmenting brass with woodwinds, sometimes substituting clarinets and oboes for violins and cellos, so that they could play romantic pieces and items from the classics just as easily.

In 1889, the year Frank Simon was born, the magazine *Harper's Weekly* reported in its September issue that there were 10,000 'adult and juvenile bands in the United States'. They moved across class barriers. Sons – and daughters – of local doctors and lawyers played alongside those of storekeepers and stagecoach drivers. Few of them were professionals, although in the big cities there were indeed bandsmen who were paid and who earned their living from parading or sitting in bandstands and gazebos. But in most of America, bandsmen – and bandswomen – usually met only for midweek rehearsals or when they worked together in uniform on Sunday afternoons. For them, they were labors of love and love rarely came any more devoted.

The names of the bandmasters were by then in the lexicon of kids who dreamed of the opportunities that they themselves might have of playing in a band and, who knows, of leading one. The Irish-born Patrick Sarsfield Gilmore, he of the impeccable military bearing (and also of the Chester Conklin cross-eyes, although the posters advertising his concerts managed to distort the fact in his favor), gained a reputation for himself for playing both 'Dixie' and 'The Star-Spangled Banner' while serving in the Civil War, a time when bands were, like their English forebears, strictly brass ensembles. By the 1880s he also had won national fame as the writer of that same 'Johnnie Comes Marching Home' which the veterans had brought back with them (a totally erroneous claim to make; as he admitted in a public statement in 1883, he had merely turned 'a musical waif' of a folk song into a popular tune). But he was an important figure, nevertheless. It was Gilmore who invented the 'concert band', which was the precursor of the kind of outfit that Simon was to head a generation later.

There were even women's bands, one of the most famous being led by a certain Helen May Butler, whose members in tight, shapely uniforms made many a young man's heart flutter as he imagined the source of the curves behind those tunics. The waxed mustaches of the imitators of Mr Gilmore – whose eyes were somewhat more symmetric – made not a few young ladies feel much the same way.

By the time Frank Simon came onto the scene there was no doubt as to who had been the greatest bandsman of them all. John Philip Sousa was already known as the March King. He was more than that: the uncrowned emperor of every bandstand in the country, presiding over what was fast becoming America's principal home-grown – if not home-born – art form, with a mixture of woodwinds and brass and even the injection of strings and vocal soloists. The art form which had imitated the Europeans had now taken on a strictly American dimension.

Reading newspaper stories of the Sousa tours is like seeing, flashing before the eyes, one of those montage scenes from a 1940s musical: 'Sousa's Band Is a Hit in Pueblo', 'Philadelphia Pays Tribute to Frank Simon in Sousa Concert', 'Sousa's Artists Bid San Francisco Farewell'. Frank was at the center of it all, even when his name was not in all the headlines. Before long, he was the giant who was a combination of Stokowski, Barnum and Bailey and Al Jolson, with your favorite schoolmaster cementing them all together.

What was already being described as 'the band movement' was so much part of American culture that it had already started enriching the language. One hundred years after they were coined, its words remained part of everyday speech – even if few now realize the origins of phrases they never stop using.

Not many pimply youths taking girls out for a 'one-night stand' realize that the expression comes from the planks laid out as temporary platforms for touring ensembles in towns that did not have permanent bandstands. 'Jumping on the bandwagon' is perhaps easier to associate. The fame – to say nothing of the status – of a band was often judged by the size and quality of the wagon on which the members rode or which carried their instruments. If you jumped on the bandwagon you were attempting to take on the kudos of its owner.

That was the bandwagon on which Frank Simon jumped and, in creating a career for himself, impressed and improved so much around him. A one-time member of the Cincinnati Symphony under Stokowski, he joined Sousa and went on to create what became known not so much as the concert band as the symphonic band. What was more, when the era seemed to be all over it was largely he who started an entirely new phenomenon: making the bands educationally respectable. Through Frank Simon, learning how to play in a band became a subject to be taught at conservatories. The newly titled Dr Simon became so influential that universities awarded him doctorates and newspapers hailed his visits to their towns with banner headlines – without now having to couple his name with that of John Philip Sousa. When a youngster won a place studying with Frank Simon it was the subject of two columns in the local newspaper. The star performer and bandmaster had become a star educator. He was instrumental (a perhaps wonderfully appropriate term for a celebrated soloist and bandmaster) in helping to foster the principal development of his educational work: the immense growth of college and high-school bands and service bands which today form the only substantive remaining link with the era of which Simon was so much a part.

It was the cowboy-showman Will Rogers who coined the phrase 'I never met a man I didn't like'. Frank Simon seemingly never met a man who didn't like him. To go through 77 years without making enemies is an achievement few can emulate. To go through those years at the top of a fiercely competitive profession is a remarkable characteristic. For Simon was a superstar in an age before people started using that now much-abused word.

More important, he was a man whose protégés became stars in their own right. No finer tribute could a teacher wish to receive, unless it was to hear the thanks of those students, and he did that, too – in abundance. Meredith Willson, who brought the days of the small-town band so vividly to life in his Broadway show and film, *The Music Man*, said in a letter to Frank Simon, the musician who gave him his first chance: 'I once wrote a song about 76 trombones being followed by 110 cornets. This is a good time to reveal to you that there was only one cornet all the time . . . they just sounded like 110 cornets because you were the cornetist.'

Perhaps unwittingly, Willson wrote an even more apt epitaph for Simon in a scene from *The Music Man*. As his central character, Harold Hill, put it to the child who fears his illusions are about to be destroyed: 'I always think there's a band, kid.'

There were no illusions for Frank Simon. As these pages will try to demonstrate, for him there was always a band.

2 · *A Life in Store*

It would be nice to think of Middletown, Ohio, as typical Small Town America – one of those *Meet Me In St Louis* places where all the girls wore crisp candy-striped dresses and had strawberry-blonde hair long enough to sit on and the boys wore straw hats, blazers and white trousers and always called their elders 'Sir'. A town where everyone knew everyone else, where the old folk reminisced as they rocked themselves in their chairs on the front porch and where the local schoolteacher was perhaps a little too sassy for her own good.

There were parts of Middletown that were like that, to be sure, but even by the turn of the century it was a bustling little place. It was a natural site for the processing of tobacco, especially that produced in the small farms nearby. It attracted tobacco workers from all over America, especially when it seemed that this area of Ohio was able to provide work while other parts of the United States were finding business to be not nearly so good.

There was a chewing-tobacco processing plant in town and the aromas of the substances (overwhelming, especially when the factory started to produce chewing plugs flavored with rum and licorice) mingled with the other more agricultural smells in the area. They called Middletown the hog capital of the world, because the farmers would go there to sell their hogs and for miles around they knew that there was no better place to buy a pig that could help bring them a modicum of prosperity.

But tobacco was what was really important there, with block after block filled with nothing but tobacco factories. There was the Middletown Tobacco Company and the firm of McCallay Wilson supplying smoking varieties, as well as Paul J. Sorg's (of whom more later) chewing-tobacco plant which was to become the third biggest in the country. It was the era before the popularity of cigarettes, which would eventually spell the death knell for that kind of processed tobacco in this part of Ohio.

The proximity of Middletown to the forests of eastern Indiana and western Ohio, to say nothing of the canal and the nearby river, meant that there was also a highly developed paper industry. The damp atmosphere as well as the canal itself which provided all the water that the producers might need (and an essential staple it was) brought a whole succession of paper firms to town – seven of them, including a cardboard box company which could later boast of having the first strike in the state. But that, too, was a symptom of that modicum of prosperity.

There can be no doubt that that slight dash of success or its promise was what brought people to Middletown – so called because it was halfway between Dayton and Cincinnati on the Great Miami River and the Erie Canal, where the flat boats and barges passed on their journey along what was then the main highway for that part of the world – the highway on the search for a modicum of prosperity. And even in a town with a name that seemed to come out of something by Sinclair Lewis or Thornton Wilder and which had a national reputation for the selling of the fattest of porkers, there was a tiny Jewish community. It was one of the things that attracted the Simon family to Middletown.

It was not until 1914 that Middletown became a fairly big place – big enough to proudly invite people from miles around to the Middletown Music Festival, under Dr Walter Aiken, head of the Middletown Society. Music had been taught in local schools since 1872. In 1890 Middleton had a population of 7681. By 1900 this had grown to 9215 (and would increase by a further 4000 ten years later and then by 10,000 more by 1920).

All through those early years Saturday was the big day of the week there. It was when the farmers from around and about came to trade and to barter, and not just their pigs. The town was surrounded by some of the richest farmland in the world, so Saturday was Farmers' Market Day, a time when more people seemed to throng Middletown's Broad Street than the 2000 or 3000 who lived in the whole place the rest of the week – which was why Broad Street was just that, it was so broad.

They sold their wares for four hours, the four busiest hours in the week. When they could not get the prices they wanted, they exchanged their eggs with the owners of food stores, sometimes in return for sugar, salt or even pickling jars.

It was here that Solomon and Bertha Simon thought they could bring up a young family in a happy, peaceful atmosphere, away from the bustle of the big city but with enough people around to help make them a living. For members of Solomon's family had already moved to Middletown and were making a very nice living from their tiny stores.

Indeed, to Bertha and Solomon it seemed just the kind of place for which they had been looking. Solomon was a small man with fairly small ideas, the biggest of which was to find a decent way of bringing up his small family. He had already had his share of adventures and they seemed enough for anyone. Now at the age of 32 he was content enough to settle down with Bertha in the Harlem Block in Middletown. For 65 years the Simons regarded Middletown as home, but that is jumping the story slightly.

To this day no one can be really sure where it was that Solomon Simon had actually been born, although the year was undoubtedly 1857 and it *is* certain that he had spent many of his early years in England. But he also spoke fluent German, which few people in Britain did, even members of the country's then-minute Jewish community. So he could also have lived or even been born in one of that collection of states which had not yet developed into the German or Austro-Hungarian Empires. (There is, however, some inconclusive evidence that his birthplace was the German town of Calvaia.) Since there were no birth certificates at the time and no one remembers his speaking about it, the mystery will never be solved.

What is sure is that before long he had emigrated to the United States, just as hundreds of thousands of other Europeans had done. Like most immigrants, after the processing procedures at Ellis Island, he landed in New York and, like not a few of them, got on the first train out of the city. Cincinnati was where he ended up. In all probability, he soon settled in Richmond Street, close to the processing and manufacturing companies which depended on people as much as they themselves depended on the firms to supply their needs. A fiery spirit who wanted to do more than simply what most other immigrants did, he soon moved to Texas. There he took a job that was totally unlike the work chosen by most of those hundreds of thousands: he drove a stagecoach.

The ivory-handled revolvers which he would delight in showing his family in years to come testified to the fact that the run made by the Duncan and Oakes stagecoach between El Paso and Camp Supply was not without its difficulties. For a time he worked as a cowboy – literally a cowhand on an English-owned ranch in the Texas panhandle.

He emerged from his time in the Wild West unbruised and wealthy only in a fund of stories he always had ready for the telling and in a collection of Western cowboy songs on his lips which he would sing accompanying himself on the accordion almost to his dying day. If that was a musical streak, it was one he plainly carried in his genes. He loved to hear music and the kind played at the Centennial celebrations of Cincinnati, the place which Longfellow had described as the 'Queen City of the Middle West' (a name that stuck; to this day there are locals who relish calling it the Queen City), was almost, alone, enough to bring him back there.

What actually made him stay on in the Queen City was the presence of a young lady he had just met at the big event. Her name was Bertha Felsenthal.

This Bertha was a very rounded young lady, the kind who, aided by the breath-defying corsetry of the day, were the admiration of those painters of picture postcards who provided the only form of mass-produced art then available to the American public. Bertha always knew her mind. She was tough at a time when ladies were expected to be demure, to stay in the background. Tough enough to have been, at 18 years of age, the first member of her immediate family to decide to leave her native town of Relsberg in Bavaria.

Unlike most Jewish families, the Felsenthals were able to trace their origins as far back as the 1600s. Earliest records were from Koblenz, but as a child, Bertha's family lived in the Pfalz, about 60 miles from Kaiserslauten, a rural area made up of a series of small villages atop the hills. The family were mainly cattle dealers, and successful ones at that. Their house was one of the most imposing in Relsberg, a tall building that stood out from the smaller structures around it.

In the wake of the American Civil War Bertha decided to come to what was still being called the New World. She arrived with her younger sister Lena, and together they found homes in Dayton at the top of the Miami River where relatives had settled. Life was a serious occupation, particularly for a young girl who had already taken the hazardous 4000-mile journey and was now starting anew.

In 1888 there was still something of the teenager about her as she surveyed that new world of hers. Everywhere she went, she took with her her autograph book, a document that still survives along with its messages – mostly in German – of welcome and friendship from the people she was now meeting. When she visited a new town she recorded it in her little leather-bound book.

From Dayton the girls traveled frequently to Cincinnati, particularly to the Clinton Street area, just west of the downtown district, where most of the Jewish community had settled. She began work there as a dressmaker and seamstress, a not unusual occupation for young Jewish girls on Clinton Street. In fact, there were dozens of them, girls with whom she could laugh and sometimes cry amid the frustrations and desperations of trying to seek a living in so strange an environment.

She and Lena went to Cincinnati for another purpose – to wonder at the events being held in connection with the Centennial. Everyone was talking about the big event in their part of the country. If you lived in Ohio, it was the only place to go.

It was a fortunate decision to go just then, for it was there that Bertha and Solomon met. It really was like a scene from *Meet Me In St Louis*. They fell in love and on 28 October 1888, Solomon and Bertha, the bride eight years younger than the bridegroom, were married by a rabbi in Dayton – which was not at all like a scene from *Meet Me In St Louis*.

They set up home in Cincinnati and Lena shared the flat with them in the Spencer House at the foot of Broadway on Front Street. It was next to the Public Landing, once the social and political center of Cincinnati, although by the time the Simons had joined other families there the place had seen its best days.

Almost exactly a year after the couple's wedding, on 26 November

1889, at the Spencer House, Bertha gave birth to a son. They called him Frank – a nice American-sounding name for a couple who already considered themselves nice American citizens. After all, could a man who had carried ivory-handled revolvers on a stagecoach and the woman he had met at the Cincinnati Centennial celebrations be anything but? True, they spoke German to each other, but then so did a lot of the people in Cincinnati and that was what America was all about. The German-Americans were just one group of the hyphenated countrymen among whom they lived. What was more, there was no more loyal group of people than those who were acquiring citizenship by study and hard work. Those who were born in the United States tended to take it all much more for granted. Irving Berlin, born in Siberia the year before Frank, would never forget how much he thought he owed the United States – which was why his proudest achievement was neither 'White Christmas' nor 'Always', nor even 'There's No Business Like Showbusiness', but 'God Bless America'.

As a demonstration of just how happy Solomon was in his new environment he spread the word among his family. He did an effective enough job of public relations for the burghers of Cincinnati. With the incentive of seeing a baby grandson, his father, Falk Simon, crossed the Atlantic and came to join son and daughter-in-law in the city. Sadly, he died soon afterwards and was buried in Cincinnati.

A year after Frank's birth the family moved to Middletown. It was not that they were tired of life in Cincinnati itself, but the smaller neighborhood had a lot of attractions in an age when things were beginning to look very good indeed for people like them. America was at peace but was still vividly remembering the torments of the Civil War, and was still, for the moment, content not to challenge Spain for control of Cuba. That was a war some eight years away.

At the Gunckel Building on East Central Avenue in Middletown – where later the gas and electric companies operated – the Simons set up a small store. They seemed to be in a hurry to do so, and were in residence and open for business even before the main structure was completed.

Not long afterward, however, they moved again, this time to a more permanent-looking Simons store, nearby at the south-west corner of Central Avenue and Clinton Street (later the site of the Middletown Gas and Electric Company headquarters), specializing, as they told customers in embossed celluloid letters firmly stuck to their windows above hanging shirts, sheets and items of ladies' underclothing that were usually regarded as unmentionable, in 'Dry Goods. Notions'.

Simons, as everyone knew it, was a long narrow store, with counters and shelves on both sides of the place, each stacked high with bolts of cloth, from which women would select material for their new dresses or for their husbands' suits. Certainly there was nowhere else to look for front-parlor curtains. If Simons did not have them, no one did.

It was a friendly place which, like most shops at the time, seemed to be as much a meeting-center for local folks as it was a store in which to buy things. No one minded the crying of baby Frank or, soon afterward, that of the couple's younger son, Leo. As the years went on there were more sounds, noises that were as familiar to the people who walked along the wooden sidewalks of Central Avenue outside the store as were the smells of the dressings on the cloth or of the chalk used to measure off the lengths being bought. Both boys had discovered the magic of what they thought was music. Frank sat on the steps outside the store, banging a pair of sticks on the ground as though he were in charge of a bass drum, singing as he did so the songs of the day or, if he did not know the words, whistling the melodies. Whistling was an art he would never lose. Leo was soon avidly copying his brother.

To Frank, at five or six, there was only one way in which to enjoy himself. For him, heaven was in the shape of a bandstand. If he could have spent every waking moment listening to the Middletown Band, he would have asked no more of life. But sometimes he had to be content with playing in the family store. Shortly before her death, his friend of those years, Alma Ritter Crowe – a member of an old Middletown family who died at the age of 101 – remembered: 'My mother regularly bought her dry goods from the Simons store and I played under the counters with Frank while she did her shopping.'

Alma's father and grandfather were in business in Middletown, running, over the years, a leather shop, a blacksmithy, an ice concern and a workshop that built and repaired wagons. As such, they welcomed the Simons as part of the local business community.

Customers occasionally found the antics of the young Simon boy quite entertaining. Others – sometimes against their will – had to admit that the most senior member of the family was himself an entertainment on his own. Solomon – by now simply Sol to his closest family and acquaintances – had a superb sense of humor, which he was adept in bringing into play when things were perhaps not going quite as well in his business as they should.

There was, for instance, the woman who came to him and asked the price of a set of linen hand towels. 'Twenty-five cents each,' he told her. 'Twenty-five cents?' she asked. 'Seiners down the street sell them for 18 cents.'

'Well,' said the brains of Middletown haberdashery, 'why don't you buy them at Seiners?'

'Because,' she explained, 'they're out of them.'

'Aha,' he came back. 'If I were out of them, I'd let you have them for only 15 cents.'

Another time, a boy came into the store and asked Simon if he wanted to buy a *Saturday Evening Post*. 'No thank you,' he said and the boy left. 'How do you like that?' Sol asked Frank. 'It's only Thursday and he tries to sell me a *Saturday Evening Post*!'

His grandson Joseph, remembering an old radio character, describes the old man as 'a sweet Wallace Wimple'.

Frank was to emulate his father in both his music and his humor – to say nothing of his approach to other people. But as a small child, playing under the counters, even sometimes tipping over the umbrella stand nearby, was nothing compared to being with the bandsmen, even if their dark-blue uniforms did sometimes give a funereal look to their endeavors, an appearance that was strictly traditional but which hardly matched the moods of most of the people who went to listen to them.

There was no better proof of how typically American Middletown was than that band, the marches and waltzes played by instrumentalists who were plainly having a good time, the cheeks of the horn players growing more and more rosy as they pushed out the notes, the rapt attention at the moment the percussionists were ready to strike, the near-angelic look of the clarinetists as they pursed their lips. Certainly, it was a perfect example of typical German America. The German bands who played on street corners throughout the United States could not have been more appreciated than they were in communities populated by their own former fellow-countrymen. Certainly, it had been that way for as long as anyone could remember. Cincinnati had had a band since 1810. Nearby Hamilton was known to have had one in 1814. When the ground was broken for the Miami–Erie Canal in Middletown in 1825 a newspaper in the county noted: 'The ceremony was greatly enlivened by many appropriate airs performed by the band.'

Now, 75 years later, the band was still enlivening society in Middletown by playing 'appropriate airs'. Real old-timers could recall the visit to the town by the future President William Henry Harrison, who had also been given a rousing welcome by a band. A generation after that, Civil War veterans led by one Isaac Worth had formed their very own Middletown drum corps.

In those dying years of the nineteenth century, when the Middletown bandsmen marched in parades up and down Main Street, occasionally a tiny figure could be seen keeping up the rear – little Frank Simon blowing into a newspaper rolled in the shape of a cornet. He made a habit of doing that. Once, he joined a parade held at a particularly inconvenient moment – when he should have been at school. When he did finally turn up for his lessons the teacher used a whip to get over the message that this was not the best way of spending his time – and sent him home making a noise more raucous than any he could possibly have produced from his makeshift instrument. But the pain apart, no one could reasonably have been expected to imagine the significance of that little boy's paper trumpet. Other kids had done similar things over the years and would do so for generations to come. Few would put the experience to such good use.

By now Bertha was a matronly looking woman. Her grandson Joseph recalled being held on her lap 'and I'd feel as if I were being sucked in between those two large breasts of hers' – but that was no more than suited her motherly guidance over Frank's activities. Bertha saw her son's enthusiasm and arranged for him to have lessons – playing the flute. Middletown could lay claim to a number of music 'conservatories', in truth, little more than a grandiose name for a collection of private teachers in town who set themselves up in business with as wide a variety of success as were their talents.

Frank's flute-playing activities were the result of fortuitous circumstances. He had found the instrument when he was nine years old, but no one knew where. But they did know he had actually taught himself to pick out a tune or two on the somewhat battered flute. Leo, meanwhile, was having his own share of musical opportunity, playing a toy drum – much to the chagrin of both the customers at Simons' store and the neighbors in Clinton Street.

There was, however, a part of his musical activities that disturbed no one – when he sat at his father's bolt table, copying music. It has to be admitted that he was happiest of all playing his flute, which caused them fewer problems than did his brother's drum. Thanks to his lessons, most people thought Frank was playing it pretty well. Except that he used his left hand and every time he played, the teacher laughed. It sounds rather like a mail-order correspondence course or an advertisement for Charles Atlas, building up the body of the weakling who is always having sand thrown in his eyes. The results were not much more encouraging.

By the time he was eleven, Frank had decided he did not like the flute all that much, certainly he did not like being laughed at. So he persuaded Bertha to buy him a cornet, which was very much more his cup of coffee, especially if it was not made from a rolled-up newspaper.

This represented a big investment by his mother, but she believed Frank when he promised to take it seriously. In fact, he took to it like a cat being offered a saucer of cold, fresh milk. He wanted lessons, but the various music academies in Middletown were not offering courses for the cornet. Yet he wanted them more than anything else, wanted them the way small boys always want things, with a total all-consuming passion. Even so, the desire to play and only to play did not totally inhibit his more conventional lessons at the North School. As he was to say, 'I was never handicapped by a formal education'.

His uncle Julius, however, might have been happier had Frank forgotten his *musical* learning. Julius was really Sol's cousin and one of the more prosperous citizens of Middletown. He owned what he liked to call a 'variety store' which he named 'Noah's Ark' and which the inhabitants of Middletown knew so well that, before long, they called it an institution. Years later, reflecting on his life, Frank Simon recalled: 'You could find anything there from fine Haviland china to a pot you set under the bed – they had everything in the world there.' In fact, if you were a child and had a chance to wander at will through a place like that, as Frank and Leo were able to do, Julius was Aladdin and this was his cave.

Julius consequently had to be one of their favorite relatives. The only problem was that, before very long, Frank's ideas and those of his second cousin would diverge critically. Nevertheless, he always said that Julius was a good man – as well as a prosperous one.

To keep such stock meant that the institution called 'Noah's Ark' was a great success. And such a success that its owner believed he was a man of influence. He decided his duty lay in persuading his cousin, and his cousin's wife in particular, that they should not contemplate giving Frank any more music lessons. Bertha, meanwhile, was not having any of it. She determined that since the boy was so keen on learning to play the cornet, nothing was going to stand in his way.

She found an ally in another local institution – one called Buckles. Mr Q. C. Buckles (what those initials stood for has long since been lost in the antiquity of local history) was the conductor of the Middletown Band, or Buckles's Band as the name on the big drum that led its parades declared. They played at two local venues: the South School and over the Erie Canal on the 'lift' bridge, so called because of the contraption which would raise it up, rather like Tower Bridge in London, whenever a tall ship needed to pass underneath. That canal, which since 1827 had replaced the river as the principal traffic route through town, was seemingly everyone's favorite spot in Middletown. It was where youths would take their girls and where small boys would look down – and sometimes throw missiles – onto the passing barges.

Buckles had not been responsible for founding a brass band in Middletown, a city that liked to think its musical heritage should be passed on to the 1400 children in local schools. A certain I. C. Fairies had actually established it in the wake of Worth's drummers. But everyone took Buckles to have been its principal influence and most could not imagine anyone else standing with his back to audiences, waving his arms with his own particular air of authority. Certainly, by the time Buckles took charge the band was fully established, with not a few performers who soon joined professional outfits.

Buckles himself was also a more than competent cornet player, so competent, in fact, that he doubled as the conductor of the orchestra of what was by then the pride and joy of Middletown: its very own opera house. Sorg's Opera House – or just 'The Sorg' as everyone knew it and still knows it today – was built and run by the tobacco baron and will appear in our story fairly constantly. Sorg was the town's leading citizen and unquestionably the biggest employer in Middletown. There were few rivals to his claims for leadership of the commercial citizenry of the place. He far outclassed the status of the owners of the Sebald Brewing Company or the Middletown Machine Company or the Palmer Milling Company. Because he headed one of the leading families in Middletown (which meant wealthiest, as his ownership of the Miami Cycle and Manufacturing Company which turned out bicycles and motorcycles along with his paper works and his directorships of the Middletown Gas and Electric Light Company and of the Middletown and Cincinnati Railroad testified), when he built his auditorium where all the greatest artists of the day would sing and dance he was finally putting his mark on posterity.

Bertha was sufficiently impressed by Mr Buckles's association with the Sorg to approach him with an idea: would he take on little Frank Simon as a pupil? He said that he would. Not only would it be useful to be paid a few cents, the mere thought of being invited to pass on his God-given talents was in itself a tribute Buckles appreciated.

Frank now practiced his horn the way he had played his flute – in the back room behind the store, although at first with results that were not totally as satisfactory. The customers were less than impressed – although seemingly with no obvious effect on their purchasing power. They still went to Simons for their needs. If they were not about to outfit themselves for the season or ready to redecorate their houses, Simons was still the only place to go for threads and buttons or perhaps for just a length of elastic, and, certainly in springtime, for a few yards of that essential staple to good housewifery: French gingham.

Meanwhile, Bertha, who helped Sol waiting on customers, providing them with the cloth or the 'notions' they required, was a good businesswoman who practiced that ideal kind of salesmanship – assuring her customers that while they were being given the best merchandise and she felt privileged to serve *them*, they themselves were being offered something of a privilege – in this case, the chance to hear a rather talented youngster. By all accounts, they believed her. Mr Buckles certainly seemed to think she was right.

He was sensible enough not to feel as though he *had* to agree with the woman who, as she served in the store, was always so immaculately dressed and was quite clearly the one who made the decisions. If you were invited to the Simon apartment above the store it was clear that beyond the sparkling white tablecloth she was the one in charge. Solomon, sitting near the stove in his rocking-chair at the back, was much easier to argue with. But when it came to young Frank's musical education there was no argument at all.

Every Monday, on the dot of 6.30 p.m., Frank rang the doorbell at the Buckles's house on Park Street, not far from First Street, for his lesson. The patrons of the store were quick to note the improvement in his playing. The first sour notes turned into pleasant little exercises which became very sweet music indeed. Sweet enough before long for Frank himself to join the Buckles Band. It was, he later remembered, at that time an outfit some 14-strong, 'when they were all there and sober', made up of men who during the week worked on farms, in factories, in offices or serving in stores like the one that Frank's parents owned.

The range of occasions for which they played was equally wide and equally tolerant. When they were not performing at their bandstand over the canal, they were playing for local politicians – Republicans' parades one week and the Democrats the next (Solomon, who voted Democrat as soon as he became a citizen, probably approved of that). Frank, who was later an ardent Republican, might not have been quite so happy to remember the fact until enough time had elapsed for him to laugh at the eclecticism of his political tastes.

No Fourth of July or Labor Day in Middletown was complete without Buckles's Band playing and Frank joining in with all the enthusiasm that other small boys showed with cheaper 'toys' – as when they were given their first baseball bat and invited to join a neighborhood team. It was the equivalent of a girl in her gleaming white dress going to her first prom.

But the most notable event in Middletown for which the band had ever played came soon after Frank joined the ensemble. At the age of 11, he marched with them down to Doty's Grove (named after Daniel Doty, who had first set up home on the plain of the Great Miami River's east bank) for a ceremony that would shape not only the future of Middletown but also the very life of Frank Simon.

The band played a stirring march while a certain Mr George M. Verity took hold of a large spade and turned the first piece of earth for what soon became the site of a huge complex – the American Rolling Mill Company. Frank could not have known at the time that that firm, which would make so much of the nation's steel, would within less than a quarter of a century determine a goodly portion of his life's work. But the citizens of Middletown would soon see what it had brought for them as a whole. On that day in 1900 a new industry was born.

Before long, an orange flame could be seen burning at the top of a tall, slim chimney – and would stay burning ever after, firing waste gases and at the same time providing Middletown with a new landmark. Alongside it, vast brick-built stacks belched smoke that mingled over Middletown with the fumes of the tobacco and the paper companies and the aromas of the pigs. But nobody was worried about pollution. 'Smoke meant prosperity in those days,' says George Crout, Middletown's much-respected historian. The thousands who found work in what was soon known as the 'mill' and the tradespeople who benefited from them had no reason to disagree.

If you were young in Middletown it was an exciting time to be alive. There were church socials – by far the main entertainment activity apart from going to band concerts. There were hay rides and oyster suppers in summer and ice skating and bobsledding in winter. Elite's ice cream was sold all over the place and in summer the company's own store – which looked more than anything else like a garage – did a roaring trade selling ices equally to youngsters who looked as spick and span as any in an Andy Hardy movie and to others who had the grime of the mill under their fingernails.

It is true that when Frank went for an ice cream it was with the children of the merchants and professional families. 'But there really wasn't much class segregation,' says George Crout. Those who did not go to the Elite store thronged together at one of the local drugstores, all of which had their own soda fountains. Prosperity had come to Middletown all right. The whole of Main Street was just one shop after another – Strauss's and the Reed-Klopp furniture emporia, the John Ross department store – before you progressed further up the road and reached the big residential homes like the Gothic Sorg Mansion and the houses owned by the other industrialists whose success and prosperity came in the wake of the mill. The town was also helped because the New York Central Railroad now went through it, heralding an era not far away when even the Erie Canal would be redundant.

Largely because of these developments, it was also fairly good to be a member of the Simon family. People had more money and spent more of it in the store, although Bertha still had to scrimp and save for things that could not totally be established as among the real necessities of life. Until his dying day, Frank talked about the sacrifices his parents made for him and once, in an untypically immodest aside, noted: 'Genius can be found in any hovel.'

Certainly for Bertha and Sol, being Jewish was never much of a handicap. They were in no way Orthodox and their religion never appeared to be outwardly very important. Their grandson, David Simon, remembers them as 'God-fearing people'. They kept the High Holidays in their own way and refused to allow any pork or shellfish in their home. But the more restrictive dietary laws requiring the consumption only of kosher meat and the separation of dairy products from meat played no part in their lives.

Neither did their Jewish background affect their ambitions for the kind of education they wanted for their sons. When Frank left the North School the Simons decided that he would do best at the local Catholic academy, the Holy Trinity School. He took lessons in commercial subjects there. Possibly the Simons were hedging bets for Frank's future. They knew that music was everything to their son, but they also knew that the chances of his making an adequate living at it – let alone doing really well – were fairly remote. The education there did stand Frank in good stead. Not only did he learn a little about another religion, he also learned to type – an ability he never lost.

There were probably no more than just ten Jewish families in the whole place in the days when the mill came to Middletown and the population hovered around the 10,000 mark. But ever since Simon Goldman – he had married a Gentile, so was immediately accepted by local society – had been the first member of their faith to settle in Middletown, they had established themselves there very well. Jewish men played sports for the local Baptist Church and no one seemed to take much notice of the fact.

The family was probably no more poor than it was rich, but to the Simon clan, Bertha's paying for private music lessons was more of a serious worry than was her brief excursion into the world of religion. They continued to think that music was a luxury use for spending money that could be more usefully diverted elsewhere.

However, no one could deny that the store was doing well and, to prove it, the Simons moved to a better part of town, away from the industrial area and far from the houses put up by the Veritys for the migrant workers and the black employees who had come soon after the establishment of the mill. Both Solomon and Bertha were well enough known in town to be asked to join organizations there and, although local historians like George Crout admitted there was prejudice in Middletown, it was mostly focused on the blacks in the area. As George Crout agrees, local blacks, who at first were mainly fieldhands working on the tobacco plantations of Kentucky and later came to work for George M. Verity and lived in the segregated housing he provided for them, would not have found it so easy to be accepted.

Being occasionally short of money was never allowed to interfere with what the Simons considered to be their priorities – their respect for education at the top of them all. They were happy living their own lives and Middletown was content to allow them to do so. Now that they lived in the better part of town and Frank and Leo went to the best schools – the poorer children went to the Central and Jefferson Schools – Solomon was highly respected in the local business community. They and the things they did were noticed in town.

As Al Block, another contemporary of Frank's, has recalled, Solomon and Bertha were good friends of his own parents and he always remembered watching Simon senior locking his horse in his barn at the end of every day. Before long, Solomon had reason to wish that everyone in Middletown drove horses and nothing else. For the time, however, he was content enough with his own life.

Everything was perfect, in fact, until the day in 1902 when Leo decided to try out his new bicycle when going on an errand for Bertha. Outside the Strand Theatre on Central Avenue he collided with a new contraption called an automobile, one that was running out of control in the opposite direction. It was driven by the man who was responsible for its being built in the first place – a New Yorker called Charles Ball, who had found a job in Middletown with the Miami Cycle Company, which had made a fortune with their Racycle machine. Ball had come to the not unreasonable conclusion that automobiles were here to stay. So he got the assembly line to switch to a steam-driven car called the Ramapaugh, named after a local Indian tribe. He boasted that the car, weighing 3500 pounds, seated eight people and had a water tank holding 68 gallons – enough for a 75-mile journey that could begin after spending only five minutes raising sufficient steam pressure. What the sales pitch did not go into was that, once the car was on the road, steering it and, more significantly, stopping it was a totally different matter.

Ball and a companion demonstrated both facts to Leo's cost. The car struck the bicycle. Ball tried to put it into reverse at the same time as he applied the brakes, but the machine's momentum carried it down the street with seemingly nothing to stop it – least of all Leo and his bicycle.

Mr Lute, the owner of Lute's Meat Store, saw the accident close to his shop. He watched the heavy new car close in on the bicycle just at the same time as he heard a voice scream 'Look out!' Leo either did not hear or, if he did, he did not manage to look out quickly enough. As Mr Lute noted: 'He turned his head to the left to look back and the wheel took a sudden lurch in front of the machine, either on account of the handle slipping from his left hand or the bar turning in its socket. The machine struck the wheel and both the boy and wheel were under in an instant, both left-hand wheels passing over the boy's body above the thighs.'

Leo was taken to the home of the local GP, Dr Logan. But he was crushed and bleeding beyond the skills of a country doctor. Logan called for a second opinion and a Dr Dell came round to the Simons' home, where Leo had been taken. This was a fundamental mistake in the eyes of the modern medical practitioners. The last thing one does to road-accident victims is to move them without expert help – and certainly to nowhere but a hospital, but they did not know much about road accidents in those days. Leo lingered until the early hours of the following morning, conscious and in agony. At 1 a.m. he lapsed into a coma. Less than two hours later, he was dead. The family – Bertha, Solomon, Frank, Julius – did not believe they could recover from the tragedy.

The Simons later found that they had made a macabre form of history. It was only the second fatal motor accident in America. The previous victim had been Edward Russell Thomas, the first husband of Linda Lee Thomas, who was to become the wife of Cole Porter, a man who wrote an entirely different kind of music from the Sousa marches and Victor Herbert operetta melodies played by the Buckles Band. It also looked as though it was going to have a tremendous effect on the automobile industry in America. If people were getting killed by these contraptions, who would want to buy them? The days of the steam-powered Ramapaugh in particular seemed numbered. As a contemporary writer noted: 'Once started, the Ramapaugh is hard to stop; to stop 3600 pounds is not easy.'

That writer pleaded for car manufacture to continue in a town that had recently added yet another new industry to its catalog of products. The New Decatur Buggy Company had come to Middle-town and was busy producing enough buggies to keep a fair number of the horses in the area in full-time work. There was also the Ling and Van Sickle Buggy Company nearby and that, with the addition of an automobile industry, 'would mean more jobs and growth for this community'. He added, quite presciently as it turned out, 'large amounts of steel would be utilized in the making of automobiles which could be supplied by the new American Rolling Mill Company'.

The event prompted the local *Daily Signal* to publish an editorial.

'It has become a favorite pastime to rush through the streets of the city with the speed of an express train and the passage of an automobile has become a menace to life.' In fact, that very afternoon, someone noted two automobiles rushed through at no less than 10 miles an hour, leaving a cloud of dust behind them.

In the end, the Miami Cycle Company produced only three of their Ramapaugh cars. When it was revealed that one of those three had gone out of control and had hit the little Simon boy, they went back to making bicycles. Perhaps because of that, the automobile was to find its natural home to the north – in Michigan, a problem for Middletown that did not concern the Simon family all that much. They had their own very personal agony.

Solomon and Bertha remained devastated for months. For Bertha there were but two choices: to mourn and lock herself away or to devote herself to her remaining son. She chose the second course. Julius, who had prospered so well that he now owned a second 'Noah's Ark'-type store, was as determined as ever. To him, the only way a bright Jewish boy could look to the future was by following his own example and trying to become a prosperous merchant. For her part, Bertha knew that that was the last thing Frank had in mind. From then on she was going to monitor his progress like a lioness watching over her favorite cub.

She watched her Frank playing in the band. She questioned him about his progress after every lesson. Nothing he did at school was allowed to escape her attention. She had good reason to be pleased with what she heard – and read. Julius, too, should have drawn some satisfaction from realizing that his second cousin's obsession with music was not to affect adversely his other schooling.

In March 1903 Frank was in the eighth grade at the Central School, writing in a neat hand from room 12, grappling with the problem of how many acres of a meadow could be mown by 27 men if it took two men to mow 16 acres. In English lessons, he analysed the anonymous poem 'From The Belfry' . . . 'Softly the Angelus sounded . . . And over the roofs of the village.' He neatly ornamented every page of his loose-leaf exercise book – with a picture of a dog at the top of a short story he wrote called 'Rab and His Friends' and with an impression of Oliver Goldsmith above a pen-picture of the writer. 'His early writings were mostly essays and a few verses that he wrote in school. At the age of 17 years, he entered college . . .'

But the most revealing of these school tasks was an exercise in letter writing – and, in particular, the note he penned to an imaginary acquaintance. 'My dear friend,' the letter began, 'I write you a few lines to let you know I have moved to East Third Street. I am attending the Central School and like it very much. My favorite studies are arithmetic, spelling, history, civics and music, but I do hate grammar.' Then came an instance of prophecy: 'I intend to remain in school until I go until [*sic*] the college of music at Cincinnati for I intend to become a musician.' For the 13-year-old boy there was already no doubt where he imagined his future to lie.

It was not, however, a simple choice that he had to make. Two years after Frank first came under Q. C. Buckles's influence, the teacher announced he was leaving town. That in itself presented two problems which somehow had to be resolved: (a) Who was going to teach his young cornet student? (b) Who was going to lead the Middletown Band?

Buckles asked if he could meet Bertha. He told her he was already sure that Frank knew as much as he himself could possibly teach him. So there was a recommendation to make – along with the name of a new teacher who could offer the boy more than he ever could; a generous gesture in itself.

As for the Middletown Band, he had a further suggestion. How would Frank like to lead it? How *would* he like to lead it? No more was this the equivalent of a new baseball *bat*. Now, he was being given his own *team*, his own *ballgame*. He was being offered a trip to the moon.

At the age of 14, Frank Simon needed to hear no more. Of course, he said yes – to both ideas. He would go to the new teacher. And when the band next went on parade, the bass drum carried the legend 'Simon's Band'.

3 · *Tooting His Own Horn*

The band was everything that Middletown could have hoped it would be. The men sometimes drank too much. Some of them did not just say 'hello' to the pretty, tightly corseted girls who lingered around the bandstands at the end of their weekly concerts. But all Frank heard or knew about was the music they made.

Others felt much the same way. More than 60 years later, Sister Francis Xavier, whom Frank may have known by the name of Hannah Welsh, wrote him a letter recalling band practice in the old South School yard. 'What a gala night was that, once a week, when all we South-enders pranced around the bandstand, devouring hot buttered popcorn to the rhythm of "The Stars and Stripes Forever".'

His own pleasure was doubled. Not only did he enjoy the music, he could also control the way it sounded – or at least make attempts in that direction. If he knew it was not good enough, he also understood that it was the finest apprenticeship a boy with ambitions for the big time (that so-apt vaudeville term which applied as much to the world of the band as to the stage acts who trooped from town to town) could wish for. The best bands in the country did that sort of traveling, too. John Philip Sousa was fully booked for the Sousa Band at least a year (and frequently two years) ahead. As he thought on these matters, Frank Simon salivated – and determined to make Middletown's band better than it had ever been.

The Erie Canal bridge was still a great spot to hear the band playing. It was perhaps Frank's own favorite part of town. In the odd spare moment when he was not playing his music he would go fishing there. But it was as a place to sound his cornet and listen to the music of the other instrumentalists that it played its biggest role in his life. People would linger around the bridge or stand on the decks of the boats that plied their trade along the water route, like *The Gambrius – the King of Beer*, owned by the brewery. That was what small-town band playing was all about.

For Frank it was merely part of the good groundwork he knew he was achieving all the time. Q. C. Buckles had been an elementary teacher, but the work he did was as important in its way as any other part of his training, and young Frank Simon knew that. He remembered it every day. Years later, he said: 'Mr Buckles never steered me the wrong way.' And the teachers who followed him echoed those sentiments. There were no bad habits that he picked up, the sort that stay with someone for life and are virtually impossible to break. He held his cornet in the correct way. He used it the way that best suited his own lips.

He learned that there are two distinct methods for playing the cornet: one was the 'bunch', where the lips are bunched together to form a cushion on which the mouthpiece can sit, the second, the 'smile', in which a player first pulls his lips together and then parts them – this makes the lips grow tighter. Buckles knew that Frank was born to use the smile system – and not simply because smiles came to him as easily as falling asleep at night. With his thick upper lip he could make a smile, stretch it and still have enough muscle left for his 'embouchure' without being tired. It was a means of playing that stayed with him for the best part of half a century.

Now he remembered the technique every time he picked up his cornet and every time he played at one of the local band concerts. He liked to think that each week his work got better, although, in truth, the people in the park applauded no more than they had done in Buckles's day, which was quite enough for most band aficionados. But every time he did play he knew he had to improve and make his fellow-instrumentalists better with him.

There was also the 'tuning fork' of his lessons, the instruction of one William J. Kopp, who had taken over from Buckles and who every time he himself picked up a horn left a sound reverberating in Frank's brain that he carried with him to his next lesson or band rehearsal. Somehow, he was sure the Middletown bandsmen heard it, too, if only vicariously.

Strangely enough, there is no record of any of them failing to take seriously young Frank, this small boy who could not yet even be called a youth. They did what he told them to do.

The fact that he was only 14 years old appeared not to make any difference at all to them, even though he was still at school and his voice had not yet broken and the other bandsmen were working during the day at mills or doing jobs in stores or in the tobacco and paper plants of Middletown. But then this was 1904, a time when people did not readily flout authority, from wherever it came. They wanted to make good music as much as Frank did and were happily convinced that anyone who had started off with Q. C. Buckles as his teacher must have been pretty good.

But in truth none of the bandsmen had the inclination to stand in his place, with the punishing round of rehearsals, individual meetings with players and organizers and with the business manager breathing down his neck most of the time. The business manager was the least of his problems: the band continued to take a few cents on Saturday afternoons – which was enough to cover what few expenses it had. The bandsmen played for the love of it all.

Kopp's Military Band was the perfect background to the lessons its conductor was giving Frank. Perhaps the most valuable thing he learned at this stage was, while playing his own instrument, how to blend it with an ensemble of musicians. It was invaluable experience even for a youngster who was already a bandmaster and who was being taught by a man who not only played a band instrument but was actually a charter member of the Cincinnati Symphony, soon to become one of the most important orchestras in the land. For a time, Kopp was even its manager.

Frank's parents were delighted with the success their son had achieved. Bertha spoke in German about her happiness and the boy replied in English, a language in which his mother was reasonably proficient but never totally confident. (When she spoke it, she never quite understood that the word 'unt' sounded better as 'and'.) It was never a problem for her son, who dutifully appeared to accept all the advice Mrs Simon could give him in whatever language she chose to use. Even while her relatives continued to try to persuade her otherwise, she thought Frank's going to Kopp was a good idea – although he was still putting in a full day's work at school while simultaneously running the town band.

But none of this was really a chore. He looked forward to his lessons with Mr Kopp more than anything else he did. Years later, he spoke of his teacher's 'brilliant playing'.

Bertha did not have a lot of money but she still regarded Frank's lessons as a principal priority and paid for both the tuition and the train fare to get him there. To her it was an act of faith which was not the sort of thing to try to shake. Once she had been sure Mr Kopp was willing to teach her son, she made it her business to provide the opportunity.

Bertha was a typical representative of her generation. There were certain things that a mother had to do – and meeting her child's teacher was one of them. So the first time Frank had gone to see Mr Kopp she went along with him. The meeting was at the Cincinnati College of Music, where he taught cornet and trumpet.

Kopp knew what he had in Frank Simon the moment of that first audition at the college. There, in front of him, was a youngster who both had the poise and could make the noise – both done beautifully and with the promise of a future to which few could ever look. And yet he also knew the problems. It was not going to be easy and he had to give a warning to the portly, anxious woman sitting before his desk. There just was not time to teach Frank Simon as he would other pupils. 'Don't register him here,' he advised. 'I could only spend half an hour a week with him at the college. Have him come to my home for his lessons.'

It was not a cheap solution, but Bertha was convinced that the teacher was not merely trying to make more money out of her. Nevertheless, it would cost at least a couple of dollars every time, two dollars of her very hard-earned money. Yet she did not have to think very long about it. Bertha just knew, she *had* to believe that it would all be worth doing. She was, after all, making an investment in her son's future.

From then on, every Saturday, Frank made his weekly trip for the lessons to Cincinnati – or Cincinnatta, as it was known to the locals and is still called by some of its older citizens. It took him an hour to travel there by train, and each time he arrived at his teacher's house it was with the kind of glow on his face most children reserved for the prospect of an ice-cream soda. In late old age, Frank Simon said:

> I'll never forget his address. Every Saturday I had to get on a train in Middletown and come down to Cincinnati and take the streetcar out to Mr Kopp's home at 1312 Broadway and have my lesson. Then I'd go home and when I got off the train I ran the ten blocks home, because I couldn't get there fast enough to practice my new lesson. I lived music day and night and wouldn't have traded places with any person in the world.

The energy of a 14-year-old sometimes makes his elders stop and wonder. The young Frank Simon had it all. There were never any problems about staying at school, taking his lessons and running the band – in roughly that order of priority.

It all tired him no more than did yet another job he was doing around this time: playing in the pit at Sorg's Opera House in Middletown, an institution which all those years later still provides opportunities for local people to see live entertainment, the occasional opera, a play or a musical show.

A century after it was built (and having just changed its name back to the original one after 44 years as the Colonial Movie Theater) the Sorg remains one of those monuments, not so much to their founders as to the age when going to the theatre was an experience to relish. Sitting in the orchestra seats with their red plush-velvet upholstery, looking toward the gilt-encrusted proscenium arch and across at the wide, deeply carpeted aisles was to be made a prince invited to a private party at the home of a neighboring nobleman. It was not for nothing that the original cinemas were known as 'picture palaces'.

It was the brainchild of Paul J. Sorg, reputed to be the second-richest man in Ohio as a result of the chewing-tobacco company he had set up which became the biggest firm in town (later to be part of the American Tobacco Company). He also owned a manufacturing firm, a paper company and a cycle factory and became a Congressman. The Sorg was a gesture of *noblesse oblige* as he surveyed his vast fortune from the study of the Gothic red limestone building on South Main Street, known to this day as the Sorg Mansion. More than that, Sorg did, of course, conceive of its being a place on which he could put his own stamp. In fact, it suited his vanity perfectly – to have his name associated with the most popular entertainment in town, apparently in perpetuity. It was the ultimate in style.

Sorg's wife, Jennie Grover Sorg, thought so too. She made herself responsible for going to New York and choosing the acts for what she had established as one of the best vaudeville houses in that part of the country. It was a fact aided by that wonder of the age, the railroad. Middletown was serviced by the Big Four Line as well as by the Baltimore and Ohio, and since it lay between New York and Chicago, Mrs Sorg was able to get all the big-time acts booked between the two metropolises. Nothing – and the significance of this will become apparent before long – matched the excitement of having the Sousa Band play there.

Al Jolson, Ted Lewis, Sophie Tucker, Eddie Cantor all played at the Sorg in the following years. Sarah Bernhardt had already appeared on a Sorg bill, although the biggest impact most people could remember in the first two or three years of the century came from the 'I Don't Care Girl', Eva Tanguay, and by a series of 'Dutch comedians' – most of whom were born in Poland but that was how they were known – Webber and Fields and Smith and Dale. Seventy years later they formed the model for Neil Simon's *Sunshine Boys*. There were, however, some people who thought that the best acts came from the political meetings held there, like the time William Jennings Bryan spoke and Sorg himself made his pitch for Congress.

It was in the more conventional 'shows' that Frank Simon made his debut at the opera house. The Sorg needed a trumpet player and for two or three nights a week, Frank and his cornet came along to substitute. His fee: 25 cents a night, playing perhaps for a new operetta, a musical comedy or a minstrel show. It was about this time that vaudeville made its debut at the Sorg, finally discarding the convention of individual acts being lightly disguised as part of the format of a play. Then something remarkable happened: the union came to Middletown in the shape of Local 321 of the American Federation of Musicians. As Frank later recalled: 'And boy! Did we stick the old Opera House – and raised the price to a dollar and a half.' Mr Kopp is not on record demanding any increase in the price of his lessons.

No one now remembers Kopp, who, with his big mustache and military bearing, seems to have resembled the typical bandmaster of the early years of the century. Nor can anyone accurately describe what his playing sounded like, but if the success of his pupils is anything to go by – and it frequently is – he was probably an outstanding musician. As first trumpet with the Cincinnati Symphony Orchestra, he had to be gifted. To run his own totally professional outfit, Kopp's Band – which has also disappeared into antiquity with no recordings or people alive who can testify to its standards – he had to know what people who enjoyed band music required and be able to deliver it. Certainly, the Simon boy had the satisfaction of believing so. Months after being taken under his wing, Frank still felt the same way about his teacher as he had the day he first met him.

Kopp knew what he was talking about when he gave Frank, first, encouragement, and then praise. His was a widely respected name in those parts and among his kind of people. The pupil, in fact, never had any doubts about the abilities of the teacher. It helped him get another one of his early jobs – as a 16-year-old part-time cornet soloist with the Dayton New Band at Dayton, Ohio.

Plainly he never thought of playing in a band as hard work. There was an air of excitement about every concert, about every step taken when they marched at the head of one of those local processions so beloved of early-in-the-century America.

Sometimes there was also the spirit of competition about it all. Alice Lytell was in her late 90s when she recalled for me running a rival band in the town of Franklin, 6 miles from Middletown. When they played on neutral territory it was always a question of which one of the two outfits could get to the bandstand the quicker, the then Alice Whiteman (she was a cousin of the bandleader Paul Whiteman, whom Frank in later life was said to resemble so closely) or Simon. They would literally race each other to the site. Even if she lost, she still made sure she had the last word. 'We would play the moment Frank stopped,' she told me. Once they played on top of a hill. When the Middletown Band finished, Alice's ensemble were there on the spot to replace him. Young bandmaster Simon did not like that. 'He raced back up the hill with his band, playing all the way up.'

It might have been easier for Miss Whiteman to achieve that feat of music on the run than for Frank himself, who already had decided he enjoyed playing more in a bandstand or gazebo. Hers was mostly a marching band, although they frequently played concerts too. 'It was a great time,' she said. 'We'd all play the best we could, while the people there thoroughly enjoyed themselves – eating popcorn while they listened to the band.'

They even competed for musicians. She knew how valued the Middletown Band was – her own father had played for it under Q. C. Buckles. 'He used to say "No one puts his feet under my table if they don't play".' That was why Arthur Lytell, the man who became her husband, was so acceptable. Arthur had been one of Frank's own childhood friends. Twenty years later he played under him in what became the Armco Band. But that was for the future. For the moment, Frank was consolidating his hold on the Middletown Band – and doing the odd bit of teaching on the side.

Alice was even one of his pupils. 'I don't want to tell you,' she recalled, her smile growing mischievously. 'No. I didn't like Frank as a teacher. He would say, "For instance, there is this way . . ." He would never say, "It *IS* that way". But Frank was all right. I liked him.'

His success was growing by the proverbial leaps and bounds. Finally, the inevitable happened: Kopp announced that he and young Mr Simon had gone about as far as they could go together – which did not mean that he had any doubts about Frank's abilities. He just thought that he had taught Frank all he knew, and that there was more out there for a youngster of his talents.

Like Q. C. Buckles before him, Kopp recommended a new teacher. He told Bertha: 'Mrs Simon, I've taken him as far as I can take him. I'm not equipped to take him any further.' The new teacher was the imposing and not a little frightening Herman Bellstedt, a man who treated his cornet the way a violinist regards his Stradivarius and who expected everyone else to cherish the instrument with the same degree of reverence.

Bellstedt was one of the leading cornetists of his time – which justified, Bertha thought, the six dollars a week it now cost her, a not inconsiderable sum; five dollars for the lesson and another dollar for fares, lunches and occasional music. Bellstedt was a former cornetist for the greatest bandmaster of them all, John Philip Sousa, and still did arrangements for him. Sousa called him 'the king of the instrument'.

Bellstedt not only had national fame, he had appeared all over the world as a soloist. Now he made Frank Simon a promise: 'Young man,' he said, 'if you play your part, I'll play mine.' The playing was work, each working for the other and producing in the course of it all an instrumentalist who would walk in Bellstedt's own footsteps.

Mrs Simon still wanted Frank to succeed quite as much as he did himself. And like Bellstedt, she offered advice that her son recalled years later when he said that he could 'still hear my mother's words as I left for the train each week'. What she said sounds a little formal, but that is what German-born mothers were like in those days. 'Make good, my son,' she said, 'you will never know how hard it was for me to get this money together.' As Frank said, along with Bellstedt's own statement, 'with these unforgettable words, I was determined that they would never regret their faith in me'.

Frank Simon said of his new teacher: 'Herman Bellstedt was a real German; very strict, exacting, but a terrific teacher.' He was 'very much the Herr Professor type of figure – although once in a while we'd get a little smile from him. But he was very exacting.' In fact, the teacher, by then in his 60s, only had to glare in Frank's direction, utter the words, 'young man', and be certain of getting what he wanted.

Frank was satisfied that the 'smile' he could get out of his own cornet playing answered most of his teacher's demands. He practiced it at home – using the back of a chair to hold his music book. It would be another year before he could afford a metal music stand.

The German-born Bellstedt may have been tough but it did not worry his new pupil. 'Mr Bellstedt fired my ambition to a fever pitch,' he recalled. 'When he played for me, I was transported into another world.' And he could also admit: 'He was a stern, exacting tutor with very little patience. In other words, he put the fear of God into me.' Frank could also say with the satisfaction of an immensely successful career behind him: 'I doubt very much that I would have met with one half the success that good fortune has bestowed upon me if it were not for [his] masterful teaching and friendly guidance . . . He took much pride in my development and closely influenced my career from the preliminary stages of my boyhood to the days of my tours from coast to coast.'

Above all, Frank respected ability. Next to that, professionalism.

Bellstedt had both in abundance. Before joining Sousa in 1905 as side partner to Herbert L. Clarke, sometimes called the greatest cornet player of all time, he had been cornet soloist with the Cincinnati Orchestra Reed Band. He had played at the world-famous Brooklyn playground, Coney Island, with the Red Hussar Band and then graduated to the Gilmore Band. In 1892 he had his own band. Later, he joined the band of Frederich Neil Innes, another eminent bandmaster who proudly announced the acquisition of his new player as 'Germany's Greatest Cornet Soloist'. There was a lot to emulate in this stern, exacting teacher. Frank never forgot his influence.

Meanwhile, Frank himself was not just a young man in a hurry, he already had a strong reputation of his own. In an illustrated history of the town, *Middletown In Black and White*, published in 1906, Harry Simms wrote about the local bandmaster:

> Frank Simon, the talented son of Mr and Mrs Solomon Simon, is the energetic director of the Middletown Band, an organization that has won the approval of the public. Bandmaster Simon has brought the band to a high state of musical efficiency and its services are eagerly sought for parades and public occasions of note. Mr Simon is a cornet player of rare ability. He has been under the tutelage of Hermann Bellstedt for some time and has made the most wonderful progress. He is a born musician and gives his art a great deal of time and hard study. He is a young man of very pleasing address and he stands second to none in point of ability. The promenade concerts given by Bandmaster Simon and his musicians have attracted attention and admiration.

Frank may have been doing well but did not forsake those who had been of help to him in the past, notably William Kopp. In 1909 Kopp thought Frank was sufficiently well versed in the art of bandsmanship to invite him to join Kopp's Band – and get paid for the privilege of being his first cornet player. It was his first professional job. There was clearly a very good relationship between the two men, one a musician of experience with a reputation that brought only respect; the other, a youngster who set his sights so far ahead, no one could see them.

There was perhaps just one thing that could drag Frank away from the sound of a band or of the instrument which would be his own very special contribution. He was a devoted fan of Middletown's own baseball team. A friend noted at the time: 'When his home team plays to suit him he leaves the ball park so hoarse that he cannot talk. And whenever there's a bargain game on the Cincinnati field, notwithstanding his home is in Middletown, O., it is a safe bet that Frank Simon and his auto are there.'

So in his early 20s Frank was doing sufficiently well to have his own car – a far from usual situation in those days. What Bertha and Solomon thought about a mode of transport which forever would be associated with Leo and his terrible death can only be imagined. But cars were becoming a passion quite as strong as the ballgames to which the automobile chugged its way to take him.

Hardly surprisingly, he also believed equally in passing on his love for his music. As a friend reported: 'When at leisure, if there are any rehearsals or engagements of home or near-home bands, he takes a solo or two with him and goes to help out. He is always a welcome guest.'

Frank stayed with Bellstedt for six years and it was an open secret that he was his favorite pupil. It was equally open that the younger man knew his teacher had a great deal to pass on. 'His cornet solos are musical gems of individualistic style and charm and his humorous compositions are inimitable,' he said.

But it was not enough for the young pupil. Now he was also looking for new opportunities.

4 · *In Two Outfits*

Frank found those new opportunities in abundance when he joined his previous teacher's organization. The audience for Kopp's Band, now that Frank had permanently graduated from conducting the Middletown outfit, waited enthusiastically for his regular solos – and then, when he had completed his performance, cheered and clapped as though the President of the United States himself had come to town.

And it was not just the *citizenry* of Middletown or even Cincinnati who had a chance to show their enthusiasm. Frank Simon was already being spoken of by other people in the band business – and always favorably. If he himself might not have known that, it could only have been that he was much too concerned with the job at hand.

It was while playing cornet solos with Kopp at the Cincinnati Zoological Gardens – there was so much more to going to the zoo than merely seeing the animals; like a visit to the circus, the band made a vital contribution to the notion of a day out – that Frank was spotted by talent scouts for another band. Immediately afterwards, he was asked if he would like to make a transfer. The invitation, early in 1910, to join Weber's Prize Band of America – so called because every time it entered a competition, it won – had to be grasped with both hands, as though holding tight a bright new silver cornet.

Weber's was one of Cincinnati's main bands. Only Smitties', under the direction of a certain George Smith Jr, competed with it and then only for the brief period before Weber's Band really got into its stride. It was under the baton of John C. Weber, one of the leading German band musicians of the day. A distinguished name in the band world, Herbert and Albert Weber were both members of the Sousa outfit and later with their father, Emil, comprised the tuba section of the famous Pryor Band. The band operated from Over the Rhine, a section of Cincinnati not delineated by any street signs and one you would not find on any maps of the city, but a place to which small children could direct visitors as though they were pointing to their own homes – which was exactly what a lot of them were doing. The name could not have been more appropriate if, by some strange quirk of the diplomatic process, the area had been taken over by Germany and the Kaiser himself had established a summer residence in town. It was as German as a slice of bratwurst and with a sprinkling of sauerkraut to add to the flavor.

Like immigrants everywhere, the Germans who came to America essentially for economic reasons still liked to retain their culture, to eat their own food, to read their own newspapers and books and to listen to their own music – while, of course, marrying among their own kind. That was why they tended to settle together in certain cities and towns, 'their' cities and towns, and then in fairly clearly defined parts. They liked to think of themselves as true Americans, but their loyalties to the old country in those early years of the twentieth century remained strong and firm. It was a brand of loyalty that would be stretched to a painful degree when events in Sarajevo in 1914 started the long process to the First World War. Even a quarter of a century after that, there were people living Over the Rhine who were not exactly ecstatic about the idea of a second war with Germany, but eventually there would be sufficient heroes in khaki and blue to dispel any serious doubts about their loyalties to America. If all of those immigrants have now gone, much of their culture remains – and so does the name of their home district.

In 1910 there seemed to be no conflict. Long before the concept of hyphenated citizens took root, those German-Americans saw no reason to jettison any part of their heritage. There was just nothing to argue about – or at least so it had always seemed.

Just one such group was the band that operated from a room above Weber's Saloon at 12th Street and Vine. It was a purely brass outfit, following a tradition brought over from the 'Old Country' that was as strong as most of its members' accents.

Many of the musicians *had* gone to schools where the day began with the saluting of the Stars and Stripes flag and most of the others had already proudly held up their right hands and taken oaths of citizenship, but they played loud, raucous German band music, the kind that flourished on street corners in Hamburg and Hanover. What was more, they spoke the same kind of language you could hear on the street corners of Hamburg and Hanover. The bandsmen were not allowed to speak anything but German – either in the room above the saloon where the band played while people drank in the beer hall below or on the trains taking them on tour all over the country. It was a period when nobody who wanted to keep a job challenged the established way – the idea of querying the way a *German* institution did things would have been even more unlikely.

Bertha could not have been more happy with her son's decision to join Weber's Band. Not only was he fast moving up in the world of his choosing – justifying that 'investment' in the boy and his career every hour of every day – but he was also continuing to live in the sort of culture that was very important indeed to her. Frank was not only learning more about music every day of his life, he was also discovering a great deal about geography – for Weber's Band was also a touring band. Not for them the complete restriction of having just one bandstand, even if it were the local prestige spot at the Cincinnati Zoological Gardens. Quite suddenly, places that may or may not have previously represented dots on the maps came alive to him.

Soon after joining the band, Frank was a featured player on their 1910 tour of the Mid-West. By Christmas that year, he was at Oakland, California. Contemporary pictures show a much stouter Frank Simon than before – a characteristic he never lost – with the first indication of the mustache which was to be another trade-mark.

But if he enjoyed the touring, which he manifestly did, it did not mean that he had in any way cut his ties with home. He was still a very good son. In the summer of 1910, just before the tour began, Solomon Simon was suffering from extreme breathing discomfort. There was nothing seriously wrong with his respiratory tract, but breathing through his nose was virtually impossible. There were so many polyps in his nostrils that the passages were totally closed. Frank could not bear his father's discomfort, even if it was not extreme suffering. So he took him to see a local doctor who soon became a family friend, David F. Gerber.

There were no ear, nose and throat specialists in Middletown, so the only thing Dr Gerber could do was to operate on his patient himself – in his own office (it was an operation he had conducted during his 'apprenticeship' as a resident surgeon at Cincinnati General Hospital). Sol was pleased with the result and Frank was equally glad to have insisted on his having the surgery. Further examples of filial concern recurred as the years went by.

Meanwhile, Sol was not slow in bringing his 25-year-old son's kind influence before the by now wide circle of friends, Oddfellows and customers. Word quickly spread of the concern the young man felt for his parents. It went far beyond what most mothers and fathers would expect of their offspring and for years afterward, people would talk of the Simons and how lucky they were to have such a good son.

Frank was also a popular figure in Weber's Band – and a highly recognizable one, slightly tubby as photographs indicate and now usually with a cigar in his mouth when there was not a cornet there. That was a habit he no longer kept to himself. He had first picked it up when he was 14, when presumably his parents were not quite so readily let into the secret. Now, as an air of prosperity developed around him, it had become a trademark.

He played the cornet sufficiently well for his fame to precede him – posters proclaimed the forthcoming arrival not just of the band but also of its principal cornetist. What was more, his fellow-instrumentalists enjoyed his company. He was already developing a strong sense of humor, seeing a funny situation in a missed train, a double-booked hotel room or a hostelry that seemed to have more rats than guests. And there were his jokes – the best that 1910 could offer, with a generous helping of the 'ethnic' variety, German and Jewish in equally strong measure.

It all fitted in beautifully with the kind of society in which he and his fellow-bandsmen now moved. Weber's Band was part of the German-American family fabric. After a hard day's work, customers would come with their wives and older children to spend evenings in the saloon, drinking beer and listening to the band music percolating down through the ceiling rafters.

There was no social snobbery. It was what people there did and Frank was happy to be part of it all – part of, in fact, what was a golden era for band music in Cincinnati. Before long, Frank Simon would be taking it all to a new, higher plane.

But people in Middletown still regarded him as their own and still talked of the local boy who had made good. Whenever Weber's Band played on 'home' territory there was always a fair sprinkling of Middletown citizens in the audience both to hear them and to cheer their favorite son.

Years later, one of his contemporaries, who was born within six months of Frank, lived on the same street and went to the same schools, Mrs Nell Blair Blackford, spoke proudly of the young man she had known; the one who, like her, had been taught 'that work was honorable, personal integrity was to be guarded jealously and that everyone – *everyone* – should give something of themselves to every task without thought of any return . . .' As she said, 'It took talent, of course, hard work, perseverance and an unwillingness to settle for anything but perfection.' That was, in one paragraph, the recipe for a Frank Simon and a description of what drew people to his solo performances.

He had many friends in the band. One of them was Charles Stacy, who achieved a fame of his own as a trombone soloist. His roommate for much of the following year was another young trombone player named Henry Fillmore. Before long, Fillmore was considered the best man on his instrument in the country and was himself among America's most popular bandmasters – to say nothing of being one of the most prominent band-music publishers.

Frank enjoyed Fillmore's company as much as that of any of his contemporaries. He respected both his musicianship and his experience. After all, his companion had already been both a circus musician (doubling sometimes as a clown) and had conducted the band of the First Regiment of the Ohio National Guard. He was steeped in music – his father had a music-publishing business which concentrated on religious works (much to Henry's disappointment; he wanted to turn out band music). And he wrote his own music, too – under a whole string of names ranging from Will Huff to Henrietta Moore. About this time, he also wrote a march that his friend Frank Simon would always enjoy playing – 'The

Victorious First', dedicated to his regiment of the National Guard. Later, he produced both a children's cantata and pieces for his own instrument, called 'trombone smears'.

Frank was always influenced by other instrumentalists whom he admired and Fillmore was in that category. Their time together in Weber's Band formed the basis for a lifelong friendship.

Frank Simon stayed with Weber's Band for five years. He was working with it in 1912 when his career took on a new and totally unexpected dimension.

The freemasonry of the music business was then and still is strong enough for word to travel along the bandstands and concert platforms whenever something or someone interesting develops. Frank was not only known to be good, he also had the reputation of being the sort of material other music outfits would go for. That was how Leopold Stokowski, on the threshold of his own international fame and then conductor of the Cincinnati Symphony Orchestra, made him an offer that was difficult for any serious musician to refuse: to join the orchestra. Frank would not be the only bandsman in the ensemble. The best musicians were delighted to be able to play for Stokowski during the winter season when bandsmen were usually out of work.

It was one of those offers that seemingly he would have been foolish to decline: the very notion of being a member of a great orchestra sounded marvelous and, doubtless, Sol and Bertha each revelled in the idea of their son, the symphony musician. It was great to *talk* about and would, ever after, look superb on the career resumé of the 23-year-old cornetist. But that would be as far as it went.

There was, before long, one inescapable fact that Frank Simon had to face: the amount of exposure available to a talented cornet or trumpet player in a symphony orchestra is extremely limited (*any* talented player, not just a super-talented one like himself). There were very few parts of the symphony repertoire calling for a trumpet solo and those that there were cannot be selected endlessly by even the most enthusiastic philohorn conductor. Worse still, the brass section simply did not have the work to do that was available to the strings, the kind of constant activity he was used to, to say nothing of the star status he believed he was achieving.

'I got fed up with just counting measures,' he said later, recalling the few moments when he would actually be called upon to play. Much more usually there were the never-ending sessions sitting on his chair, waiting for the point where he would at last be able to blow for a few minutes – and sometimes just a few seconds. As he said: 'I didn't want to sit and play a few notes and then count measures again.' On another occasion, he explained it in greater detail: 'I was dissatisfied with that job because in those days, they only played the great classics – Mozart, Beethoven, Brahms, Schubert and so on.'

His elder son David Simon now recalls: 'He was a born soloist. He wanted to sing.' It was something that William J. Kopp had probably warned him about, but it was also an experience he now had to try out for himself.

Herman Bellstedt had taught him enough about professionalism, which was no less important to him in his band than it was to Stokowski and his orchestra. Bellstedt, despite his sense of discipline, was 'interesting and entertaining'. But it was his devotion to work that really registered. On tour with Sousa in England, he had worked standing up, leaning on a high mantelpiece 'with his heavy overcoat on, writing music with the aid of the bad light of the short candle'.

Frank knew the stories and also knew that there were no compromises. He was now taking that old knowledge to his own new world. He went on tour with the orchestra – no symphony, even then, could exist entirely on the support of its own townspeople. But he somehow was not affected by the snobbery of being one of the Stokowski musicians. He always said that a good band could play as well as any symphony and he started saying it at this time.

In truth, he was a whole lot happier playing with Weber and when the band made its two trips to the West Coast, it was joy unbounded. He was no less ecstatic to know they were going to play at the Canadian Exhibition and at the Chicago Electrical Exposition.

The bandsmen worked in the sure knowledge that people traveled to hear them, sometimes as much as 30 miles, driving in open cars in their long white coats, goggles under tightly strapped caps or beneath the brims of the big hats worn by their wives and sweethearts (no self-respecting lady would dream of driving an automobile herself).

That had to be satisfaction – especially when Frank also had those opportunities with the band to brush up his German. Bertha liked that even more than he did. Now he was *speaking* the language, instead of merely understanding what his mother wanted and replying to her in English. But that was a mere incidental to his professional work. When he was making the kind of music he liked, the word 'satisfaction' had to be an understatement. It was all he wanted from life.

After two seasons he left the symphony orchestra to concentrate on being a bandsman. But there *were* problems in his life – or rather problems in his family's life. This time, much more serious than a mere case of polyps in his father's nose. In 1913, the Ohio River did something it was occasionally prone to do – it flooded. Not just a little water breaking the river banks but a deluge of a kind virtually unknown in most other parts of the United States. When it rains in the Cincinnati–Middletown area in winter it does so with a force strong enough to defeat an army. In the winter of that year it seemingly defeated the Simon family.

The traditionally below-zero cold and the snow in its wake were given the accompaniment of the most severe storms in living memory. Streets were awash when the banks of the river were breached, and buildings tumbled or were wrecked without actually falling down. One of those was the Simons' store. The family had virtually no insurance – or at least not enough of it to make any difference. They were ruined. Or rather, they would have been ruined had it not been for the earnings of their son Frank. Without giving them time to think about the situation any further, Frank made the downpayment for a new store – and bought sufficient bolts of cloth, cards of buttons and reels of thread to set them up in business again. Before very long, with their new premises over the railroad on First Avenue, they had an apartment above the store – which was soon to do better than the old one ever did.

Naturally, Frank was happy – as much for what it represented as for the achievement itself. 'I'd like to say,' he recalled in old age, 'that I came up the hard way, which I've been grateful for all my life. I had a lot of ambition and a lot of dedication. I worked hard.'

But in the course of that 'hard way' he had relieved his mother and father of the sort of pressure that would have been unbearable to them – and he had a job that was the pinnacle of success for a Cincinnati musician. Even in a band there were fewer opportunities for a soloist than for a mere cornetist in the line. But there were consolations. There was only one soloist, and that soloist *was* allowed to sing. For an emotional young man like Frank Simon, singing with his cornet was the best way he knew of expressing those emotions. He was an artist who felt he now had all that he needed; all that he had worked for.

Or so he thought. He soon got to know that there was more to come – a fact that came to light the moment he was called to Middletown's only telephone, a hand-cranked instrument in the care of the Libee Block at the corner of Central Avenue and Main Street. It was Herman Bellstedt on the other end of the phone.

'Hurry up down here,' he instructed his young pupil, 'I've got good news for you.'

That was all that Frank needed to know. He took the first available train to Cincinnati and walked over to Bellstedt's home in Clifton. It was as though another fairy had waved her wand in his direction. His old teacher asked Frank a simple, direct question: 'How would you like to join Sousa's Band?'

5 · *Marching Along*

Sousa *was* American band music. He was the Beethoven of the band – and the Irving Berlin and the Jerome Kern, too. He represented both the culture of band music and its popular appeal. To be invited to join the Sousa Band was the equivalent of a doctor being appointed to the staff of one of the world's great hospitals, a reporter offered a job on the best newspaper of the day, a lawyer being told he would appear before one of the most outstanding judges in the land.

John Philip Sousa was known throughout the world as the 'March King'. He had followed the example of Gilmore and set up a military-style band and had now far surpassed his mentor. Sousa's Band was originally called the New Marine Band. After leaving the US Marines where he had conducted the most famous military-style outfit in America, his agent and General Manager, David Blakely from Chicago, suggested the new name.

By the time the invitation to Simon to join the band arrived, Sousa had already made several international tours, had played before the crowned heads of Europe and had composed the best-known marches to which anyone in the world had ever tapped their feet. A Sousa tour was as much a part of the scene as the seasonal weather.

All over America, and in a great part of the world besides, Army and Navy bands led troops to the strains of 'El Capitan' and 'The Washington Post', and they had been doing so since 1892, when Sousa had directed his first concert on 26 September at Plainfield, New Jersey (two days after the death of Patrick Gilmore, with the old bandmaster's musical ode, 'The Voice of the Departed Soul' beginning the performance by way of tribute).

The troops in the Spanish–American War went into battle with 'The Liberty Bell March' ringing in their ears above the sound of gunfire. In more recent years there had been 'The Glory of the [Yankee] Navy' and, as befitted a man who had been the most eminent leader that the United States Marine Band had ever had, the official anthem of the corps, the 'Semper Fidelis March'.

Years earlier, in December 1904, *The New York Times* asked the question: 'Why is John Philip Sousa so popular in New York? The answer is, because he gives the people the music they want. Sousa is never afraid to play what is called "popular" music. The result is that he is always listened to by cheering crowds.' An anonymous critic, reporting a concert at the Metropolitan Opera House the previous April, had noted: 'A concert for the common people was what John Philip Sousa offered last night – that is a concert for the masses who have no inherent objections to an occasional strain of ragtime or a dashing, swinging march of modern vintage.'

Sousa wrote marches for high-school cadets and marches for the Shriners. He wrote marches with threatening, militaristic titles like 'The Thunderer' and gentle pieces like 'The Bride-Elect March'. He wrote operettas and novels. He also ran a tight business, helped along the way by Blakely. In a November 1892 programme for a concert at Boston, Massachusetts (tickets, 50 cents, 75 cents and $1), Blakely wrote:

> I am introducing to the American public by far the finest military band ever heard in the country. This is not my own assertion alone. It is endorsed by the enthusiastic encomiums of the press and people wherever the new band has appeared, and every person glancing at the testimony of the following pages, cannot fail to be convinced that by hearing the programme to be given by this band in this city, he will listen to what the *New York Herald* characterized after listening to its first performance in New York, as 'without exaggeration, the best concert of the kind that New York remembers'.

Overseas, people were saying much the same thing. In 1903, the same newspaper reported from London:

> The audience at the concert given yesterday at Windsor Castle by Sousa's band numbered about 60 persons, including the King and Queen, the Prince and Princess of Wales, Princess Victoria . . . His

> Majesty [Edward VII] asked for several encores, which included the 'Washington Post' and 'Hands Across The Sea.' He desired as the final piece, 'The Star Spangled Banner', throughout the playing of which the King and court stood.

But it was at home that the real Sousa impact was felt. Single-handed, he changed the look and the sound of the traditional American band. After Sousa, it was no longer a mainly brass outfit, like the industrial bands in England and the German ensembles which had been so influential on his side of the Atlantic. He reduced the brass and the percussion and introduced many more woodwind instruments. He it was who first brought a harp into the band world. Through him, the concert band came into its own – and became his own. More important still, he became everyone's idea of what a band should sound like.

But above all, John Philip Sousa epitomized patriotism – which was typical of so many people from immigrant stock. (He himself was born in Washington, DC, but his father was Portuguese and his mother German.) When bands played 'The Stars and Stripes Forever', audiences stood to attention. In years to come, it was declared by Congress to be the National March. By the time Frank Simon came on the scene it was already the *magnum opus* of all the Sousa band concerts – with the instrumentalists taking their places at the front of the platform, standing to attention and looking for all the world as though they were about to exchange their instruments for rifles.

The band always appeared to be a military organization. Out of respect and the custom of the time, Sousa's men always referred to him as 'Mr Sousa' or 'The Governor'. According to Paul Bierley, 'Because of Sousa's kindly concern for his men, while demanding their best musically and personal conduct of the highest standard, the bandsmen developed a loyalty towards him that could be found in no other musical organization.'

They wore military-style uniforms, and had to wear them whether they were 'on duty', playing or not. Once fitted and worn, psychologically the plain dark tunic became like a second skin. Herman Bellstedt, for instance, was so acclimatized to his that the regime and the discipline of Sousa would stay with him for the rest of his life. He still kept in touch with his former colleagues in the band, and when he wrote his arrangements it was always as a result of direct talks with John Philip himself.

Then, one day in 1914, when the world was beginning to assess the consequences of the great powers eyeing each other over the precipice of war, a war that President Woodrow Wilson promised would be a foreign conflict in which the United States would never get involved, Bellstedt presented Frank with his great opportunity. Frank himself recalled how it all happened: 'He said to me: "Mr Sousa's first cornetist and assistant conductor, Herbert L. Clarke, will retire soon and I told Mr Sousa you could step into his shoes".'

It was a very satisfying thing to hear. It was also a great compliment. He was not only recommending his pupil for a great job, he was recommending the job to his pupil. More significantly than anything else, the recommendation was for what had been his *own* job.

Once Bellstedt himself had retired, Clarke became perhaps the finest cornet player in the world. Even Frank himself admitted that he could never *quite* reach his standards, no matter how much he aspired to them. Now he was being invited to, as Bellstedt said, almost literally step into Clarke's shoes.

This was an offer that seemed to come straight from heaven. Herbert L. Clarke could play a chromatic scale of three octaves four times through in one breath. That was an achievement which made people sit with their mouths open. That Frank Simon could be compared with someone of that standard – and compared, he knew, he would be – was a kind of praise that didn't come frequently to any musician.

Clarke was so conscious of his role as a – no, as *the* – cornet virtuoso, he was determined there should be no sour notes to spoil that status. He had already decided that when he reached the age of 50 he would put down his horn before people started asking him to do so. The time to go was while he still had the stamina and ability to play his cornet – perfectly. He was wise and conceited enough to realize that he himself would probably be more distressed by anything less than that perfection than would his audience, but he was not going to give anyone the chance to hear him when he was anything but at his peak. He estimated that the hill would have been climbed and the downward trek begun in three years. That being so, at 47 he felt the obligation to find a successor and spend those 36 months ahead planning for the future.

For most people who knew anything about such things that sounded more like whistling in the wind than cornet-playing in a theatre. It was certainly easier said than done. Sousa himself would have been right to think so. He honestly believed he would never be able to replace Clarke – who, in addition to being the mainstay of Sousa's Band as an instrumentalist, had also written a much-requested composition called 'Bride of the Waves'. But Herman Belstedt convinced the 'Governor' that he had a worthy candidate in the youngster from Cincinnati called Frank Simon. Whether from contentment or desperation, Sousa took the advice and offered the job.

The greatest compliment of all was that the invitation to Frank was unconditional. It was extended, via Bellstedt, without an audition. Yet even in those circumstances, Frank was not going to dance any pirouette and shout from the Cincinnati rooftops. He did not exactly play hard to get. But he was the one who was insisting on the conditions. He had sufficient confidence – some might have defined it as chutzpah – to say he would accept. But only if the financial arrangements could be sorted out first.

The truth of the matter is that it was not only Frank speaking. Julius Simon stood in his Noah's Ark store and insisted that Frank negotiate a deal before accepting. The young man was clear in his own mind about it, he wanted the job so badly he was ready to take it for nothing. But that was not the sort of language you spoke in Noah's Ark – certainly not when you were the one doing the buying. As far as he was concerned, Frank was up for sale and there was no reason why he should not get a top price for the merchandise.

Sousa offered him $35 a week. Frank asked for $75. That was no more than he was earning already. It was a convincing argument and he won. The weekly $75 was his. Sousa could easily afford to pay it. He was already a millionaire, probably a multi-millionaire, a club that did not have too many members before the First World War.

Even so, few people before had ever had the temerity to argue with a pay offer from John Philip Sousa. Being taken on without an audition had never happened previously either – and the only time it would ever happen again would be as a result of a Frank Simon intervention. Now, however, in 1914 it was Frank himself who was being offered the chance of a lifetime, although initially not to take over from Clarke but to sit by his side and to act as his deputy.

That chance began with the first rehearsal. Frank had never been to New York before, but now, at Carnegie Hall, it was all happening. The Sousa practice was to rehearse there for four weeks at the beginning of each season and then to move off on tour. The hall may have been more used to echoing to the sound of the New York Philharmonic or the symphony orchestras from other cities in the United States and from abroad who played there as a sign of their prestige, but when Sousa was at Carnegie Hall, no one thought about that other kind of music. Once there, the hall was all his.

The 'Governor' would have been insulted had it been any other way. He frequently found himself compared with a symphony orchestra, if not always flatteringly. He always had a ready answer:

> Believing . . . that entertainment is of more real value to the world than technical education in music appreciation, I would not accept the symphonic orchestra as my medium. Of course, the cabaret orchestra's limitations were too great . . . [and] the military band was too vague in its instrumentation, but a new combination, unhampered by tradition, which could get at the hearts of the people, was my destination.

Frank knew it was his destination, too. Carnegie Hall was merely the railroad station on the way. But he had to be sure his suitcases were packed. They were, but not just with his cornet and the clothes and shaving gear he needed for the outward journey. He took with him to that initial 'blooding' a photograph from his mentor. It was inscribed: 'To my pupil Frank Simon with the best wishes of Herman Bellstedt, August 2 1914.' Two days later, Europe was at war. But as he mounted the platform at Carnegie Hall that day, the only war that really bothered Frank Simon was the one with his nerves.

He was given a show to watch and hear before being called on to perform with Sousa for the first time. (He knew that, appointment or not, if he failed to deliver now the promised contract would never be signed.) 'I listened spellbound,' he later wrote, 'to the great Mr Clarke play a solo. When he had finished, Mr Sousa, a perfectionist, said to me, "Young man, would you like to play now?"'

What went through his mind as he contemplated the task immediately before him, the 'young man' revealed years later to his sons. It was the simple matter that his whole future depended on this performance. He *had* to make good with it. Not just because he was afraid of that contract being rescinded, more because of all the sacrifices of his mother. Like a drowning man seeing his life rushing before him, as he went up on the stage everything Bertha had ever done for him came to the surface.

It was the most important day in the band's rehearsal schedule. Sousa took three days to rehearse his band before he got around to the cornet soloist. When at last it came to Simon's turn, Sousa asked him what he was going to play. 'La Mandolinata', he said. It was a piece that had been written by Herman Bellstedt and was dedicated to his pupil Frank Simon, but it was already a favorite solo piece in the Sousa repertoire and the perfect test for the man whom he had apparently employed on trust – and who could almost as easily have been fired without playing a good note. But it was not to happen.

Sousa might or might not have noticed Frank's legs shake as he took his instrument from its case and put it to his lips. As he stood up, he glanced into the serried ranks of the (for the most part) empty seats in the auditorium. He might have preferred it had these seats been entirely empty but they were not. The composer and the bandmaster Victor Herbert, the impresario Mr Naon Franco and the conductor Walter Damrosch were all friends of Sousa's, who together founded ASCAP, the American Society of Composers, Authors and Publishers. They were among the top names in popular American music and had come to hear Sousa's final rehearsal.

Frank went on: 'I put my cornet to my lips, closed my eyes and played "La Mandolinata". I finished in a trance like a punch-drunk fighter and was snapped out of it by the bandsmen stamping their feet.' Plainly, his new colleagues more than approved of what they heard. Sousa certainly did. Immediately after the performance the 'Governor' said to him, 'Young man, you have a lifetime position with this band.' At which point, Frank collapsed. He had fainted. Sixty or more years later, the eminent violinist Isaac Stern said: 'No one is a real artist unless he falls on his face in Carnegie Hall.' So Frank was proving his artistry very early on in his career.

In Frank's case, it was worth all the trauma – but for three days he was in hospital suffering from shock. It was a typical Simon reaction. Again and again in his life, the important events would be followed by an almost complete collapse. But he always recovered in time and he did so on this occasion, with one ambition – to achieve all his other ambitions.

Three days later, Frank caught up with the Sousa tour. The March King was a born showman (and, as we shall see, sportsman, too; he was national amateur trapshooting champion of the USA). But he was also a consummate musician – in his own peculiar way. He was the kind who regarded everything he did as a tribute to his patriotism. Perhaps that was only to be expected from a man who had joined the Marines at 14 and later conducted its band – soon to be given the title it would carry thereafter, 'The President's Own'.

Frank saw a great deal of that militaristic influence in the next few years, like the time two years after he himself joined the band when his conductor volunteered for the Army. A war with Mexico was expected after the raids of Pancho Villa's bandits across the US border, but it never amounted to anything and the 'Governor' was not called. In 1917 when America did finally enter the First World War, Sousa became the Navy's oldest ever recruit. At 62, he was welcomed by his band playing their hearts out for their newly commissioned lieutenant – salary \$1 a month. His principal job, he was told by the Navy department, was to train young bandsmen.

But the war lasted just over a year and he had his eye on the 'real' Sousa Band all the time. Frank Simon needed no convincing just what a great opportunity it was to play with Sousa; not just to play but to have the promise of a future at the top with him.

But nothing could alter the fact that it was an exacting life. Frank began touring – the first of five transcontinental tours. He learned the routine of the most prestigious outfit in the band business. More important still, he learned from Herbert Clarke. 'Twice a day he would play one of his own solos,' he later remembered, 'finishing on either an E flat or G above the staff. Never once in five years did he ever fail.' But his relationship with Clarke at first was just part of the picture. 'To play with Sousa,' he said soon after joining the band, 'was heaven on earth'. As we shall see, however, sooner or later heaven would come down to earth and he would have to partly rethink that notion. He never changed his mind about Clarke, however.

Almost immediately on joining the band a close friendship developed between the 47-year-old and the newcomer just about half his age. More than that, however, Frank Simon could add a new name to the roster of teachers who had guided his career. Q. C. Buckles had given him the groundwork. William Kopp had allowed him to grow up. Herman Bellstedt had paid him the compliment of treating him as favored student along with the ultimate award of the recommendation to Sousa. But it was Herbert Clarke – 'Bert' from then on, a gesture of equality he would never fail to appreciate – who provided his first real on-the-job training. Never before had he been so close to a man he admired more than anyone else in his profession, and never before had he been able to observe every lip movement, every touch of the valves, measuring the length of each note and acknowledging all the time that this was the sweetest music he had ever heard.

Twenty-five-year-olds, if they are any good, have all the confidence they think they are going to need. The doubts come later. Whether at this stage Frank knew in his heart that he might find it difficult to become Clarke's equal or simply that he was being given a never-to-be repeated opportunity to study the man he would soon replace, no one can now be sure. What is certain is that he felt he was improving with every concert, benefiting from imbibing an atmosphere that he loved.

This was a time for changes in the band world and Frank Simon was well aware he was in the midst of them. Only two years previously, Edwin Franko Goldman – who was equally a great rival and great friend in times to come – had changed the name of his Goldman's New York Band to simply the Goldman Band and was exciting an ever-growing body of fans. But there was nothing anywhere to compare with Sousa, playing with him and receiving the plaudits of his unique number of enthusiasts.

To Frank, it was not the easiest job in the world, playing sometimes four concerts a day in a far-away town, sometimes two in different places, a matinee in one city, an evening performance in another, frequently with a totally different program for each. Sousa was a demanding taskmaster, although those who knew him always denied he was a martinet. He was just as much a taskmaster to himself as he was a bandmaster to his audiences – and he expected nothing less of his men. It was not enough that they should abstain from both womanizing and heavy alcohol – 'drunkenness disgusts me,' he said – but they were required to have a work ethic as strong as his own. He himself, however, had both a will to work and a talent that few others could be expected to emulate. Frank had joined the band soon after Sousa had completed his 1914 march, 'Columbia's Pride'. In the next few years he produced 'The Chantyman's March' (1918), 'America First' and 'Boy Scouts of America' (both 1916) as well as 'Anchor and Star' (1918).

In between concerts and tours Sousa wrote 15 operettas, 15 suites, dozens of songs – including 'Boots' (1916) and 'The Toast' (1918) – 14 waltzes, and a whole slew of incidental music, suites, humoresques and fantasies. There were arrangements and transcriptions, articles and even seven novels. In his first, *The Fifth String*, which sold 50,000 copies after its appearance in 1912 he told a story about a violinist from Tuscany ('A tipsy man is never interesting . . . He isn't a bad sort for a violinist'). It was clearly a good platform for Sousa's various philosophies. It also made him a great deal of money. As he once said, he 'kills time by sprinkling gold dust on paper'.

His instrumentalists had to be content with the money they earned while playing. The men would get on a train in the morning, go to an hotel in the afternoon (two of them to a room) and then go on immediately to the concert hall. Exhausted, they would climb into their temporary beds – after having placed their trousers under the mattress to ensure the kind of creases Mr Sousa required of his bandsmen – and wake up early enough to shine their shoes to what the 'Governor' regarded as his minimum standard before breakfast and the next train to the next town. (There were times when Sousa brought a trunk full of shoe blacking onto the stage so that his men could shine their shoes before their rehearsal.)

There were precise Sousa standards. His marches had to be played the Sousa way. Nothing else was acceptable. Just before Frank's own death he wrote a series of what he described as 'rehearsal techniques', illustrating both how the marches should sound and the more usual mistakes.

Frank had soaked it all up in his earliest sessions with the band. Nevertheless he was not sure that he could cope with it all. It was not the pressure, that never-ending grind that always seemed hardest at the beginning, when there was only more of the same to look forward to for months ahead and which his more senior colleagues knew so well. It was the physical pressure on his mouth.

After three weeks, he was ready to pack up. 'I can't stand the pace,' he told his senior colleague, Herbert Clarke. He really believed he had no choice but to go home. After all, what use was he to the band with lips so swollen that his whole face seemed distorted? In addition, there was a corn on the inside of one lip. 'Yes, a real corn,' he remembered. 'I was pulling it off my lip every morning with a pair of tweezers.'

There was nothing to do but report to Sousa. The 'Governor' would be the first to spot the trouble – a man who could sense a flute coming in a fraction of a second too early was not going to miss a wrong note emanating from the front-row second chair in the cornet section. Clarke's apart, there was not an instrument more important in the whole outfit.

Sousa was no more sympathetic than should have been expected of a man whose sense of duty and discipline sometimes made him seem close to a slave driver. Frank might have made the mistake of appearing to ask for sympathy. 'Mr Sousa,' he said with no more thought than asking a fellow-bandsman to pass over the sheet music, 'I'm afraid I'm a failure.' That was a terrible thing to say. No one who had made the Sousa Band could have possibly been a failure. To say that he was one was almost to impugn the integrity of Sousa himself in bringing him into the fold. But he went on to explain his situation. 'My lips are so tired, so swollen and dead that I can't play.'

Clearly Sousa did not like to hear that. Simon never forgot his 'Governor's' reaction – to the point that, in one of his few asides about another musician that was not entirely laudatory, he described it as 'one of the most nonsensical and inane things I ever heard him say'. What Sousa did say to his new man was 'I don't see why a cornetist can't play as long at one time as a violinist'. Sousa thought he was speaking from experience. In between being an apprentice with the US Marine Band – his father was a member of the band at the time – and later conducting it himself, Sousa had worked as a violinist in theater orchestras in Washington and Philadelphia.

To Frank Simon the conductor's reaction was not just insensitive, it was painful – and stupid. 'I thought it was ridiculous,' he wrote in his commentary on the Sousa rehearsal techniques (subtitled, *My Years With the Sousa Band*), 'I went to my chair on stage and cried tears of sorrow and despair.' Frank never lost that emotional response to what he considered the really important things in his life.

It was Herbert Clarke who made him see reason – and accommodate the 'Governor' at the same time. He gave him what he later described – *à la Reader's Digest* – as 'the best advice I ever had'. Clarke told him: 'Now, don't you play a note tonight and in the morning come over and see me. I want to talk with you.'

They did meet the next morning. Clarke told him: 'Frank, I want to tell you that you are a beautiful player when you are fresh, but you will never be fresh in this band.' He was not referring to Simon's mien and certainly not to his sex life. 'You know,' he said, 'I have gone through everything you are going through and a bit more. You see, I had to go through this same experience to be able to find a way to build up my endurance to do this work.' And then came the advice. 'It has taken me years to do this. In the first place, Frank, you play with a little too much pressure on the lip.' So he promised to show him what he had in mind. For the first time, the colleague became the teacher – and the friend. He took the young Simon to his dressing room and gave him his lesson. He showed him how to develop the lip muscles and to strengthen his embouchure 'so that you can withstand this work'. It was, Simon later reported, the greatest cornet lesson he had ever had. 'He showed me how to exercise the muscles of my face, just like you would the muscles in your arms, to make them firm and strong.' And he did something more, something that Sousa would certainly not have appreciated. He told him to sit in on the next concert but not play a note. It was as though he were inciting the youngster to go on strike – three weeks after joining the band, an act of professional suicide. 'If Mr Sousa looks at you, just ignore him, pay no attention to him.'

Frank was no fool. He said it would be difficult. To him, Clarke's advice was like saying that if he saw his mother falling over in the street he would not go to pick her up. But he took that best advice he ever had. 'You do what I'm telling you,' Clarke cautioned, and Frank did. For 24 hours, he did not play a note. The swelling started to go down while the lip turned black and blue.

After that, he gradually started practicing techniques, Herbert L. Clarke style. 'I used to hear him do it himself for about 30 to 40 minutes a day in his dressing room. Mr Clarke had developed a warm-up that was terrific. I used it myself and later I taught it to *my* students.'

Gradually his lip muscles strengthened – and were better than they had ever been before. 'A strong embouchure was in the making and I stayed on the rest of the year without any further lip trouble,' he said. As he also said: 'I owe a lot to this man, Mr Clarke. Endurance is 90 per cent of the skill of playing well.'

But there was more of the advice to learn. He *had* been a little too ambitious. 'Most young people,' he explained, 'will put the mouthpiece up to their embouchure and set their mouth in one position and try to play all over the register of the cornet. That was my trouble.' So Clarke had a suggestion for him. 'Pronounce your vowels,' he said. He was not giving him lessons in elocution. Not Herbert Clarke. 'A, E, I, O, U,' he said pronouncing the sounds perfectly. 'Isn't your mouth in five different positions for each sound?' he asked his colleague/pupil. Frank had to agree that yes, it was. 'Now try to say your vowels without moving your mouth.' Even Frank Simon, who had learned to do remarkable things with his mouth, could not manage that.

It was a lesson he would never forget – and he practiced his vowels every day that he played his horn. As he explained: 'In many respects you don't eat the same things at every meal; you change the diet from meal to meal. It gives variety and helps the appetite. Thus, by doing these different vowel constructions and the exercises that he wrote that went with each, you could really build an embouchure.'

From that time on, Frank loved every minute of his first years with Sousa. Older bandsmen might have begun to feel a little jaded, but young Mr Simon was still excited by every performance and by all the attendant activity. It was a chance to see more of a country's energy he had only just begun to tap. Even if he did know a city only by its main band arena and by the hotel in which he stayed, it provided him with the start of the fund of stories with which he regaled his friends for the rest of his life.

Bertha and Solomon were more proud of their son than ever before – even if secretly, they might have been happier to have him constantly closer to home. But they knew that this was precisely the kind of success he had always sought.

Clarke became the greatest influence of all in Frank Simon's career as a cornetist. Sousa, far and away, was the mentor as far as conducting a band was concerned, although he had learned much classical conducting under Stokowski. From the day he first heard a crowd of musicians play a Sousa march, it achieved in his mind a position close to holy writ.

They were rehearsed and taught meticulously before ever reaching the public. There could be *only one* way of playing a Sousa march – and that was the way Sousa played it. Not the way Sousa wrote it but the way he played it. Sousa wrote his marches and then decided, on the field, how they should be played. The written score was little more than an outline of the piece as it was supposed to be performed by his bandsmen. This was one reason why he did not like using the printed scores of other musicians' work. He did not like their instrumentation and hated the way the Germans arranged their music. It was altogether 'too brassy' for his tastes.

Certainly, there was a distinct Sousa timing as there was a distinct Sousa sound, a certain stress on notes that could be imperceptible to the people who paid for a deckchair at one of his concerts or who cheered as the band marched by in a parade. But Sousa knew when a note should be played long or short, when the flutes had to come in a fraction of a second before the drums and *precisely* how and when they interacted with each other or overlapped. Just before his own death, Frank commented: 'I doubt if any contemporary performance could match the original composer and his band. You don't have the dynamics, the accents as they should be, the notes, the difference in the volume of tone, when the brass drops out, where the clarinet section drops an octave and then they reverse it. So many things that they did to make it colorful.'

Not that Sousa did not appreciate another musician's interpretation of a piece. If he thought it was sufficiently 'artistic' he was frequently happy to adopt one as part of his repertoire. But what he was really concerned about, his almost fanatical interest, was his own work. Writing in his *Rehearsal Techniques* about the 'flagship' march, 'The Stars and Stripes Forever', Frank wrote:

> At the beginning, the band is full and fortissimo, noting that the last two measures are marked with a black marcato [strong accent]. In the downbeat of the first strain is another black marcato. Be sure to observe the eighth rest that follows; this is important. I have heard some bands do it without the rest and I am sure that if Mr Sousa wanted it played that way, he would have written it so.

For seven years, Frank would play that march with Sousa – 'and he always insisted on this rest being observed. The rest actually increases the weight of the preceding note.' Then he added: 'Believe me, it is the little things about this march that make it great. Piccolos are tacit on this first trio. At the last half note of this strain for the lower brass (before breakup) the full band enters solid and full . . .'

Simon was thrown into the midst of it all from the moment he put on his Sousa uniform for the first time and picked up that cornet. He enjoyed hearing the applause of the audience, stronger and more powerful than he had ever heard with either Kopp or Weber. It all had a quality about it he could not have anticipated.

But he was also fairly quickly involved in the problems of sitting in the front row of a prestige outfit like Sousa's. They could not contemplate getting away with certain practices that other bands might have considered unavoidable. Nothing was unavoidable to Sousa. He took perfection as a matter of course. Anything less was never acceptable.

Frank had discovered that early on, when he found himself in the middle of a crisis that required fast thinking from both himself and Herbert Clarke, and with which they coped better than during the previous 'unfortunate' incident. This involved one of the two sopranos Sousa always had in his team – women whom he treated with the kid gloves of a headmaster suddenly put in charge of a convent. The girls were given respect and every consideration – which principally amounted to keeping them away from instrumentalists who were barely allowed to be close enough to smell their perfume. Where women were concerned, the bandsmen were not given a moment of indulgence. Swearing was forbidden and the very notion of their touching a girl was not even considered. It would result in their never again touching an *instrument* – not in Sousa's band, at least.

On the other hand, the 'Governor' himself quite liked to be seen with his girl singers, who had to be as decorative to look at as they were beautiful to listen to. But whether this was simply because he was concerned for their safety or for his own, one cannot be sure. Certainly, he always insisted on bringing a chaperone along when he took them out for an evening – which he almost invariably did when he was on tour.

Frank came face to face with this in his first season in the shape of one Grace Hoffman, the band's coloratura soprano. 'She sang just like a nightingale,' Simon recalled. But in Pittsburgh, on that first coast-to-coast tour, the nightingale was not giving out the notes Sousa decreed – as severe a sin as a band failing to take a rest with 'The Stars and Stripes Forever'.

The stage manager had come out as the band was assembled on stage and announced that the vocal solo that evening would have to be cut somewhat. Neither Frank nor Herbert Clarke had previously accompanied this piece or the violin solo that was to follow, so they studied the music closely and followed it totally – omitting the pieces to be cut. The rest of the band did, too. The only person who did not do that was Miss Hoffman – who forgot. Or at least, that is what she claimed. As Simon recalled:

> There were 5000 people in the auditorium and when we heard what was happening we all stopped playing. She was singing all by herself and she kept it going. And [he added] I thought, 'My God, where will this ever end?' Apparently, she wasn't a bit flustered and kept right on singing as though it was supposed to be that way. Finally, Henry Heidelberg picked up his flute and started to play. Then Maurice Prague, who was first horn with Toscanini, started and finally everyone was in and we all finished together. It seemed like an age that she was singing all by herself. I'll bet it seemed longer to her.

Just what Sousa thought of it is not on record. But what he thought of indiscipline most certainly is. Sometimes this extended beyond the footlights to the audience. One of the great successes of Sousa's Band was the fact that its appeal stretched across the generations. Just occasionally, however, his audience did not show quite the deference he expected, if not for himself, then for his music. That was all too clear to him one evening in 1915, when the band gave a matinee concert in the University of Colorado at Boulder. Two young boys were in the audience for this show, taking place on the return trip from California to New York. Throughout the performance the boys talked. This was sacrilege to both the 'Governor' and his players. Other members of the audience felt much the same way about it, too. Since Sousa could hear pins drop when he required silence, the discordant sound of the constant chat could not be missed, and he did not miss it. But he did not lose his temper or even embarrass the youngsters. He simply turned to them, smiled and said: 'Would you two young boys come up here, please?' As Simon recalled: 'They came up very boldly, right on stage, when Mr Sousa said to them, "I want you to go straight out that door over there and do it right now." You know, that was it. They marched out and that was the end of that.'

Soon afterwards, Frank Simon stepped into Clarke's shoes for the first time. The soloist was sent to hospital suffering from ulcers. There was nothing for it but for Frank to take over his solo spot that day – 'The Floral Waltz' by Cunnard seemed a good piece to use. There was no sense in simply doing what Clarke himself would have played. He had his own repertoire which would have been impossible to replicate, so Frank chose a piece he had performed many times with the Weber Band.

Unfortunately, as the pieces were handed out, it was obvious that this was new even to Sousa. The piece was played. The audience clapped and Frank sat down – but not fast enough to miss the 'Governor' saying to him: 'Young man. I want you to dig a hole six foot deep and put that waltz in it.' That, as he noted, was the end of the 'Floral Waltz' by Cunnard. But he still had to play an encore – this time, one chosen by Sousa himself. 'This kept you on your toes. I had 66 solos memorized and I didn't care which one he picked.'

Of course, the 'March King' – a title bestowed on him by British impresarios on his world tour on which they embarked before Frank joined the band – was constantly keeping his instrumentalists on their toes. Frank, like every other member of the band (even those who were older than he was), was always 'Young man', a title Sousa bestowed at rehearsals or when he walked down the trains carrying the band to their next engagement. Frank seemed to appreciate the high and sometimes severe dedication to work demanded of him. Most of the time, by all accounts, he and Sousa got on like a concert hall on fire.

In 1915, Frank's first full year with the band, they played at the Panama Pacific Exposition in San Francisco, when Sousa proudly introduced his new cornet player to the French composer Camille Saint-Saens, a great admirer of the American band movement. To be fair, the person the Frenchman had really come to meet was Herbert Clarke. He had taken time off from his own concert – the performance of a major work written specially for the Exposition, played by the city's symphony orchestra and directed by one of the conductors of the Metropolitan Opera – to hear Sousa, and was amazed by the precision of what he termed the 'piston soloist'. He asked to meet Clarke and his assistant, whose skill he watched with the kind of admiration reserved by one brother professional musician for another.

'Neither he nor I understood a word of French,' Frank remembered. When he finished, the interpreter said: 'Mr Clarke, the master has never heard a piston played so magnificently, so artistically. Never in his life has he ever heard that last note you produced on any brass instrument.' As Frank also recalled: 'Well, the band broke out in applause. It was a thrilling moment. You know me, I sat there and cried for joy and the glory that had come to my friend, a very modest man, Herbert L. Clarke. Mr Clarke was also thrilled, I am sure.'

There could not have been much doubt about that. For Herbert Clarke, it was just praise. For Sousa and for every member of his band, Frank Simon included, it was the perfect example of the obvious link between two distinct branches of the music business.

The way Clarke was being fêted was no more than was just, Frank believed. Everything that Herman Bellstedt had been to him, Clarke now was, too, although the relationship was more one of colleagues, if not equals. It did not mean that he was not constantly learning. 'He took care of me like a father would a son,' Simon later wrote about this 'very modest man and . . . fine gentleman'.

Frank was constantly learning at Clarke's elbow, if not his feet, and it was Clarke who introduced him to the work of McCoy, a particularly important composer in his field at this time; a piece called 'Lala Rook'. As much trouble came from playing this as from a chorus line of sopranos all suddenly deciding to sing different parts of the score simultaneously. They were playing in an open-air bandstand, 100 feet from San Francisco Bay, in the area known as 'the Court of the Universe', when help came to hand. A gust of wind blew over the music stands and sent the sheet music floating away into space.

Until that point, no one had really been able to do very much with the music which, despite hours of rehearsal, remained almost impossible to play. Frank remembered turning to his senior partner as they both saw the papers sailing away into some blessed void, and saying: 'Mr Clarke, the Lord is sure with us here, isn't he?' And when both men laughed, neither was thinking entirely of the fact that they themselves had not been blown into the bay along with the impenetrable music.

It was while at this exposition that Sousa composed his 'Pathfinder of Panama' march, and then prepared for a tour of the North-West and West before spending a month at Willow Grove in Pennsylvania. Then there were two more weeks at the Pittsburgh Exposition and finally several months playing in the musical spectacular *Hip Hip Hooray* at the New York Hippodrome, sometimes giving a full concert on stage, part of the time doubling for the pit orchestra. It was sufficiently significant for Sousa to take a whole page in his publicity brochure featuring the event – headed 'Sousa's Unparalleled Engagement at the New York Hippodrome'. 'Sousa's band,' declared the brochure, 'enjoys the distinction of being the only musical organization that ever played for an entire season in New York City and also [had] the distinction of playing for this period in the largest theatrical structure in the world.'

The stay at the Hippodrome was divided over two years between September 1915 and June 1916 and again between October 1916 and

March 1917, and was then followed by an extensive tour. There was perhaps just one feature of the tour which Frank Simon himself did not appreciate – Sousa's own tribute to the theater which was plainly doing him and his band so much good. 'The New York Hippodrome March' was played twice daily for one and a half years. 'I got tired of it,' Simon later reported. 'If ever Mr Sousa wrote an uninspired march, this was it. He wrote it on the train in about half an hour. I saw him writing it down.'

So when the Hippodrome March was laid to rest, Frank for one was delighted. He always said that the 'Bride Elect' was a much more polished work of which he *never* got tired. 'One of my favorites,' he declared.

Even if the music tended to pall, certainly the stay at the Hippodrome, which was the largest theatrical structure in the world, was important. During the run the band accompanied some of the greatest singers in the world, among them the Dames Nellie Melba and Maggie Teyte and the Japanese prima donna Tamakio Miura. Other times, it played for as diverse an assemblage of talent as Bert Williams, the black comedian (who had to make up his face with burnt cork like a minstrel because his skin was not considered dark enough) with whom Frank shared a dressing room, Mary Pickford and Charlie Chaplin and Anna Pavlova and the specialty dancers Vernon and Irene Castle (who were immortalized in the film of their life by Fred Astaire and Ginger Rogers). This was one of the most spectacular performances in which this band of spectacles was ever involved, although with Charles Dillingham (who, along with the Shuberts and Florenz Ziegfeld, was one of the outstanding stage producers of his day but with the reputation of being the nicest human being of the lot) in charge of the whole thing, that was hardly surprising.

One of the most remarkable features of the show was the 'March of the States', which in turn became the 'Sisterhood of the States' and then the 'Ballet of the States' – with dancing girls wearing what were thought to be appropriate costumes for the states they represented. Miss Ohio, for instance, was dressed as a black-eye pea; Miss Kansas was a sunflower. The imagination did not have to be extraordinarily stretched to work out the other designs. The music sounded as good as the girls looked – written especially by Sousa himself.

Frank was delighted to be part of it all – as was the audience, who loved the final embrace from Sousa for his featured soprano. The man who was very proper and straitlaced adored the theatricality of public affection. His 62nd birthday came during the show's run and the employees of the theater and the band gave him a present they considered suitable. Frank was among the subscribers to a loving cup made up of dimes – 1200 of the coins, one for each employee. During the show's second year Sousa himself completed his last operetta, *The Irish Dragoon*, and still found time to volunteer for war service.

If he could do all that, why should his musicians have any easier time of it? But he did encourage them to play sport – like helping to make up Sousa's own baseball team. The luckier members of the band sometimes joined him on his trapshooting and horse-riding expeditions as well. A healthy body, he clearly believed, was the best instrument of all.

What he did not do a great deal of was recording. It was, he said, 'canned music' (coining the term is a credit Sousa does not usually get). He hated the artificial atmosphere of the recording studio and detested the tinny results. It was nothing like the noise he made in a live performance and he did not think it did his reputation any good at all. In later years, the Sousa Band would play for records, but in few of them did John Philip Sousa have any active participation.

Probably his greatest contribution to the kind of music he made was to influence his men. Frank was one of the principal beneficiaries of this. Sousa encouraged his young cornetist to play as well as he knew he was capable of playing – always holding out the promise that when Herbert Clarke did finally decide to go, Clarke's job and his chair would be Simon's own.

6 · *The First Chair*

Frank was ready to take what he was offered, both the first cornetist's chair in his own right and all the opportunities it brought. It had been largely recognized that Herbert Clarke had no peer. With all the enthusiasm and self-confidence of his youth – his parents might have dubbed it 'chutzpah' – Frank Simon was going to take Clarke's place metaphorically as well as in fact. Instantly, on his appointment, he had new notepaper printed. It proclaimed at its head: 'World's Premier Cornet Soloist.' And he went on to prove it.

He knew there was no other way – from the moment he got the letter telling him that the 'chair' was his. It came from Edwin Clarke, who in addition to being Herbert's brother, was now manager of the band. 'Dear Frank,' the letter began, 'Herbert has resigned the Sousa Band to take a position at Huntsville, Ontario, Canada, conducting the band of the Anglo-Canadian Leather Company. Who would you like as a side partner?'

He did not really want to be asked or to hear anything else. 'Well, you know, that was a moment of greatness for me,' he later wrote. 'At last I was to become solo cornetist of the Sousa Band. I hated to see Herbert go.' There was a little white lie to accompany the words. 'I would have been satisfied to sit with him the rest of my days with the Sousa Band, but now that he was gone this was a tremendous opportunity, a high honor for me.'

He would not have been satisfied with anything of the kind. He itched to take on the chair and all it represented. But there were probably mixed feelings. Clarke was going to be missed – by Frank along with everyone else. Once Clarke actually stopped sounding his horn, it became a matter of simple fact. There *was* no other cornetist who was still playing to match him, and that was the case abroad as in America.

If Frank caused less of a stir than might have been anticipated, it was simply a question of degree. People at Sousa concerts went in the certain assurance that they were going to see the best. There was no room in the outfit for anyone who was not at the peak of his profession, and at the same time it was assumed that players who were at that peak would automatically find their way into the band, as sure as swans found their own lakes after their seasonal migration thousands of miles away. Frank Simon was a fine swan and the Sousa Band his very own private waterway.

It was also a highly profitable one. The solo cornetist was the star of the band. Accordingly, the star had a star's salary – the biggest of any performer playing under Sousa's baton. Frank enjoyed the fruits of his labors. When he was not in uniform, he dressed well – suits well tailored, coats immaculately fitted, hats that gave him the air of a successful executive, comfortable shoes perfectly shined, spats that always looked as crisp as bandmaster Sousa's white kid gloves, the ones he always wore when he conducted and which he discarded the moment they looked in the least bit soiled. And those cigars, which were now more of a trademark than ever.

He had the money to pay for them all. But it was not in his nature to waste it. Some people called him frugal, but he thought it nothing less than sensible to save all that he could. Who knew when there might be another disaster like the flood which had all but wiped out his parents? He had to be ready for it. Sousa paid him enough so that he could be ready. In return, he not only had to play better than anyone else in the band, he also had to accept Sousa's sense of discipline and good order.

Joining the Sousa Band was like living in a new country without getting citizenship. You were proud to share the privileges and just as honored to be part of it. But there was no opportunity to vote. Sousa was king of his own empire and no one was allowed to question him – either in the marches they played or in the way the band played them. Certainly, no one was invited to doubt the various rules and regulations that the 'Governor' had instituted. The way the men wore their uniforms was one of those – without bulges and with those trousers neatly pressed. According to Sousa's award-winning biographer Paul E. Bierley, he had a valet for himself and a shoe-shine cart for his men. They always took the hint.

The quiet-spoken Sousa, with his Baltimore accent and the dry stories he liked to tell at luncheon clubs, was an exceptional man in every respect. He may not have looked or sounded like a showman if you met this patrician figure in the street. But that was precisely what he was. He may have been the March King, but, as we have seen, few of his performances were actually 'on the march'. The band performed in concert halls that were cavernous and in other centers where conditions on stage were so cramped that some of the bandsmen actually sat in the auditorium.

According to Bierley, in the 31-year history of the outfit it performed as a marching band only seven times. It had its favorite venues – like Willow Grove Park in Philadelphia, which would earn a hallowed place in Frank Simon's own individual story – but most of the time the band was on tour, playing at the Pittsburgh Exposition one week and at the Southern Theater in Columbus, Ohio, the next and then going from town to town, theater and bandstand to theater and bandstand day after day, sometimes playing in two different towns in one day.

Fred Bayers, a bandsman who played with Sousa after Frank Simon's time, put the experience, which in the 1920s was no different from that ten years earlier, into verse:

> First you play a concert
> Then you run and jump a train
> Stop to get a bite to eat
> And then you play again.
> Chase around and look for rooms
> Gee, but life is grand
> For there's always something doing
> In the Sousa Band.

Less poetically, in his biography, Bierley recalled a never-changing situation: 'It was not unusual for them to play in a dozen different towns a week. There were no air-conditioned trains and diners. Meals came irregularly and each night was spent in a different hotel.' And he added: 'The men became highly efficient in arranging for their meals and sleeping accommodations, because the trains left on time and the concerts were begun promptly at the scheduled times . . . The Sousa Band man was a hardy man, one with stamina and fortitude.' As the author noted, no bandsman of the 1990s would accept that sort of regimen.

Frank remembered times when it was the norm to play 14 concerts in one week. 'I want to tell you, that was traveling.' The bandsmen carried their itineraries in their caps – but that was of no great significance. The band's manager would give instructions on the times of trains and the number of the track and the men would follow. It was not their responsibility. But as Frank also said: 'I couldn't tell you where I was yesterday, we went so fast.'

They played for thousands of people, hundreds of thousands of them. But if it was a hard life, that was what the band did – and what the bands*men* expected to do. For anything between six and ten months, the men in the navy blue and, after 1919, black uniforms – now each wearing a patriotic badge, an eagle on a stars and stripes (what else?) background or a globe with the word 'Sousa' inscribed on it – went from one town and city to another, each containing audiences with little more in common than the fact that they appreciated the best band music they could hear.

But it was all hugely profitable. Sousa himself would say that in his career running his own band over 40 years, traveling expenses alone accounted for more than $15 million – which was $2 million more than he spent on salaries. Even allowing for the hyperbole of showbusiness – and there is none like it – and for the memory of an old man, quite clearly the money spent was formidable. The money raised from ticket sales was equally vast, particularly bearing in mind the period covered a time when $10 was a very reasonable weekly salary indeed.

Just as demanding as the concerts themselves were the rehearsals. If John Philip Sousa required perfection when he and his men were 'on parade' for their audiences, rehearsals had an additional dimension – the threatening presence of a conductor who did not mind barking his instructions if he did not like what he heard.

The rehearsals were not just opportunities for new music to be tried and old marches to be perfected but also rare moments for the organized band to let down their collective hair – frequently under their fedora hats or derbies which they seemed to wear with as much regularity as their uniforms at virtually all other times. They were the only occasions when the men were allowed to play – or indeed to be seen in a group – without their uniforms.

As much for the Sousa Band as for any symphony concert, most of the rehearsing was done in advance of a tour – there just was not time to rehearse any more than they would while actually playing in a performance. But when there was organized rehearsing to do, it was done with the precision of a military operation; which perhaps was no more than was appropriate for a man of Sousa's background.

The men practiced scales and tuned their instruments and the conductor himself listened to every sound with as much care as if he had been waving his baton for 'The Stars and Stripes Forever'. When it came to the marches themselves or to one of the other pieces in his repertoire, he listened to every note as precisely and critically as if he had (perish the thought) experienced the displeasure of hearing a concert by some other and, inevitably, inferior band.

Not that Sousa himself conducted every concert. There had to be a deputy. As soon as he took over Herbert Clarke's chair, Frank Simon also stepped into his second role with the band – as the assistant conductor. Everyone knew they were watching the Sousa Band performing in all its finery, but on the occasions that Frank Simon took over the podium he could be forgiven for feeling that at that moment, the greatest band in the world was, in all but name, the Simon Band. It was a thought that concentrated the mind exceedingly – and an opportunity to show that he knew a great deal more about band music and the band business than merely how to blow into a cornet and operate its valves.

There was more than mere physical endurance and stamina that was being demanded of him. Sometimes it was simply a matter of doing the impossible – and making it sound perfectly normal. That was why playing off the cuff was more than a phrase for Frank Simon.

It was while the band was playing at Willow Grove that he

was put to the kind of test no professional musician enjoyed contemplating. There was a one-and-a-quarter-hour break between two concerts. This was a beautiful day and Frank was enjoying what he had a right to consider his just due. He was sitting under a tree. That was when his peace was disturbed – by Sousa's valet. 'Mr Simon,' he said, 'the Governor wants to see you.' If you were a professional musician working for John Philip Sousa, you did not refuse a summons like that, no matter how inconvenient or how much you were enjoying the sun and the scenery. He walked to the bandshell where the leader had his dressing room.

'Young man,' Sousa barked (and when this dog did bark, you did not contemplate how much worse his bite might be; you reacted by saying 'yes sir'), 'young man, do you know a song I wrote called, "I Wonder"?' Frank saw an opportunity to save himself some trouble. 'No sir,' he said, telling nothing but the truth, 'never heard of it.' 'Well,' Sousa replied, 'I have a request for it to be played right after the intermission.' 'Very well, sir,' Frank said. He was a good sight reader. With the sheet music on the stand in front of his chair, he would cope easily enough. 'Have Mr Russell,' said Sousa indicating the band's librarian who was nearby, 'give you a piano part.' Frank had the temerity to mention that he would be happy to play it from his chair. 'Oh no,' said Sousa. 'I want you to stand up and play it.'

That made a huge difference and Frank was not merely talking about his comfort. There was a little matter of the Sousa concert style. A soloist never, but never, used sheet music when standing up. But what was the cornetist Frank Simon, who had a certain reputation for excellence but not for performing miracles, going to do? There was now only about half an hour before the performance. He was being asked and was about to ask himself to learn a new piece in an impossible time frame and then play it, but also play it well – as if he could dream of playing it any other way. Three or four generations later, another Frank, Frank Sinatra, would say that he had to go 'out on the field intending to make a home run' at every performance; Frank Simon had had that philosophy before Sinatra was born. It was an impossibility.

That was when the Simon philosophy of pragmatically dealing with situations as and when they presented themselves came into its own. 'The intermission was then half over. I had my coat off, it

Part of a program for a Sousa concert at Willow Grove Park, inspiration for Frank's most famous composition, 'Willow Echoes'. Note (*overleaf*) star billing for Mr Frank Simon, cornetist, and his cornet solo, 'Airs from Carmen'.

e secured in advance
Park or by telephone,
Bell, Willow Grove 21.

EVENING

MR. JOHN PHILIP SOUSA, Conductor
Miss Florence Ffrench . . . . Soprano
Miss Ruby Helder . . . . Vocalist
Miss Susan Tompkins . . . . Violiniste
Mr. Frank Simon . . . . Cornetist

3d Concert, 7.45 to 8.30

"THE STAR-SPANGLED BANNER"

1. "HOMAGE TO PITTSBURGH" . . . . Sousa
   (Written for and dedicated to the Pittsburgh Exposition)
2. CORNET SOLO, "Airs from Carmen" . . . . Bellstedt
   Mr. Frank Simon
3. EXCERPTS from "Oh Boy" . . . . Kern
4. VOCAL SOLO, "The Trumpeter" . . . . Dix
   Miss Ruby Helder
5. *a.* MORCEAU, "The Butterfly" . . . . Bendix
   b. MARCH, "El Capitan" . . . . Sousa

ELECTRIC FOUNTAIN DISPLAY, 9.30 O'CLOCK

4th Concert, 9.45 to 10.45

1. OVERTURE, "The Diamond Jubilee" . . . . . Kappey
2. VIOLIN SOLO, "Deep River" . . . . Burleigh
   Miss Susan Tompkins
3. NAUTICAL FANTASIA, "A Life on the Ocean" . Binding
4. SOPRANO SOLO, "Somewhere a Voice is Calling" . Tate
   Miss Florence Ffrench
5. *a.* MORCEAU, "La Gipsy" . . . . Ganne
   b. MARCH, "Imperial Edward" . . . . Sousa

was very hot, and I thought, "Oh . . .!" (He presumably thought something a little stronger.) "I can't memorize this solo in 20 minutes. That's ridiculous!"'

But there had to be an answer. His solution was to go into his locker and get out a fresh pair of cuffs (there is something to be said for the days before progress is supposed to have begun and changing fashions consigned the idea of transferable celluloid cuffs to the history books). On those new cuffs he wrote down the notation for Sousa's melody.

On stage, Frank Simon playing 'I Wonder' was note-perfect. And Mr Sousa never allowed himself (in public at least) to 'wonder' how he had learnt it. Fortunately, the soloist always played with his back to Sousa's own rear. He did not notice the fact that *this* soloist seemed to be spending a rather long time looking at the end of his sleeve. As he sat down Sousa whispered, 'Well done' – with a 'little wink of his dark Spanish eyes'. (Sousa usually liked to say he was of Portuguese ancestry: indeed he was but his father was born in Spain although of Portuguese parentage.) As Frank commented, 'I know darn well Mr Sousa couldn't have memorized it that fast.'

There was undoubtedly a certain sense of power in standing in front of the Sousa Band, playing a solo. But despite that instant feeling of authority, there was a greater consideration he had to bear in mind – his innate respect for the music and the way he knew Sousa wanted it played. He would no more try to play Sousa's 'Imperial Edward' – named after the late King of England, Edward VII, who had proved himself to be such a Sousa fan – without the 'Governor's' instructions firmly in mind than he would have suddenly switched a concert's program to include 'Alexander's Ragtime Band'.

There was another aspect to Sousa's demand that all the music sound a certain way. The band not only had to play the music he chose, the way he chose to play it. They had to play it on instruments that he himself chose, too. This was *not* simply for the sound the music made. In this instance Sousa had simple commercial thoughts in mind: he was endorsing the instruments, all of which had to be made by the C. G. Conn company of Elkart, Indiana. Now, to a man who not only knew what was right for his music but also for his career, Frank had no difficulties with that. The fellow who paid the piper – in this instance, the cornetist – had a right to call the tune. But then, in 1917, Frank Simon succumbed to temptation.

The band was playing in Chicago. Even in the Sousa outfit there were occasional times when they would not be totally restricted to the auditorium theater and to either performances or rehearsals there. There were those rare times when they were entirely off-duty. It was during one of these interludes that a fellow-bandsman, by the name of Cory – what his first name was is now lost in the antiquity of band records that have gone to a far better place – suggested that the two of them might be welcome at a local musical instruments factory. Holton was a hallowed name in the band world, but strictly taboo among Sousa's players. But Cory wanted to go to see their firm at work and Frank could not resist the opportunity.

Obviously, as members of the most famous band in the world, they were treated as honored guests. Who knew what influence they might have? Frank picked up a cornet and started to play it, a cornet that had never been played before and had not yet left the workshop. 'In fact,' he recorded in his *More of My Years with the Sousa Band*, 'it was so new that the rough solder wasn't even cleaned off nor was the horn burnished.' It was a moment of truth.

'That was a fine instrument and I fell in love with it from the first breath I put into it. I told Mr Holton this and he said to take it with me and give it a more thorough tryout.' He knew that was easier said than done and, more reluctantly than he could probably adequately express, he decided to leave it behind in the factory.

Holton was not going to give up quite so easily. It was not the possibility of a sale to Frank Simon himself that he had in mind, much more the possible publicity value of a Sousa member breaking the bonds connecting the band to Conn instruments and choosing one of his cornets instead. That afternoon, a messenger arrived at the theater dressing room with an enticing package for Frank – the Holton horn he had tried that morning, but this time burnished and shiny and resting in a velvet-lined case.

'It looked as good as it played,' he recalled. And that night, he put both the cornet and his own reputation to the supreme test. He was due to play Herman Bellstedt's 'The American Boy' in a solo.

He did it – just before the band went into what had finally reached its destination as 'The Ballet of the States', accompanying a troupe of dancers dressed in what was now their accepted suitable attire for the states they represented. At the end of the performance, Frank walked off the stage, pretending that everything was as normal as anyone might imagine. Anyone that is, except John Philip Sousa, who had spotted the deliberate mistake.

'Are you playing a different instrument today?' he asked.

'Yes, sir,' said Frank, probably sounding like George Washington admitting he had just taken an ax to that cherry tree.

The response he got at that moment was perhaps rather more encouraging than the one Washington had received. 'Well,' said Sousa, 'you keep right on playing that horn. It is beautiful. I like it very much.'

But, inevitably, there was one further question: 'Is it,' he asked, 'a Conn?'

'No, sir,' Frank admitted. 'It's a Holton.'

Having already committed himself to liking the sound of the Holton, Sousa could not easily ban its use. But he kept the information to himself – and everyone else used a Conn. Eventually, Frank was endorsing the Holton in the same way that Sousa was kept on the Conn payroll.

Herbert Clarke liked the Holton enough to add his name to the instrument. It became the 'Holton-Clarke'. But the advertisements in magazines like *The Musical Enterprise*, headed 'A Sweeping Victory of Holton Quality', had a picture of Frank in his Sousa uniform playing the Holton cornet. 'The velvet tone, wonderful flexibility, extreme power and the most delicate pianissimo combined with perfect intonation make the Holton-Clarke in my opinion the finest Cornet ever built.' It was signed 'Frank Simon, Cornet soloist, Sousa's Band (First chair)'. And then he went on to tell the story of how he came back to the band with his Holton. 'The boys complained they could not get the results I was getting and prevailed upon me to let them try the extra Holton-Clarke I carry with me and they are simply wild about it.' When he ordered a Holton the firm also quoted his letter in their advertisements.

The Holton revolt was an aberration. Normally Frank toed the Sousa line completely. He usually wanted, as much as the

'Governor' himself, for every note to sound the way it was supposed to sound, every piccolo to come in at the precise point Sousa wanted it to come in, every solo performance to last exactly the time that Sousa had decided it should last. The 'Governor's' reaction to the soprano's lapse of memory is not on record, although it can (within the reason dictated by his chivalry and good manners) be imagined.

The sopranos represented part of the paradox of the Sousa philosophy. He knew what fitted into a band concert, which, he still continued to insist, owed nothing to the symphony orchestra and was certainly never its inferior. And yet into his concerts he could quite happily introduce a solo violinist – usually a woman and when it was, always a good-looking woman at that. He chose his artists as though every member of the audience had a ringside seat or was perhaps sitting on the platform with the players – whom he also expected to look as good as they sounded.

The nicest part of it all for Frank was that even now, at this early stage in his career, he was getting the support of his musical peers. In 1917 his old friend Henry Fillmore put his feelings and his opinion of his former colleague on paper. He wrote:

> Mr Simon is a musician through and through and commands a wonderful cornet technique. He can play anything written for the cornet and anything within human possibilities that may be written for the instrument.

And then he went on to gild the lily, evoking a name from the recent past: 'Mr Herman Bellstedt is known among musicians as the writer of the most difficult cornet music, yet Mr Simon plays it with apparent ease.'

He did not say anything about the music of Mr McCoy. His 'Lala Rook' continued to be on the agenda – and continued to bring problems. Three years went by before Frank was invited to play it again – an invitation that could neither be turned down nor enjoyed any more now than it had been previously. This time, Frank's current side-partner, identified only as 'Mr B', was the one having the real problems. Fortunately for Mr B, as Frank recalled, he had a sense of humor – which, of course, had to be a prerequisite for a satisfactory relationship with a man called Simon. It also meant a chance of surviving a relationship with Sousa himself – who still had the slightly irritating habit of making up his mind about the music he wanted played at something very close to the last minute. This was how Frank described his colleague's introduction to what was undoubtedly not the easiest piece of music he had ever seen:

> We were not permitted to go to the stage until the bell rang, then the brass and reeds would file on to their places on either side of the stand. I walked on with my partner, sat down and opened the book. Lo! and behold! There was my old friend, 'Lala Rook', staring me in the face. I knew Mr B had never seen this work, so I called his attention to the number and showed him the possible pitfalls. By the look on his face, those pitfalls were staring at him the way a cat does when it gets caught in the headlights of an oncoming car. 'Frank,' he said, 'can you play this?'

Frank did all he could to try to ease the passage of the next few minutes. He told him the pitfalls, in more detail this time. Mr B had a solution: he would not play at all. Let Simon over there deal with this problem. Speaking from a degree of personal experience, Frank let him know that that did not seem a terribly good idea. As he said: 'I reminded him that Mr Sousa took a very dim view of people who did not play their parts.'

There was not a great deal of time to think that one out. Almost instantly, Sousa arrived on the scene accompanied by his wife – 'and we were off with "Lala Rook". When we came to the *allegro vivace* in five flats, Mr B laid his cornet on his lap. Mr Sousa noticed it immediately and kept looking daggers at my partner.' But the daggers could not pierce 'Mr B's' determination not to be caught in a trap that seemed even more deadly to him than the wrath of John Philip Sousa, the like of which hell held no fury. He kept staring at his number-two cornetist. 'I could feel it,' Frank recalled, 'and it made me nervous.'

Finally, 'Mr B' made his first move. He turned, pointed his finger at Sousa – a gesture which alone could have been conceived as playing with fire or firing – and told the 'Governor': 'It's just as easy for you to conduct in six flats as it is in two flats.' Frank said it broke him up and he was unable to continue playing until he managed to regain his composure.

Apparently, the man survived, which was perhaps another paradox in the Sousa story. Sousa himself now had other concerns in mind. He had actually done the deed and joined the Navy as the oldest ever recruit and from then on, the erect, white-mustachioed figure of John Philip Sousa liked best of all to be photographed in his Navy uniform. It seemed to confirm the fact that playing in his band was in itself a patriotic gesture and that if there was ever such a thing in the United States as a private service organization, the Sousa Band was fairly close to being it.

Sousa's own patriotism was beyond question, but he could not always be sure that that applied to all his musicians. He made it very clear that what he himself was doing was precisely what he expected of his men – providing, that is, that they could arrange it so they would not be disrupting the Sousa schedule.

After the 1917 autumn season Frank Simon offered his own services to his President and country. Could the Army use a bandmaster? They decided that they could – leading the band of the US Aviation School at Fairfield, Ohio, not far from Cincinnati and conveniently close to his family roots. Dayton was the centre of the American aircraft industry and so the base had become spectacularly important. Morale had taken on new dimensions and the band at the base had become a vital feature of its activities. It had been going for some time, but there was no proper bandmaster.

Frank let everyone know how proud he was to have been enlisted – Sousa's commission was unique at the time; bandmasters were until then never officers – into the 42nd Aero Squadron at Wilbur Wright Field – and waited for the call. It never came. The idea was scuppered. Sousa wrote to say how sorry he was that his cornet soloist had become a victim of a not-unfamiliar kind of military confusion.

He had made a point. Strangely and, again, paradoxically, the man who had such fixed ideas about everything could sometimes be swayed away from those notions. Also, even though he liked to be the first to play his own compositions he was happy to play the work of other people, provided it measured up to his own standards. And that was how Frank Simon himself entered the roles of the big band-music composers.

What he did was to remember Herbert L. Clarke's advice to get out and compose. The result was called 'Willow Echoes'. It is perhaps one of the sweetest, most lyrical pieces that a solo cornetist could choose to play or to which an audience could listen. Half a century after it was written, the solo had gone into 15 editions which sold about 3000 copies each. That alone was satisfaction to Frank Simon. More so, though, was the simple fact that he had written a piece that Sousa welcomed his playing – and before long had the joy of other people playing, too. It was a new career and a new life for the young man who, hitherto, had not really thought of doing much more than tooting his own horn.

7 · *'Willow Echoes'*

Frank Simon was never afraid of giving people credit for the things they did for him. No one else put the musical thoughts behind 'Willow Echoes' into his mind that day in 1917, but he went to his death saying that had it not been for Herbert L. Clarke, he would never have written it. Clarke had told him that the best soloists were the ones who played their own music. It was almost because he needed to prove to himself that he was in that league that he got out his new Horton cornet and started, in his own words, 'to noodle about'. A great deal has been accomplished from such 'noodling' and when Frank used the term he was not thinking about the spaghetti and its sauce, which was beginning to play such an important part in his dietary life.

He was inspired by Willow Grove, that pantheon of good band music, to say nothing of some of the best-ever Sousa performances. But he wrote it at his parents' home at Middletown. It was a nice day and fairly obviously the muse was working well. In half an hour he had the opening cadenza, that sweet start which was to rocket his name and the tune that went with it far above the Sousa bandstand. Almost instantly after that, the entire movement and the triple-tongue strain accompanying it was down on his sheet of manuscript paper. Before long, there was the second strain and the finale. 'No tuttis, yet,' he recalled. 'Just the main solo parts.' As he did so, he thought of Herbert Clarke again. 'The way to tell about a solo, Frank,' he remembered his saying, 'is to imagine you are sitting in the audience and someone else got up and played the solo. The tone, the taste, the style, the musicianship that you put into a solo is far greater than the techniques you can put in.'

He looked at what he had written and heard it in his mind. He heard, too, Clarke's further advice that now was jumping to the front of his mind: keep it short. He began to realize that for all he had learned from his various outstanding teachers, none of it compared with the Clarke one-man advice bureau. Four and a half minutes at most was all that an audience wanted from a soloist. Go over that time and there was a risk of losing its attention span – and its enjoyment. There was a purely pragmatic reason for curbing its length, too: the sensible bandsman had to think of all the hard work he had to do and not give himself an even tougher burden. From then on, it was a matter of cleaning it all up. 'I made a short introduction and smoothed out the cadenza. I wrote a tutti that would fit in between the solo parts – not too difficult to detract from the solo. Finally, I got the whole thing on paper.'

Once down on that paper, it had to be arranged. He wondered about that. Like all professional musicians, he knew what a good arrangement could do. Like all professional musicians, he knew exactly how he thought it should go. But like all *good* professional musicians, he also realized that he needed another eye on it – to say nothing of another ear.

He took the piece to his friend Augie Schaeffer, who had already done a lot of arranging work for Frank with the pieces he played for Sousa. 'Augie,' he asked, 'do you think this sounds corny?' He said he wanted it to be playable by high-school bands which were already developing as an important element in band music. Schaeffer did not have to tell any untruths. He genuinely liked it – providing it was kept, to use his words, 'light and commercial'. Corny it was not. The band parts were arranged, copied and Frank Simon packed them away in his trunk ready for the first rehearsals of the late 1917 New York Hippodrome show.

Now going further than that was easier said than done. It was one thing to convince himself that he had written something valuable, another to prove it to his arranger, but a quite different matter to get Sousa to accept his judgement. What was more daunting, Sousa had already selected the Simon solos, and while he might look indulgently at the work of one of his young men, upsetting his own previously ordained schedules was a whole new band game. Sousa wanted him to play two Bellstedt pieces 'Student Sweetheart' and 'La Mandolinata', the tune for which, if he was human, he had to be extraordinarily grateful. It was playing that which touched Sousa sufficiently to say there was a job for life for Frank Simon.

He could not be sure whether or not Sousa would like it, even though it was not quite like the days when his knees shook at the idea of performing in front of the March King at Carnegie Hall. Now there was the confidence of the professional soloist who knew that if he was going to succeed, he had to put his own stamp on his work. Summoning up perhaps more courage than at any time since his disaster with the 'Floral Waltz', he approached the 'Governor'.

'Mr Sousa,' he said, 'I wrote a new solo. It's my first one for cornet. I have it with me and I wondered if you would like to hear it.' All in one breath.

'Yes,' said Sousa, probably to Simon's not inconsiderable surprise. 'Have Mr Russell [the librarian] put it out.'

The music was put out. Frank Simon took his cornet in his hand, adopted his standard playing poise and played 'Willow Echoes' – from memory, of course. The music was engraved on his heart, he needed nothing scribbled on his cuff. The sheets were for the other, seated, players.

Frank was pleased with his performance. He was even more pleased with Sousa's reaction. No suggestions of digging a six-foot hole this time. Now, America's top bandmaster was telling him: 'This is it, this is exactly what I've been looking for, this is what I want. You play it at the night shows.'

What could Frank say to that, the answer to most of his current dreams? He said 'Very well sir' – and went on to play it every night of the show and sometimes twice a day.

Sousa would have said that he was merely recognizing the ability of one of his men, a perfect example of his own ability to choose the best men for the best band. Sousa himself was never modest and rarely allowed himself the luxury of letting a good word go unrecorded. But it was good public relations to extol the abilities of one of his 'boys'. As Sousa wrote in *Marching Along*, his autobiography: 'The leader who doesn't watch for outbursts of genius in his men in the playing of a phrase makes a sad mistake.'

To Sousa, bandmasters were entertainers and as such, commercial figures. But they were also educators, and no serious leader of a band ever doubted or forgot that. For Sousa, it was a *cri de coeur* and an example to set his successors like Frank Simon. Sousa saw it as an essential part of his patriotism and so did Frank – who always loved telling stories about his 'Governor', not least of them the time President Grover Cleveland asked Sousa how he liked being a musician. 'Mr President,' he replied, 'I'd rather write the country's music than make the nation's laws.'

Frank thought about that when he had finished 'Willow Echoes'. The commercial success of the piece was merely on the way. He took it to his old friend Henry Fillmore, who had by now got his music publishing business under way. Henry instantly agreed to distribute and sell it. When the first of those 15 editions reached the music shops, Fillmore told him: 'Frank, if we had ten more of these, we would be in business.'

Frank Simon began to write more music. He had a talent for it. But he never produced another 'Willow Echoes'. He was in real business all right – but it was the solo cornet-playing business and that was all he really cared about. He once said: 'Fate will direct your course if you work hard enough and try to steer it.'

He worked every hour that was provided for him by the source he always called 'the good Lord' and he always did a little steering along the way. And he always said that the years he was spending with Sousa were the proudest in his life. As he also said, hearing a Sousa march being played properly was the most thrilling sound he knew. 'It raises the hair on the nape of your neck.' He was doing a lot of hair-raising himself at about that time.

Fillmore was a contemporary, a man who also made, to use that Simon phrase again, the hair at the nape of the neck of every follower of the band movement stand on end. There were others at this time. There was no more respected name in bands in the early years of the century than that of Arthur Pryor, another trombone virtuoso as well as a composer of operas, marches, rags, songs and 'novelties' like his 'The Whistler and his Dog', with which funsters would entertain partygoers for two generations. In the band movement, he was a star to say nothing of being a hero.

He had been offered a job in Gilmore's Band but turned it down. Two years later, in 1892, he joined Sousa and stayed with him until 1903 – the star attraction when the March King played before the crowned heads of Europe. He later formed his own band, and as such became a one-man pilgrimage destination for the younger musicians who followed him. Frank Simon followed his band and Pryor followed Simon's progress. He had long before vowed that if he could become as great a name with the cornet as Pryor was with his trombone, he would be a happy man. Pryor was not the only one to assure him that it was a dream he was fulfilling every day of his life.

Just as much as Frank worshipped at the shrine of respected older colleagues, he was also looking out for talent – with Sousa as the principal recipient. Except that that was not entirely true. The more talented people who joined the band, the better it became – and the prouder he was to be a part of it. He also had to recognize that it was through a recommendation that he himself became part of the ensemble.

For that reason, he took it upon himself to be a kind of talent scout for Sousa. Every now and again he heard an instrumentalist who he thought could benefit – and the band itself would also benefit – from a Sousa connection. But he did not limit himself to fellow horn blowers. There was the time he heard a soprano sing – and instantly imagined her on the Sousa bandstand. It says a great deal for the Simon status that his tastes would have wider repercussions, but for the moment that is jumping the story.

It happened most notably when he was staying with Sammy Harris, a fellow-member of the band, during an extended stay in Boston. Harris lived at Lynn, Massachusetts, renting rooms from two elderly ladies. One of them had been in her day a famous opera singer who had sung for the Italian court. Now, in old age, as Madame Balch, she was working as a voice teacher. Just how impressive her credentials were Frank discovered when he went to the house at Lynn for Thanksgiving dinner.

Well fed and equally well satisfied, he went to bed – and woke to the sound of singing. As he later said, it came from 'one of the most beautiful coloratura voices that I can ever remember hearing.' It was a voice no one had yet heard in public and he knew how remarkable it really was. Frank asked his friend who was doing the singing. He told him her name was Marjorie Moody, 'Madame's star pupil'. The Simon musical antennae were working at full thrust. There was something there to note, he was sure.

'I want to meet her,' Frank said. Harris could only agree. They dressed hurriedly and, before breakfast, knocked on the door of 'Madame's' studio. Ever the most polite of men – Bertha had taught him well – Frank apologized for interrupting. 'Madame, please pardon the intrusion and the interruption of the lesson,' he said, 'but I don't think I have ever heard this aria done more beautifully.' And at that he moved from teacher to pupil. 'Miss Moody,' he said (it wasn't necessary to wait for introductions), 'did you ever sing professionally?' 'No,' she replied. 'In church. That's all.' Frank's mind was racing now. There were more people than her church congregation who ought to hear her, he thought. And he knew where they could do that listening. 'If I can arrange an audition for you with Mr Sousa, would you consent to sing for him?' The formality was catching. 'I'd be happy to,' she said as Frank Simon bowed and left.

Frank could not have been more excited. As soon as he got back to Boston that afternoon, he told the 'Governor' of his discovery. He told him that he had not heard anything like this 18-year-old Marjorie Moody since Grace Hoffman – he ignored the trouble that she had brought. The idea of the voice impressed Sousa. But he wanted to know more. 'Is she good-looking?' he asked. 'Yes,' said Frank who considered himself an expert in such things, 'she is a gorgeous-looking girl – and, Mr Sousa, you will be missing something if you don't listen to her.' Sousa was willing to be convinced. An audition was arranged. Marjorie Moody prepared two of her specialty numbers – an aria from *La Traviata* and 'One Fine Day' from *Madam Butterfly*. Frank coached her in what he thought were the essentials for a Sousa performance, not least an ability to sing songs that blended well with the background of a Sousa band. The band was there to accompany her, but no one was allowed to forget that they had principally gone to hear a *band* concert.

There was more than that to learn, however. The two men knew there was a speedier route to Sousa's heart – via one of his own songs. As Frank noted, 'Mr Sousa was a vain man. He just loved to hear people sing his songs.'

After Frank had coached her, Miss Moody sang Sousa's own 'The Card Song' at noon the following Sunday and John Philip pronounced himself captivated. As Frank remembered: 'Now with this great accompanist playing, this young lady just sang her heart out. She just stepped out there like a fairy.'

Once finished, Sousa beckoned the girl to walk toward him. He gave her a kind of back-handed compliment. He did not say that he thought she had a beautiful voice. Instead, he left the generation gap . . . gaping. 'Young lady,' he said, 'you have a most remarkable teacher.' He not only engaged her to sing with the band but to start the following night.

As Frank said, it was not the easiest time to debut. It was Irish Night in Boston, an occasion not noted for its sobriety or, for that matter, for delicately behaved hushed audiences. But the paying customers were as won over as Sousa himself. 'She sang like a bird,' was the Simon memory of that remarkable performance. 'Boston took her into their hearts.' That appears to have been the case. The city's toughest critic, Philip Hale, recorded the fact. He said she stopped the show – and she went on doing so at Sousa performances for the next 14 years.

Frank helped her arrange her repertoire. He would always say that bringing her into the Sousa orbit was one of the things that helped make his life worth while. Sousa also thought so. She adorned his band both in sound and sight. He loved the way she looked as much as he was thrilled by her voice. If he had a chance to be seen out in her company, at a restaurant or out driving, he was happy – providing, that is, he had a chaperone with them.

Sousa always enjoyed fostering new, young talent – and not just girls with beautiful voices and equally beautiful faces and figures who would do well with his band and whom he would treat with the delicacy of a mother superior. When he could, he went to schools to hear their bands play and to offer a few words of advice. Frequently, he took Frank with him. Sousa was an intuitive teacher, and he was able to recognize the fact that Simon would be one, too. Frank always remembered the advice the 'Governor' offered the students at one school. 'When you play, 'he said, 'please never cross your legs. That prevents your thinking.' In another such lesson, he instructed the youngsters: 'Always keep one eye on the music and one eye on the stick. If you have only one eye, watch the stick.' Frank always said he thought that was 'pretty good advice'.

Simon indeed passed it on to his own pupils. Glenn D. Bridges, a younger musician, would later pay tribute to Frank the teacher in the days when he was officially assistant conductor and cornet soloist with the Sousa Band. As he said: 'He was always very easy to talk with and never at any time pompous. He was always willing to help young players particularly.'

The people he helped most, though, were his audiences. Helped them have enjoyable matinees and evening performances which many of them would never forget. The success of those shows and those definitive performances was obvious from the press reactions. Those press clippings were mounting up now. 'Lavish Menu at Music Fete' declared the Ithaca *Daily News* on 18 June 1919. 'An audience most liberal with merited applause' was how its critic described reaction to the show in the city. It talked about the most notable number in the concert, '"Beneath thy Window" by E. di Capua as encore of Frank Simon to his cornet solo, "Willow Echoes" by Simon'. Then there was the Newark, New Jersey, *Star Eagle*: 'A cornetist who ranks with the virtuosi devoted to that instrument is Mr Simon. To a remarkable executive facility, he unites a pure and steady tone, more mellow and ingratiating than most players of the instrument produce. Furthermore, his breath control is astonishing as it was revealed in a long, sustained tone on a naturala trumpet.' The Cortland, New York, *Standard*, at about that time also mentioned Frank's playing of 'Beneath thy Window': 'He delighted the audience with both solos.' In Plainsfield, New Jersey, the city's newspaper illustrated a story headed: 'A Sousa March Heard Along The Rhine' – how the defeated Germans in Koblenz (nobody appreciated the Simon connection) heard without protest an American band play 'The Stars and Stripes Forever' – with a double-column picture of Frank playing his cornet. The band was playing at Plainsfield that night.

And so it went on. The Duluth, Minneapolis, *Herald* talked about his predecessor, Herbert L. Clarke. 'Comparison would be virtually impossible. Clarke was a wonderful cornetist, but so is Simon. His playing last night was undoubtedly the best of that instrument that has been heard in Duluth in many years. Authorities, local and away, declare it to be wonderful and to the lay ear it was all of that.' And so it was. The owners of those 'lay ears' were buying tickets for Sousa shows – so that they could hear Simon perform – just about as quickly as they could be printed.

8 · *Discovering Another 'Music Man'*

It was not just an interesting life, for Frank Simon it really was everything he could have wished for. He was playing the kind of music he liked above all else with the finest outfit of its kind anywhere in the world. What was more, he was doing it in the public eye – even if occasionally it might have seemed that that eye was the one in the center of the storm. Sousa was demanding and Frank was the first to admit the fact. If his principal success was avoiding the hurricane, that in itself was no mere achievement. But really it was not. He was successful in proving his own talent and in being able to give it full expression.

In many ways it was a time of establishment and, once becoming established, of consolidation. With the Cincinnati Symphony Orchestra under Stokowski, if nothing else, he had learned how to watch a conductor and appreciate his true value. Now, under Sousa, he was not only learning the same thing but, in his own milieu, he was also getting actual experience at doing it himself.

The symphony orchestra had enriched his knowledge of the classics. Now there were opportunities with Sousa's own brand of 'concert band' music, to be able to play it the way he liked to hear it. Sousa only played what was right for the band. That, too, was a lesson Frank did not forget in a hurry.

Perhaps the most important lesson of all from Sousa was in the field of programming. It was a successful formula and he remembered it for the future, tucking the notion if not under his cap with his schedule, then firmly into his brain. It made a lot of sense to do things the Sousa way, starting with an overture (were they not there simply to open programs?), continuing with some light music, suites, polkas and always having a march for encores. Perhaps he also learned a sense of concern for the welfare of other bandsmen, because, for all his strictness, Sousa always gave the impression of trying to seem, if not fatherly, then at least paternalistic to his 'young men'.

By the spring of 1918 Frank was already thinking of the future. Had the time come to try to branch out on his own? The thought was in his mind and Sousa knew it. He also knew that his young cornet player was not feeling terribly well. So from his favorite base at the New York Hippodrome, writing on the theater's patriotic red, white and blue banded notepaper, he sent Frank a note of consolation and encouragement:

> My dear Simon, I am greatly pained to hear of your rheumatism. I sincerely trust that you have recovered and are as strong and healthy as ever. Certainly, a man whose habits have been as excellent as yours deserves to enjoy most perfect health.

There was a message there for other bandsmen who might not have been quite so excellent in their 'habits'. Oh, the problems of women and those demons smoke and alcohol! Frank Simon may have been extravagant in his talents, but he was moderation personified in most other things. But then the note addressed itself to the question of the Simon career:

> It seems to me if you will make an application for a position as bandmaster, I would make it to take effect after you have completed your summer work with the band, especially as you have been ill and should not tax your strength too much in the strenuous work of organizing a band during the hot weather.

The really important part of the note was at the beginning of the second paragraph. 'Sousa's Band,' he wrote, 'wouldn't be Sousa's Band without you in it.' That really was generosity. Even if the signature was formality itself: Simply, 'John Philip Sousa'.

Working with Sousa was still like living in a separate country and Frank recognized its advantages sufficiently to shelve his plans for independence for a time. He was fascinated by the 'Governor's' methods, enthralled by his working schedule, writing music on the train, with only a pillow to support the manuscript paper.

The band was still having an enormous impact on audiences

and on the press, in particular. In October 1918, during the flu epidemic that was sweeping the world, a writer in the Detroit *Journal* advised:

> Girls, you needn't put your muffs up to your mouths or turn away when Sousa's Great Lakes band boys go by. And don't start worrying about old Spanish influenza. They haven't got it. In fact, they rather worry that they may contract it from you if you cheer their playing too loudly. Sousa's boys are total strangers to flu germs. They wouldn't know how to comport themselves if they saw a germ coming toward them. But the doctor with them would. He'd wring the germ's neck and throw it over the fence.

The band had arrived at Detroit on a special train at 8.30 in the morning and were ready to give a concert in Cadillac Square at noon. For the moment Frank was going to stay with the band. He was, after all, being treated well. When Sousa played at the Toronto Exhibition in 1918 – one of Frank's earliest associations with the neighboring country that would become an important part of his career – he was given the full treatment, star billing and the center attraction when it came to his solos.

The 49th Parallel may have been the border between the United States and Canada but, as far as his music and its fans were concerned, there was no line between them. Canada loved that kind of band and the band loved Canada, even if it did mean the beginning of another one of those hard-working tours. It would prove to be busier than ever before, from New York City to Calgary, then returning, town by town – including Montreal, where there was a fire immediately after the concert and 12 people were killed – 'resting' at Willow Grove before continuing west to Seattle, Los Angeles, Salt Lake City and the Deep South.

Willow Grove was Sousa's home from home. It was there that he went riding on a horse brought to the park every day by his groom. 'He rode at breakneck speed,' Simon later remembered. 'He was up there as solid as Paul Revere, I guess, on his famous ride.' Once the tour got under way again, however, there was no time for riding. As far as Frank was concerned, Canada was the part of that particular trip he would remember most clearly. They played at open-air fairs all over the country, even during a gale-force wind at

Calgary. Sousa did not want to disappoint children from a nearby blind school who, despite the weather, had come to hear the performance and were sitting in their places even though the wind was now accompanied by heavy rain.

So the band played the *William Tell* overture as best they could – there was no way they could use sheet music – and followed it by whatever marches came into Sousa's head. '"Semper Fidelis", gentlemen,' called Sousa and the brass instrumentalists played while the water poured down their horns. All shows must go on. Sousa's shows never came off. It was an important lesson Frank would never forget; a rehearsal for even more hair-raising days to come.

The newspaper critics were impressed, but mainly with the performances they heard. The Winnipeg *Telegram* reported: 'A cornet solo by Frank Simon, "Willow Echoes", was a very clever and most satisfactory performance, which showed the cornetist to be a real artist with deep musical feeling and wonderful technique.' The *Evening Bulletin* in the same city noted: 'Mr Frank Simon displayed exceptional ability as a cornetist in Bellstedt's "Polka Caprice", its plaintively sweet passages contrasting beautifully with the gayer interludes of the accompaniment.' Then there was the Regina *Daily Post*: 'Sousa's Band Making Big Hit At Fair' it said. But there was something more significant than the show's contribution to the city fair. 'Thousands simply lost their hearts to Frank Simon, cornet soloist, who played "Popular France" and for an encore, "Annie Laurie".'

The band went to Hartford, Connecticut, in September 1919. 'In passing, it would seem remiss not to mention the work of Frank Simon,' said the *Daily Times*:

> Mr Simon in his cornet and trumpet solos won the house from the very start and his wide range and the sweetness of tones produced convinced those present of the rich mellow notes that brass instruments can possess when in the hands of an artist. His opening number, 'Willow Echoes' written by himself, was one of the finest pieces of cornet solo work that a Hartford audience has ever been privileged to listen to. The echo effect he produced as the mellow tones softened and disappeared into the distance from whence faint echoes could be heard before entirely disappearing, was a rare display of the cornetist's art.

The same month, the Columbus *Journal* was thrilled by a Sousa concert at the Hartman Theater in their city: 'Mr Frank Simon, cornetist, played several solos – his "Willow Echoes" written by himself being particularly filled with melody.' And at Bridgeport, Connecticut, the band in general and Frank Simon, in particular, were a huge hit. 'Frank Simon's cornet solos,' reported the *Musical Courier*, 'were a leading feature of the program, in which he was given ample opportunity to display the rare perfection of his art.' From Rhode Island, the *Providence Evening Bulletin* called Frank Simon 'a great favorite here' and said he played with 'fine effect'.

The stories multiplied with the tour. Sousa was always in the headlines: 'Sousa's Band Delights Crowd' (Albany *Democrat*); 'Sousa Receives Rousing Welcome' (Vancouver *Daily Sun*), 'Sousa Concert of Rare Charm' (Newport *News Record*). And Simon was always quoted in their reviews.

The fast-maturing Simon was now extending a talent that had become apparent when he first spotted Marjorie Moody and commended her to his 'Governor'. He knew precisely what was right for the band. When he heard the 19-year-old Del Staigers at this time he knew he would be the ideal side-partner for him – so much so that when the band made its 1918 visit to Willow Grove he was happy to share solo honors with him, just as Herbert Clarke had shared them with himself. With the additional participation of Eugene LaBarre, Frank was not afraid to allow Staigers to join him in a cornet trio – an extraordinarily generous gesture from a man like Frank who, above all, liked to 'sing'.

What he would also have liked a great deal would have been to sing on his home turf. Sousa referred to this in his letter from the Hippodrome. 'I can recall at former times of being indirectly approached about engagements in Cincinnati and $1000 a day has always been the stumbling block.' Sousa, of course, had to pay all his instrumentalists, fund travel and accommodation, but in those last months of the First World War $1000 a day represented a fortune. It was the equivalent of about $100,000 in the 1990s, the kind of figure most people never saw in their whole lives and Sousa was using it as the starting point for a *day's* fee.

But before long, the money obstacle would be overcome. And, as far as Frank was concerned, he did even better. Sousa came to

Middletown and the audience there on 3 October 1919 saw a Frank Simon in his element as never before. Sousa's performance was, inevitably, at Sorg's Opera House, and Frank, equally inevitably, was there as principal soloist and assistant conductor. Solomon and Bertha could not have been more proud – and perhaps bathed in the reflected glory of the local boy made good. That day, Frank Simon was Middletown's favorite son, and he enjoyed it all quite as much as if he had single-handedly just routed a nest of German machine gunners and had been awarded the Congressional Medal of Honor. Middletown knew how to treat its heroes, and that day Frank Simon looked as though he were destined to have a statue put up in tribute.

If nothing else, it was an opportunity for Frank Simon the patriot to come into his own – to say nothing of Frank Simon the baseball fan. For this was World Series time, an occasion when even the band music seemed to take second place to what was going on in the ballpark. Frank had by now joined the Sousa baseball team himself, so he could be forgiven for thinking his enthusiasm would be respected. This was one time when the Sousa boot was on the Simon foot. Now it was Frank's enthusiasm that was infecting the 'Governor'. Thirty-five years later, Frank wrote: 'In mind, I can still hear the shouting, deafening ovation [given Sousa] by a wild and cheering throng that filled the stands to overflowing.'

The day after the Middletown concert, the band played at nearby Hamilton. A lot of Frank's old friends were in the audience. One of them, Ed Reed, could not afford a ticket. Bertha got to hear about it and took Ed along with her for the evening show. It was a well-planned visit, although Sousa's road manager could not have known just how well planned when he first scheduled the date. It was the precise moment when the Cincinnati Reds were playing the Chicago White Sox. All through the performance, Sousa's valet was standing in the wings, writing down the score for the conductor's attention. The band had some idea whether Sousa was pleased or not with the results. They saw it on his face in just the same way that they always knew whether or not they were pleasing him with their playing.

Yet the pressure of the ballgame was too much, even for John Philip Sousa. The following day, the band did play Cincinnati – but only for the evening performance. That afternoon, Sousa conducted 'The Stars and Stripes Forever' on the center of the baseball diamond – not by the Sousa Band but by the ensemble got together for the occasion as if they were a mass of cheerleaders. 'I never heard such thunderous applause,' Frank Simon recalled. It was Frank who had made the arrangements – again as part of the local-boy-makes-good status – and so the previously planned matinee was cancelled. (Sousa later paid tribute to baseball with a new march that he called 'The National Game'.)

The performance that afternoon at the Cincinnati Music Hall was just about the only concert anyone could remember Sousa calling off, although the reason had probably more to do with the fact that there would be no one left in the audience than, as he claimed, to give his musicians a chance to see the game. That night the players were at the Music Hall, as scheduled. But it was the baseball everybody had in mind.

No one was happier with that game than was Frank Simon. His home team beat the White Sox, five games to three, and so won the series. Other games were much more personal to Sousa. There was no pennant for trapshooting, although he had become, during Frank's tenure with the band, one of the finest practitioners of the sport in America, with guns worth $1000–1500 apiece – and that was before America went to war in 1917. It was just another example of his fabulous wealth.

In a way, Sousa had himself come home. Frank told him that, as a child, he remembered hearing the 'Governor's' music every day of the week. 'He was so popular that I couldn't walk a block here in Middletown when I was a boy without hearing a Sousa march being played on a piano. Being in the area was also a superb opportunity for Frank to discuss his own family and, in particular, its financial situation. Bertha was not altogether happy with the money her son was earning – not that she did not think he was getting enough; more that perhaps he was not going to spend his $120 a week sufficiently wisely. So Frank, ever the dutiful son, agreed to a way of putting her mind at rest. He decided to send his mother half the money from every pay check which she then banked on his behalf.

Sousa paid his men well because he demanded so much of them.

A 'shiver circle' soloist – so called because the men like Simon in that favored group were said to need nerves of steel – sometimes regarded his salary as being close to danger money. Certainly, paying well suited everybody concerned, to say nothing of the bandmaster himself, who would be able to point once more to the obvious rectitude of his soloists.

Sousa was quick to pick up what in the 1990s are called the 'vibes'. If Frank Simon made people think about the Sousa Band, he was only too happy to let Sousa be the focus of attention. It was a sound philosophy and one that countless entertainers in other media have adopted over the years when bringing in guest stars who, on the surface, seem to take all the attention. Just the same, like the perfect Christmas dinner always prepared to the recipe of the cook, everything the band played was according to Sousa's own instructions. He was the chef and the concert hall always his kitchen.

The years 1914 onwards were the ones when the Sousa trademark was more heavily emblazoned on the things he did than ever before. Up to then, there had been a certain flexibility. Now the marches began to sound the way he had always planned them to sound – the same on each occasion. This was now an old dog who was not prepared to learn any new tricks and he saw no reason why any of his musicians – or his audiences – should either. Now every piece of music he played was, like every one before, done with a Sousa stamp. Frank would remember being in at the birth of many a Sousa march. He saw him write the music first, add the piano parts and then finally orchestrate the whole piece, never to be changed. Although, as we have seen, that was never quite so. The playing style would be established only once a piece had actually been performed. It was when the 'Governor' was satisfied with what he heard that he established the way it should be played thereafter.

It was Sousa's musicianship which allowed him a certain degree of generosity. He always claimed to appreciate talent for talent's sake. The March King in a moment of monarchical condescension once wrote (although the truth in the statement needs to be taken with a pinch of Sousa salt): 'The leader who doesn't watch for outbursts of genius in his men in the playing of a phrase makes a sad mistake.' And he went on to add in his autobiography:

> I would hear some fellow going over a portion of the piece and playing with it – trying it this way and that until finally I would hear him play it in a certain way and I would say to myself, 'That's the way it *ought* to be done . . .' If I were not open-minded, I could not improve as a director – I am a better director than I was last year and I hope to be a better one next year.

But then his men always knew what to expect, even when there was not time for rehearsal. All Sousa had to do was to tap his baton, lift his immaculately white-gloved hands and say 'El Cap', and the band could do the rest. They could play the 'Governor's' 'El Capitan' in their sleep. They knew how he wanted the drum and cymbals parts to sound and when the horns came in – even if the sheet music said it differently. All Frank Simon and his fellow-musicians had to know was that 'there would be a big *wham* there, then it would be soft until the cornets and trombones came in, fire and tongs about six measures before the break-up strain – and we'd play that with all the fury we had.' That was what was required of a Sousa march like 'El Cap'. It had to be played with all the fury the men had (unless there was a heavy raincloud overhead: then he would tell his men to play fast and not worry so much about the noise). It was the 'Governor's' second-favorite march (after 'The Stars and Stripes Forever') and had featured in his operetta of the same name. The show was never the success that the march became and by playing it often, he somehow felt he was helping to keep the operetta alive.

It was mostly played as an encore to the opening overture, and Sousa took those overtures particularly seriously. When his wife arrived late at one of his concerts he was quick to tell her: 'You do know that the composer wrote that overture to be heard.' He expected everyone to hear what he played, as carefully as he heard if the trombones did not come in on time.

Just occasionally, he would vary his routine – as when the band played four concerts a day, and Sousa liked to offer his customers variety. Some of them might have come to every performance. So they had to wait to see what their conductor wanted. When he required the base drum to come in he would point with his foot. Every other musician knew what his own particular signal would be although he only ever talked to the first-chair men. He was a great believer in the chain of command. It was the first-chair soloists' job to speak to the lower echelons. If the second cornetist was required to play soft, Sousa would not tell him. It was up to Simon, the man sitting in the first chair, to tell the luckless man.

But then there were always the general's commands from above. 'Post' meant it was time for 'The Washington Post March', 'Eagle' was 'The Invincible Eagle'. As Frank later wrote: 'There was never time to look up the marches. You had to memorise them. The stick was down and everyone was in. You had no time to hunt music. He just worked us to the limit. There was never time for emotion.' In Frank Simon's eyes that was perhaps Sousa's greatest sin. An emotional man like Frank expected nothing less of everyone else. It was an essential characteristic of a person's humanity, to say nothing of humility. But he had to concede that John Philip Sousa always got along without humility, just the same.

These days, there are people who say that perhaps he was not the greatest conductor in the world. What all have to accept is that he was a superb organizer, able to play almost all the year round and so uniquely able to bring in audiences. The arrival of the Sousa Band in a town was like the coming of the circus. There were posters everywhere, the newspapers were full of it and the lines stretched from the box office to the corner of the next block. It was as good a recipe for success as anyone else has been able to dream up.

One of Sousa's best marches was 'The Diplomat'. Frank said of that: 'The moment I heard that march and the style that he put into it I said to myself, "I can just see a diplomat in my mind's eye. A very distinguished man in perfect clothes".' Perhaps that was the real secret of the Sousa marches. They were always in perfect clothes. 'You became inoculated with the spirit of the marches and with the intent that they had had in the way they should be played.' The inoculation came into play at every concert, but it only made the infection of Sousa fever that much more serious.

A typical day at Willow Grove – detailed in leaflets showing the same stern, white mustachioed Sousa in his naval uniform – would include five different items for each of the four performances. All would begin with 'The Star-Spangled Banner' but that was all that they did have in common. The 2.30 to 3.15 show would begin with the tone poem, 'A Day In Venice', followed by Frank's cornet solo,

'Youth of America', written by Herman Bellstedt. Then there would be Percy Grainger's 'British tune', 'Mock Morris', after which there would be a soprano solo of 'The Lass With the Delicate Air'. Before the final encores the band would play a Swedish wedding march and Sousa's own 'The Man Behind the Gun'. For the 4.30 to 5.30 concert there would be a Saint-Saens 'divertissement', 'King Harry', a violin study, a suite called 'Three Quotations' which Sousa had written, a vocal solo and finally an intermezzo and a march, 'The Bride Elect', by Sousa. The first evening concert would begin at 7.45 and last until 8.30. Sousa's own 'Homage to Pittsburgh' would be an opener for Frank's cornet solo, 'Airs from Carmen', arranged by Bellstedt. There were then excerpts from the Jerome Kern show *Oh Boy*, a vocal solo, 'The Trumpeter', and finally, 'El Capitan'. There was, after that, the longest show of the day, the 9.45 to 10.45 concert, beginning with an overture, 'The Diamond Jubilee', a violin solo, a nautical fantasia, a soprano solo and the finale 'Imperial Edward'. It happened every day and the musicians took it as much for granted as they did blacking their shoes and putting their trousers under the mattresses.

Off-duty, Frank in particular would know what was expected of him. He was there to ensure that no one dared accuse his boss of immorality – the complete reversal of the situation many aides-de-camp had to perform for their employers. The nation was full of yes-men; men whose role in life was to protect their 'governors' from the prying eyes of a public who might otherwise see things they were not supposed to – like the company of women to whom they happened not to be married.

Sousa never had any such plans with the opposite sex – and did not want anyone to think that he did. That went for his men, too. Sousa always insisted on the women in his band having their meals in public – and with *him* so that there would be no suggestions that they could be having intimate relationships with an employee. For the same reason, he insisted that the ladies, and only the ladies, traveled with him in his Pullman car.

In Latonia, Kentucky, on a balmy night there was an essential extra-mural activity that could never be turned down. In those surroundings, in that kind of weather and at that time of year there was nothing Sousa liked better than taking a horse and buggy ride.

But he would never go alone. That was the time when he would take his prized female soloist out for the evening. He liked her company; was certain she adored his; and was convinced her presence made him look good to the crowds. Like the subjects of some other kind of monarch, they would, of course, always doff their hats as he and the lady processed among them. But Sousa, as Frank knew, would never compromise himself by going alone with a woman. So Simon's job was simply to play chaperone for the evening. He took it in his stride along with playing 'El Cap'.

For Sousa, this was a unique relationship with one of his bandsmen. He saw his connection as strictly one of commanding officer and enlisted men. That was why he never went into their 'mess'. He would not shoot pool with them or play cards. Because he never swore – the worst he would do in a fit of temper might be to utter 'Christ and all his brethren!' – he permitted no profanity from his musicians. When he walked into the room he all but expected them to salute him. But 'Good morning, Mr Sousa' and occasionally – for the 'non-commissioned officers' – 'Good morning, Governor' had to do.

Frank and he had a closer relationship. The two men, senior bandmaster and young soloist, seemed to have an innate respect for each other. It was not corny in those days to talk of being 'gentlemen' and that was the way both men behaved. They did so in matters of the pocket as well as of the heart.

In all his years, just as no one could ever suggest any impropriety on Sousa's behalf when it came to his female employees, neither could anyone pin any financial misdeeds on him. They would have had great difficulty in doing so. He was earning enough without needing to resort to dishonesty, although the very idea was probably furthest from his mind. He never had a sponsor, never required a grant from a worthy institution and could earn as much as $60,000 a month in royalties – in the days before income tax.

All these factors – the success and the road to that success – combined to make Frank Simon determined to follow in the footsteps of his idol one day. He loved every minute of every day with Sousa – enjoying the rewards but having none of the responsibilities that would be his before very long.

Between seasons, he would come home, and the customers to

the Simons' dry goods store would once more be entertained to the sound of a practicing cornetist echoing down the street. It was like a story in the *Saturday Evening Post*, the concept of which Sol still failed to understand, illustrated by some imaginary Norman Rockwell.

Those breaks were times to recharge the batteries as well as to absorb the thorough knowledge of the geography of the United States they had picked up on the way. Frank might not have thought he needed to put any charge into *his* batteries. All he wanted to do was to play, and every performance was a practice, a rehearsal for the next one; a honing of his talent. But he was also intelligent and worldly-wise enough to know that there were no half-measures to count when playing with Sousa. His 'Governor' was an actor-manager who stayed in business because he knew what he wanted and what his customers demanded.

Frank knew too. He was, after all, Sousa's star. He was a carded player. When he got up to play, a card was placed at the side of the stage announcing that the man with the horn was 'Mr Frank Simon'.

There was a kind of telepathy between bandmaster and bandsmen. All he had to do was flash his dark Portuguese – or Spanish, depending on the mood he was in – eyes, Simon repeatedly said in old age, and his musicians would know what was required of them. It was like a mother who never had to raise either her voice or her hand to chastise her children; one look was enough to tell them they were running out of favor.

These were the peak years for Frank Simon. He was an athlete who could do a four-minute mile or contemplate an Olympic long jump simply by looking at the track. He practiced long and hard, but the results were as natural as drinking a cup of coffee or lighting up one of those cigars.

He managed to give the impression that he did not have to labor over his work. It just flowed out as if produced by some exceedingly well-oiled machine or like a meal concocted in that mythical kitchen, but a steamy one that was never seen by a table of satisfied diners who only knew that it all tasted wonderful. The diners at a Sousa concert hungered for a Frank Simon solo and, when it was over, wiped their lips perfectly satisfied.

Probably the greatest satisfaction of all was in not just being good but in knowing that other people also thought he was good. Which was what landed him in Mason City, Iowa, at the age of 31.

It was another case of Simon, the talent scout, at work – after having himself been spotted once again. One of the sponsors of the town's Municipal Band was Harry B. Keeler, Vice President of the Mason City Brick and Tile Company. He was a Sousa fan – if not a fanatic. He was one of those people who believed that the sun rose and set to the spirited sound of 'El Capitan' or 'The Stars and Stripes'. If he could bring a Sousa-type band to Mason City, he would die contented. When the band did come to play at Mason City's armory, it was the happiest day of the year. The brass all but rattled the rifles racked up around them, but nothing vibrated like the emotions of Mr Keeler.

Anyone who knew his band music also knew that it could not possibly depend on one man, although if a band, like an orchestra, could possibly speak – if not sing – with one voice, that voice had to be that of the conductor. He also knew that soloists were fairly important, too, and when he heard Frank Simon standing in the front of the bandstand playing 'Willow Echoes' he was dispatched into realms of glory.

Frank also enjoyed the experience. The little town with its 20,000 population showed its appreciation and there was nothing else like that to make a band happy. They left next day for Des Moines, the nearest big city, with the applause ringing in their ears. There was no more gratifying sound.

But there were even more gratifying results of that concert – most of them summed up in the 75 words of a telegram from Mr Keeler. He had a proposition for the man who had seemingly so electrified him: Come and join the Mason City Municipal Band as principal soloist while Sousa is laying off between seasons. The temptation was huge and the money was not bad either. It was another one of those offers Frank neither could nor wanted to refuse – even if, as on all the important occasions in his life like that first meeting with Sousa, there were, as he put it, 'negotiations' to complete before officially accepting.

Keeler stressed the advantages once more. Frank did not have to work too hard. No one played at all on Mondays, and during the rest of the week there was an hour's concert in the afternoon and another one lasting an hour and 15 minutes in the evening. Oh, yes – and there was a beautiful lake eight miles away. It was indeed impossible to resist. He took the trip to Iowa and the little place which, in its way, was so much like his own Middletown. It was also Middle America with Middle American-type people who prided themselves on loving their Middle-American (and middle-class) neighbors – sometimes a little too freely, as anywhere else, but on the whole a nice, wholesome place where people were proud to walk down the main street.

Not that this mattered to Frank Simon. There was a much more important event on his agenda. In the weeks in which Simon was playing with the Mason City Band it took on an undoubted Sousa style. The band had an eminent Boston-based conductor, but Simon used his influence and, by all accounts, it was accepted. He recommended programs that were distinctly Sousa, even if Sousa programs those days had a distinctively Simon sound. Frank it was who had introduced the post horn into Sousa concerts and the 'Governor' constantly thanked him for it. In Mason City he did all he could to make the music sound the way Sousa wanted it to sound – how could it be any other way? Not for him – of all people – to tolerate a Sousa march played the way every other band in America played it. He knew when the drums came in and when it was time for a resounding clash of cymbals, to say nothing of just the right sound for the brass section.

As he said, it was engraved on his memory for ever after. 'Gee whiz, I remember the town,' he said over and over again. 'Very little playing' and the lake eight miles away was ideal for swimming, boating and fishing.

Frank and Harry B. Keeler got on well enough to keep them both happy. Writing about his new patron, he recalled he was a 'very fine gentleman and incidentally a fine musician'. (Keeler was a graduate of the New England Music Conservatory in Boston and played both trumpet and piano, as Frank reported, 'beautifully'. It was enough to commend him to Frank as being a man to respect.)

The band, Frank told his Sousa colleagues, had 25 musicians. Except that he said they had '23 musicians and two drummers'. It was a lack of respect for the percussion members of the band which he was later to regret. There was no one he claimed to respect more than Sousa's principal drummer August (Gus) Helmecke, who he said was a 'fine artist', but it took some time to get used to the idea. Even so, drummers were not his principal preoccupation while at Mason City.

Above all, perhaps, he now had an opportunity to study the talent at his disposal. Most of the musicians played well, although if compared with Sousa they were, at best, mediocre. But there was one instrumentalist who was exceptional even if he was not always able to correctly stretch a note the way that he should. But when he played his flute or his piccolo – Mason City had just one man on both instruments – he 'sang', and that was all Frank asked of anyone.

The youngster was 18 years old. 'Your name?' the new cornetist asked him. 'Meredith,' he replied. 'Meredith Willson.' The two 'l's in his name were important and not to be forgotten. Frank never did forget.

Three weeks into his stay at Mason City, Frank received the kind of invitation always extended to celebrity newcomers in town. The three service clubs there – the Kiwanis, Rotary and the Lions – invited him to a special meeting at the local country club. It was a meeting right up his own street – actually, a band concert. A concert of solo performances and one in particular that stood out from all the others. Meredith Willson on flute sang his heart out and the audience loved every moment of it. 'I thought he was simply great,' Frank later remembered. 'I was astounded at this young man's artistry, how magnificently he played. I wondered how he got it, but he did play like an angel. I was knocked off my feet.' The young Willson was accompanied by his mother on piano and she was very good, too. 'You could see where he got his background of good manners, good looks and great musicianship.'

Frank was the first to congratulate the flautist. 'Young man,' he said – it was not just the art of conducting a band that had rubbed off onto this 31-year-old. He adopted Sousa's mode of speech as easily as his programming choice and his march style. 'Young man, you play the flute very well. You are a very talented young man. I have noticed your work in the band.' And then came the punch line that was almost that – it all but knocked the young musician out: 'How would you like to go with Mr Sousa?'

Willson could not quite take it in. 'Are you kidding me?' he asked.

'No, I'm in dead earnest,' Frank replied. 'You're just the type of young American boy that Mr Sousa wants for his band.'

He did not add that Sousa had himself told him that he hoped to see the day when every one of his musicians would be a 'real American'. It was not the sort of thing to mention at the turn of the century, but by the 1920s, when there was an assortment of German, Spanish and Italian-born musicians in the Sousa Band, it was a different world. As a first-generation American-born citizen Frank thought there was as much merit in this Sousa philosophy as in most others.

Willson had to steady himself to regain his composure. He laughed. He had never been out of Mason City in his life. 'You know, Mr Simon,' this polite young musician told him, 'I didn't believe this could ever happen to me, but I would give my right arm if I could get in.' He would have found it totally impossible to get in without that right arm, but Frank understood his sentiments. 'I'll see what I can do,' he assured him with a smile that people with a longer acquaintanceship with the Simon personality would easily recognize.

That night, he sat down to write the 'Governor' a letter. 'Mr Sousa,' he wrote, 'you will be pleased with this young man. He is a fine reader, he is a handsome-looking boy. He plays well and is an excellent musician.' The order in which he expressed his appreciation of the youngster's qualities gave an astonishing indication of Sousa's own priorities. He was not interested in ignoramuses and could not abide the thought of anyone ugly on his bandstand. Once those qualifications had been satisfied, the question of his musicianship was ready to be considered. Frank's letter went on: 'He has style, taste and technique. He has everything.'

Sousa was about to look a gift musician in the mouth. From the DuPont hunting preserve in Carolina he wrote back, 'Have your boy send me two pictures of himself,' he instructed his soloist. 'One in playing position and one standing holding his instrument.' Sousa was casting his mind ahead to how a Meredith Willson in his band would look in front of the customers and, perhaps even more significantly, on his posters and in his publicity leaflets.

The letter arrived by return of post. Quickly enough, indeed, for Frank to take the youngster aside and advise that he would have the photographs taken as quickly as he could get to the neighborhood photographer's store. And then to Sousa he sent a second letter, with a little plea along with the flattery. 'Don't pass this boy up, Mr Sousa,' he advised. 'He's got it and he's going places. He has the dedication, determination and the talent.'

Clearly, one of Frank Simon's greatest qualities, the fostering of young artists, was now in full swing. When he heard that Sousa had ordered his manager to prepare a contract for the youngster from Mason City it was as though he himself had just been told that the 'Governor' was about to retire, had nominated Frank Simon to be his chosen heir and was forwarding an engrossed agreement for his signature by return. Certainly, he could not have been more happy. The sun was undoubtedly shining above Mason City. 'This made me feel pretty good,' was as far as he would go in admitting the fact. '[Sousa] had never heard the boy but had taken my word and hired him for the next season.'

Meredith appreciated the opportunity he now had. 'Sousa was a genius,' he said in the 1960s. 'He had the ability to make the illogical inevitable. He was like Beethoven. He put the emphasis on all the unexpected parts, like Beethoven did at the start of the *Eroica*.' The Beethoven of the March appreciated Willson just as Frank had predicted he would. He told him never to be falsely modest.

For two years, the young mustachioed Meredith Willson was the 'star' attraction in the Sousa flute section and then went on to other things – the main one of which was to write a musical show about life in a small town called River City, where the population's entire life was lived around the sound of a band and 'The Music Man' who had brought it there.

9 · *Love and Dissent*

Meredith Willson was not the only discovery Frank Simon made in Mason City. As he said so gleefully – which was perhaps out of character for this man who seemingly would rather play his cornet than eat and drink – Mason City was not a demanding place. Because the demands of the locals were few, he was able to indulge his other pleasures, showing that his kind of man did not live by playing a horn alone. He did like to eat – although drinking held little interest to him – and he also liked to socialize. Now he was having as many opportunities to take advantage of these pleasures as he had ever had in his life – his adult life, at least. There was no Sousa breathing down his neck. Neither were Bertha or Sol around to ask, just in passing, if there were a teacher he needed to see. Now, he was interested mainly in meeting people who were there just to be entertaining, whom he would meet solely for the chance of a chat, a meal or the other human things of life.

It is perhaps surprising how easy it is for a man in a community enterprise like a municipal band to become part of that community. He gets to know people who know everyone else. That was how he came to meet the proprietor of the local newspaper, a Mr McKay.

Frank and he were talking after a concert on the white-painted veranda of his hotel. As he later remembered: 'I went there to do my job. After the job was done, I was bored and there was nothing else to do. So I said to Mr McKay, "Are there any young people I can meet?"'

Mr McKay told Frank: 'I'll get the Wolf brothers to come to see you.'

The Wolfs lived in town and were, as people liked to say at the time, the gay young blades of Mason City – 'gay' in the dictionary definition of the term. The two Wolf brothers, Louis and George, came to meet Frank, driving up while Frank sat on the white porch. They were in a Stuts Bearcat, which was just about the best status symbol any man's magazine of the time could have recommended.

They suggested that it might not be a bad idea for Frank to join them in the Stuts and drive off to Clear Lake, ten miles away, which was not only a temptation for a visiting bandsman but was where every young person who was any young person in Mason City would go for laughs.

They made the trip and it became perhaps the most important visit of Frank Simon's life. There, the brothers introduced Frank to two visiting young women who had rented a cottage there. One of them was pretty enough to attract Frank more than he would have imagined possible.

It was George Wolf who made the introductions. 'Frank Simon,' he said, 'this is Mary Chapman.'

Neither the name nor the appearance of the young girl who seemed to knock Frank off his feet rather like a Herbert Clarke performance of 'Willow Echoes' seemed to indicate that they had anything common in their background. But, as the Wolfs explained, Mary was Jewish – although she usually only admitted it to please her more Orthodox grandmother. But she was not denying it either.

Frank was 31. Mary was just 23, and engaged to be married to a man named Mike Baker. This fact was no more going to put him off his next move than if he had been told he had to retire from playing the cornet at that moment.

Three days after that first meeting, Frank proposed. He was head over heels in love with the girl from Des Moines. She was 'flabbergasted' (a generation later, their son Joseph Simon was to marry Louis Wolf's daughter). 'Here was this successful musician proposing marriage to me,' she kept telling friends. Really, she did not know what to say. She was engaged to someone else, but Mike Baker did not have the charisma of a Frank Simon.

Mary's one trouble was that she had no one at home with whom to discuss it. Her father had died when she was tiny, her mother had remarried – a man with whom she never got on – and so she lived with uncles who had a large furniture business in Iowa.

But Frank was, she later recounted, 'a very persistent fellow'. A persistent fellow who would not go away. But this was 1920 and decent young ladies could not rush into marriage just like that any more than they could jump into bed with a stranger.

She solved the problem by consulting her family doctor. It was the usual way in those early post-First World War days. The doctor was also a friend of the family, so he knew their standards. He asked her: 'Do you respect this man?'

'Yes,' she said. 'Out of respect then,' said the doctor, 'love will grow.'

But she still was not ready to give Frank Simon an answer. They corresponded. He waited patiently. But he had to get back to the Sousa Band. A new tour was on the way. The best he could do was write to her – every day.

Falling in love can be a somewhat painful undertaking – if there is nothing else to worry about. But Frank Simon did have something else to concern him. Just as he was determining that he was going to marry Mary Chapman, there was trouble in the band.

This did not happen very often. As should be apparent by now, one did not join the Sousa Band and argue with the 'Governor'. You were paid by a man who had very dogmatic ideas about the way things were carried out – and not just about the way the music was played. On the other hand, you did not join that band if you were not prepared to abide by the rules – *Sousa's* rules.

Yet suddenly, the fabric of the band started to crack. There was dissent in the air and, quite unintentionally and equally unexpectedly, Frank Simon was in the center of it all. It was a time when musicians newly out of the services were looking for jobs that were no longer as regularly available as they had been before the conflict. The band was coming to the end of its tour in the Deep South. They had played at a Shriners concert at Nashville, Tennessee. As usual, one of the men had been assigned the job of getting the hotel reservations at the next town. The problem was that he did not do so. As Paul Bierley says, 'He fell down on the job. He really screwed up.' He did not get the train seats the men needed either, although Sousa and the 'talent' – the men's name for the women in the band – were comfortably ensconced as usual in the Pullman car. Most of the journey was spent standing up. Even those playing cards – mostly poker, although some of them played pinochle – played in a standing position. There was no diner on the train either. By the time they got to Winston Salem, South Carolina, they were hungry and exhausted – and had nowhere to go.

The real difficulty was that there was a convention of tobacco salesmen in town at the same time. *Their* advance men had been nothing like as neglectful and had found all the rooms the delegates needed.

But there were none for the Sousa musicians in Winston Salem. Despite the lack of comfort on the trains, the problem of hotel accommodation did not become apparent until they got there. There were no beds anywhere for men who, after a hard day's traveling and playing, needed their rest as much as did a small baby. The trouble was that whereas babies can sleep anywhere, irrespective of the surroundings, hard-working men in the Sousa Band could not. Those who could find accommodation in private homes did so. The others ended up sleeping in lobbies, on pool tables, on any flat surface in any available hall.

Sousa had no such trouble. The only accommodation which *had* been reserved – and, admittedly, in a second-rate hotel – was for Sousa himself and the girls. That did not exactly commend him to his men who took the view that if this ship was going down, the captain ought to sink with the rest of them. The few who did manage to get a room there shared their beds with two other instrumentalists, who were now having to play the brass bedstead as well as they had played the drums or the trombone. The musicians decided to do something about it. They held what they called a 'gripe session'.

'What are we going to do?' was the one subject on the agenda. The result was a decision to take action by not playing at the next matinee performance. Only 19 of the 64 members of the band turned up for the concert, Frank among them. For the first time, there was a strike in the Sousa Band.

The audience was invited to ask for their money back. Not one person did.

Frank described seeing Sousa waiting to go on, standing in the wings in his best uniform, his crisp white gloves on his hands, his eyes blazing with anger.

The band played a Massanet overture and 'El Cap' as an encore. Frank played 'Twilight Dreams' by Herbert Clarke as his overture. There was a coach-horn solo and a vocal performance.

'I was in at the gripe session,' Frank later recalled. 'But that was all.' Even so, his participation in the events tended to cause a degree of confusion. Was he involved in the strike itself? Frank always denied it. But just before his own death, he revealed that Sousa believed he had a great deal to do with this unique brand of industrial action.

The truth is that the men doubted Frank's loyalty. They did not know if he was on their side or the 'Governor's' – a man who, for once, was not being called '*Mister* Sousa'. They thought that Frank was too close to Sousa for comfort and did not invite him to the final meeting, which called the strike.

That was not good enough for their conductor. Sousa was convinced that Frank was the ringleader.

The striking bandsmen were immediately fired. They all turned up for the evening concert but were banned from going on-stage. Simon did play that night, as he had at the matinee. He continued the trip for the next six days and at Richmond, Virginia, the tour was over. But when Frank went back to New York for the start of the next season's tour, Sousa told him: 'Mr Simon, we won't need you this year.'

Frank was not happy with either the news or the mood of the man conveying it. He later remembered: 'If ever I saw fire in a pair of black Spanish eyes it was then.' The reference suited this situation as much as it did every other occasion of Sousarian anger. Once more the place name was interchangeable but the phrase was repeated and, as before, totally appropriate.

He had played his last notes with the Sousa band, which was now virtually a totally new outfit. Most of the other members of the band had been sacked. (In fact, only the drummer, August Helmecke, and possibly one other striker, although this has never been officially confirmed or denied, remained.)

For ten years, John Philip Sousa harbored a grudge against his sometime favorite soloist. Later, Sousa realized that Frank was not involved in the strike plans, and apologized. But after seven years, the Simon–Sousa connection was broken. Frank might have been broken too, except that he still hoped that Mary might come to see things his way, and just a little earlier he had had a call from Middletown – offering him a job.

'Why should I take it?' he asked. 'I've got the greatest job in the world.' And he added for good measure that he had just spent the happiest seven years of his life with the greatest bandmaster in the world.

But strike or no strike, the band was not what it had once been. Sousa, who started it as a young man, was now growing old. The caliber of the musicians had deteriorated. Very few of the good ones stayed with the band very long. What was more, the industry was changing. The real money was in the 'symphony orchestras' in the pits of cinemas and that was not going to last very long either.

Frank Simon wondered for some time about the offer being made to him – and then, conveniently, decided to take it all rather more seriously. It came from the American Rolling Mill Company in his old home town, where they knew it simply as Armco.

10 · *Armco and Marriage – The Story of Two Loves*

Armco by now *was* Middletown. The war was over. Peace was the norm and bit by bit, Middletown was rationalizing its industry. The paper firms were still there, but the tobacco companies were beginning to get smaller – they could not help doing so with most smokers turning to cigarettes – and Armco was getting bigger. It was as if a new Industrial Revolution had happened, and in a way it had. People in America were buying more and more cars and more stoves and more central heating radiators and there was talk that, before long, those newfangled things called refrigerators would be coming into people's kitchens, too.

To the people at Armco this meant just one thing: they would all be needing more steel. More steel meant more workers. Even if there were the seeds of unemployment already being sown in other parts of the United States, in this corner of Ohio – a corner stretching way beyond the horizons of the boom-town centre, Cincinnati – it was prosperity time.

Workers were needed the way carts needed horses. And now the company was taking to heart the first notion of industrial psychology – those workers had to be kept happy. 'Why not have a band?' thought George Handley, a senior company executive.

That was how Frank Simon came into the picture. It was a few weeks before the Sousa strike. Handley ran the Armco Association which was responsible for health and sickness insurance for the workers at the Armco plant and organized their sporting activities, their baseball, football, tennis and swimming – all top attractions for the citizens of Middletown. Every Armco employee was automatically a member of the association. They paid 50 cents a month into the funds and the company matched the figure cent by cent.

Handley thought of Frank Simon because he simply seemed the obvious choice. He invited him to Middletown during a break in the Sousa Band season simply to discuss the matter, just as a businessman without a lawyer would call on the attorney on the next corner, the one who had got into all the newspapers after successfully defending a seemingly lost cause, or simply because he had been to school with his brother. To the folks in Middletown, Frank Simon was the local boy who had made more good than any of them could have thought possible for someone from their area. Teachers at the local schools talked about him when they tried to instill standards of industriousness into lazy students. Tradesmen discussed him as though the fact that he had once gone into their stores to buy a cigar or a newspaper automatically presented them with a social cachet all of their own.

Handley did not know that this was just the right time to net his quarry. Nor did Frank, which made it a lot easier for him to get the best deal – if he wanted it. And when he expressed his reservations, he could not have been more sincere. Did he really want to exchange the fame of the best band in the world for a new organization which, as far as he could see, had few temptations to offer?

Handley invited Frank to a meeting at the association's headquarters in the old US Hotel in Middletown on Main Street. 'You know,' he told him, 'Armco would like to have a band in this town. I don't know a bass drum from a clarinet, but could you help me or give me some ideas how we could have a band in Middletown?'

It was a subtle approach. He wanted Frank Simon to run the band, but he also imagined he would instantly spurn an invitation to do the job himself.

Frank knew he was being wooed. The temptations that he could see, he kept to himself, with thought of what Julius, now the serious businessman, might advise ever in mind. They were, in their way considerable: Bertha and Solomon were getting on and, devoted son as he was, he found it difficult to contemplate spending years separated from them for all but a few days of a year. But most important of all, there was Mary. They were going to get married and she had already made it very clear that she did not want a husband who was away on tour most of the time. It might have been good enough for Mrs Sousa. Not for Mrs Simon.

Frank told Handley there was a way to get his band started and would help him to do so. He promised to get out a questionnaire which Armco could send to all the people working in their plant as well as in the office. Who, it asked, had ever played a musical instrument – what kind and where had they played it?

Only 22 replied, which, as Frank commented, was 'far from encouraging'. Most of the respondents said they had played in college or town bands, which was why they were interested in joining an Armco organization.

As for Frank himself, he had to consider his own position – and the alternative side of the picture was a lot less attractive. Here he was having to put into the past the camaraderie of the Sousa outfit, and – to quote a song from a later period – all those far-away places with strange-sounding names.

Middletown was home, but it was also still very *Small*town. It was not a totally exciting prospect. But much, much less enticing was the notion of what he was being offered in terms of his musicians: there was no guarantee that any of them were musicians at all, apart from those who had reasonably impressive experience. Some of those who answered were just Armco employees who happened to own a trumpet or a trombone. Not necessarily men who could *play* a trumpet or a trombone – there was not even the guarantee that he would have the right number of each to balance the operation.

He really did not want the job and said so. The Armco people, however, were persistent. What Frank saw as a huge disappointment, a 'gloomy picture', they insisted was a great beginning. They could not understand the Simon reluctance and he could not begin to comprehend their enthusiasm. But the firm kept up their interest. Surely, they mused, there must be *some* satisfaction in starting a band from scratch? He told them that was precisely what worried him – and how could he even consider giving up the best job in the world for . . . what?

On a Sunday morning in December 1919, he thought he had the answer: for nothing. He got the 'musicians' together for a rehearsal – and the results were as dreadful as he had predicted.

Then he went back to the Sousa Band – and the strike. No one knew that when he next had an approach from Armco he was not at that moment in the best job in the world. In fact, he had left Sousa and had been doing a job that offered no satisfaction whatever – setting up home in an unimpressive flat in Chicago from which he had started giving lessons to enthusiastic but, on the whole, untalented pupils.

So plainly there *were* ways to persuade him back home to Middletown. He could have what he wanted, provided the ensemble was called the Armco Band, a prerequisite for what the firm also judged could be quite good public relations. Frank was not so sure. If the band was as dreadful as he anticipated it probably would be, what it would do to the Armco name was not worth thinking about. The one thing which was assured was that it would not exactly enhance it. The effect on his own name hardly bore thinking about.

The temptation was stronger (or so it seemed, but not nearly as strong as his present position indicated, should anyone have realized it) when someone suggested this was going to be the first great industrial band of the nation. Of course, the people of Middletown thought they knew what they were getting, even if Frank himself did not. Sunday afternoon concerts were as popular in town as they had been when Frank himself was leading the Middletown band.

Frank fronted the band on its first unofficial airing and wished with all his heart that he had not. He was determined not to make a habit of it. It was the first of what were before long to be billed as 'Armco Friday Nights', restricted to Armco employees and their families. Which in itself was fortunate. The ensemble had had just five Sunday-morning rehearsals – and sounded like it.

Frank would not have wanted any of his musician friends to stray into the Elks Hall in Sorg's Opera House, hearing the amateurs playing what Frank called 'a lot of little baby music – the kind you would teach little kids, four, five and six years old. It was God-awful, believe me.'

The only one who was worth listening to was Frank. The smile on his lips was reserved strictly for his embouchure. He could bear neither the sound his outfit made nor the thought that he was conducting it.

Frank had a band of sorts. He chose the best available to him. If he had let slip that he would have preferred to have musicians who worked in a steel mill rather than steelmen who played music, he would have been told that was not the idea at all.

Frank took on the responsibility of buying the instruments – second-hand trumpets and tubas, clarinets and cornets – on trips to Cincinnati. He still had not agreed to take on any position with the ensemble and, strangely, no one asked how it was he had time to do all this.

There was one huge problem after another. As Frank later remembered: 'Most of them wanted to play drums. They had the idea you don't have to read music to be a percussionist. All you have to do is just beat it. That's a long way from the truth.' But it had been a mistake he had made himself, so was in no real position to criticize amateurs. But he stuck with it and doubtless the less than sympathetic comments from more knowing members of his audiences stuck in his gullet. 'I wanted to do anything I could to help make the town better because man does not live by bread alone. You have to have some culture in a community. That's life.'

Part of the frustration was being expressed in telling himself he still had his job with Sousa – even if, in his heart, he knew that he had not – and that it was still the world's greatest band. By now it was a fair bet that Goldman's Band was much better, even if it was less well known.

It was Charles R. Hook, the company's vice president, who changed everything. Hook was married to Leah, the daughter of the same George M. Verity whom Frank as an 11-year-old boy had seen cut the first turf for the Armco mill at Doty's Grove. When Hook married Leah, a national magazine reported he had wed the boss's daughter. It was not a clever thing to print. Hook was so angry that he immediately canceled the firm's advertising contract with the paper. Now Hook took it upon himself to hoist Frank ashore – to Hook him. 'I want to thank you for what you have done to help us to try to have a band in Middletown,' he told Frank. 'Every town ought to have a band and I love a band – and we want one in Armco. Now, what is the next step that we do?'

Frank did not know he was walking into a trap. He told Hook it needed a full-time director. Without one, it would founder. As he said on numerous occasions afterwards: 'A band is no better than its poorest musician.' The most important musician was its conductor.

So to whom should that voice belong? Frank told Hook: 'I can't think of anybody at this moment that might be interested in coming here and assume a job like this in building something.' Did Frank at this point see the gleam in Hook's eye? It is possible that he did, for he went on – perhaps weakening, perhaps willing the steel executive to take the next step. 'It would require a man with more patience than I would think I would have,' he continued, sounding not a little like the girl running away from the man she hopes will quickly catch her. 'Secondly,' he added, stating his own qualifications for the job he was protesting he did not want, 'it would require a man of great knowledge about all the instruments, who could help all these men to perform and come on.'

At that point, it seems Frank realized how far he was going and he held back – but positively. 'Maybe I can come up with a name in three or four days that I could recommend to you.'

Frank knew musicians all over the country, he explained years later. But was that what *he* wanted? Hook came straight to the point: 'What's the matter with you taking it?' he asked.

'Oh, I wouldn't be interested, not for one minute,' he said, not allowing himself anything like a minute to make his statement. And again, he said: 'I'm sitting on the best job in the world for a man with my instrument at the present time. It is a position that every talented man on my instrument hopes to get some day. It is with the greatest bandmaster and the finest band in the world.'

Now *that* leads to a degree of speculation. Did Frank in his heart still *really* believe that the Sousa job was still available to him, even though he had gone to Chicago, even though he had spent weeks training the Armco amateurs? It seems unlikely. Shortly before his death, he told the Sousa biographer, Paul Bierley, that he knew he was wrongly held responsible for the Sousa strike and had, in effect, been fired. Plainly, the protestations to Charles Hook were a ruse.

But by now he was warming to his theme – and carrying the game a stage further. He repeated that his was the best job he could possibly want. The subtlety was, however, fading slightly. Hook asked him why yet again he was turning down the offer.

'I'll give you three reasons,' he replied. He still repeated: 'It would be a terrible mistake to leave the top job in the United States – or in the world for that matter – to come back here to Middletown where I started as a boy and assume a thing like that.' So far so good – and so consistent. But he plainly had started to weaken, even if Hook did not see it that way. 'It would depend upon how much support you gave me and a lot of other things.' Now he was saying that he really was interested.

But if he saw the smile on the executive's face, he had to retrench – and he endeavored to do so. 'It would take me 20 years to build the type of organization that would please me, give me any satisfaction for all the hard work [and] thought that I would put into the thing.' Then came the final thrust: 'Besides, I don't think you could afford to pay me enough to do that.' So there *was* a price to compensate for all the inconvenience and loss of prestige he would inevitably suffer in moving to an inconsequential outfit like an unheard-of amateur band. After all, he told Hook he would have to give up a 'tremendous salary' to take on the job. There would be two branches to the compensation tree – the company would have to make up for the lost prestige *and* the salary.

Possibly even to Frank's surprise, the bait was taken and Hook was biting (the fact that the man's name was Hook should not be allowed to confuse the metaphor). 'Suppose it does take 20 years to build what you want,' said Hook. 'Isn't it better to take that long to really build something than to have it great right off the reel?' (Hook was either adopting the same metaphor or was using a steel term.)

At that point, each of the two men, Frank Simon and Charles Hook, decided that the fencing had to come to a stop and that, equally, each of them had won. Frank was allowed to admit (to himself as well as to the man from Armco) that he had been presented with an exciting challenge. 'I realized that immediately.'

Hook on his part could say: 'We're willing to support you with every reasonable request that you make of us. We know it's going to take equipment, we know we're going to have to buy instruments and a library of music and all these sorts of things. We know this and we're willing to spend the money if we have some reasonable assurance that it will not be a *bloomer* – something that will be enthusiastic for about a month or two and then fold up.' Frank could fairly promise that this was not going to be some new toy that would quickly be discarded – if he were interested, that is.

But there was still that question of money – and here Frank had been more subtle than perhaps he had realized. He had struck a nerve. If his own prestige had been on the line hitherto, now he had put Armco's own reputation there, too. Could not afford him? 'How do you know we can't afford to pay you what you think you ought to have?' Hook asked him.

Plainly, Hook *had* hooked him – at just the time when he needed it most. But Frank Simon still wanted the last word: 'I'll tell you, Mr Hook, I'll think it over. But don't be encouraged. I don't think I would ever want to give up what I have.'

What he thought over was a strictly business arrangement – one that fitted in quite perfectly with the sort of negotiation standards to which he had been introduced by his relatives in Noah's Ark. The cousins would have been very proud of Frank's stance as he contemplated the Armco offer. Yes, he told Hook, he would take the job. But he framed his acceptance into a proposition.

'I will try this for one year,' he told him. 'If at the end of one year both of us are satisfied with what has been accomplished, we could continue. If either of us are dissatisfied, we can quit without any ill will.'

'That suits me,' said Hook. 'You'll never find me unreasonable in anything.'

Frank said, 'But there are certain things I am going to have to have.'

'I know that,' said Hook, contemplating all the instruments that Frank would require. 'We will supply them.'

But all that was in truth a mere formality. Frank knew that once the money had been settled there had been no reason for his turning down the opportunity. He could think to himself that he knew his duty – to his parents who would be so glad to have him around, to Mary who would have a solid base and a marvelous salary in her husband's hands every week and to himself. At the same time, he could publicize that his real duty came from that challenge – to make Armco's band better than anything else that had ever come out of a factory.

To be fair, the company was happy enough with the results of it all to decide that the band was an official organization, and on the following 21 April Frank was promoted to musical director of the company.

There were duties and obligations to the holder of what the other directors assured him was a highly prestigious post. He was obliged to give free instruction to any member of the association who provided his own instrument (either privately or in a class). Anyone could join the band once they assured Mr Simon they could play, which must have been a hard condition for him to swallow. Given the chance, he would have been as strict on his entrance requirements as Sousa had been with his.

But one obligation was left to the steel mill company itself. It would buy all music and uniforms out of association – i.e. company – funds.

Of course, there was a considerable amount of personal pride involved. Even 46 years later when addressing a meeting of the Middletown Optimist Club, he maintained the pretense. He said that the decision to leave Sousa's Band 'nearly broke [Sousa's] heart'. And to illustrate this, he quoted the letter that the 'Governor' had sent from the Hippodrome long before the dispute between them, saying, 'Sousa's Band wouldn't be Sousa's Band without you'. Alas, Sousa had decided – to his own ultimate cost – that it *could* be the same. Of course, it was not. But it assisted Simon's idea of literary license.

His reasons for the protestations were totally understandable and indeed had taken a great deal of heartsearching. In a way there was also snobbery and he would probably never have denied that. He knew he was above what this group of amateurs could do. Way above, in some kind of musician's stratosphere these players would not even have imagined existed. He could dream of having a Herbert Clarke at his side or a Henry Fillmore. But they were just dreams. He would not have wanted them at an Armco concert. He would not have wanted them within anything that could possibly be imagined as listening distance.

Quite suddenly, he was thrust into an alien world. The wining and dining to which he had been subjected in the wooing process dried up soon enough for the Armco plant to become no more than an uninviting business center. There was no one to call 'Governor' and no cap in which to insert an itinerary, even an imaginary one.

He practiced his horn every day, but for weeks on end he was, it seemed, simply an administrator, another Armco executive, except that his responsibility was men playing musical instruments, not machines making yard after yard of molten steel, pouring off the line like the protruding tongue of a prehistoric mammoth.

It took very little time for Frank to dread the sound of another machine minder trying to get a recognizable note out of a cornet, or an accounts clerk tooting his flute hoping he was not sending the neighborhood cats scurrying for shelter. The whole concept, he knew, was fundamentally wrong. Yet it had to be accepted that works bands in England, for instance, were a tradition – and it was one that produced prizes. The best brass bands in Britain were drawn from the ranks of men who spent their days working with blackened faces in coal mines. The miracle was that the same people who before long would be wracked with the coughs of silicosis could blow horns better than anyone else in the country. Where they had competition, it came from skilled laborers at motor works playing in their own bands.

He later described it all as one of the most frustrating experiences of his life. 'The results were so discouraging that many a night I would slink home [through] back streets and alleys ashamed and bored at what I had to endure and bewailing the fact that I had lost or rather given up a position in the world's best band to conduct the world's worst.' The only consolation to it all, professionally speaking, was that when it came time for a cornet solo, he knew he was providing the best in America. He played 'Willow Echoes' and the customers had their money's worth. Everything else was peripheral – if not to him.

On 7 January 1921 the band played together officially for the first time to an invited audience – playing the 'Chicago Post March' and 'American Patrol'. But the main honors went to a piece specially written for the occasion by Frank's friend Henry Fillmore, 'Armco Spirit'. George Handley, signing himself 'Manager, Armco Association', wrote in the *Armco Bulletin* listing Frank's accomplishments:

> With this record of achievements behind him, Armco can well be proud to have Mr Simon direct her musical activities and Armco offers Mr

> Simon a wonderful opportunity to develop the latent musical talent of Association members. This will give the Association one of the greatest industrial musical organizations in the United States. All Armco can look forward to some real musical treats in the very near future.

Yet by 30 April 1921, the band was really in its stride – with just a few non-Armco players in the team. It played its first public performance for the opening of the baseball season and Armco's own team's first game of the year on its own field. Simon the baseball fanatic – who had the comfort of knowing that in this at least, the 'Governor' would have approved – was beginning to feel a little happier.

For the first time, the Armco Band led a parade to the field, marching down Curtis Street, a parade still made up of men who during the day drove locomotives or cranes or worked behind desks in the offices, the white-collar staffs who considered themselves a cut above the industrial workers. In the band, they were all equal – if, at times, Frank could be forgiven for thinking that they were all equally bad.

By the end of 1921 the firm was proclaiming their band to be one of the best amateur outfits in the land, a status that was not guaranteed to bring much pleasure or pride to the bosom of Frank Simon, who considered himself the finest *professional* cornetist in America. He held his rehearsals on the first floor of the Main Street building. As he later remembered: 'I want to tell you that in the first year that I put in that organization, I nearly was sent to an insane institution.'

The good human being in Frank Simon was being sorely tested and tried so often that he said he felt he was 'destined for the insane asylum'. But he also now knew that he could forecast the onset of a temper tantrum. Fortunately, because he knew it, he was able to warn his band *before* they started that they could be sitting in a tornado. 'Now gentlemen,' he told them as he tapped his stick ready for the initial downbeat, 'I like you all. I think you are a fine group of men. Now if I get hot under the collar, don't pay any attention to me.' And he added, as if he knew that a confrontation was a distinct possibility, 'Don't speak back to me. I'll cool off again.'

If professionally, he was having precisely all the trouble that he had prepared himself for, his personal life was happier than it had ever been. He and Mary were married at a ceremony at the Hotel

LaSalle in Chicago on 28 August 1921. They chose the place because Mary's mother then lived in the city. The service was conducted by Rabbi Charles A. Levi, who had traveled from Milwaukee to officiate. There was just a handful of guests. In addition to Mary's mother and Frank's parents, Julius was there along with his aunt Carrie, who lived in Dayton, and a few other close relatives. Mary's sister Ruth and her friend Tillie Haskell were bridesmaids. Lillian Jacobson of Des Moines sang 'Oh Promise Me'. The couple went to Niagara Falls on honeymoon. They delighted in the first months of wedded bliss. Frank and his 'Maryla', eight years his junior, had never been happier. The other consolation was the one he had also anticipated as he signed his contract with Armco; his frequent visits to the town to see his parents were no longer luxuries but as much a part of life as going home to Mary every evening.

The younger Simons now had a home of their own on Arlington Avenue in Middletown, which must have signaled a sense of family continuity if nothing else. On their first night in their new house the local children delighted them with a ceremony that has mercifully died out. In California, it was known as a chivaree. In Ohio, they called it 'tin-panning' the young couple. Boys and girls of about seven or eight stood under the windows literally banging tin pans – loudly enough to wake the neighborhood and to encourage the couple to initiate peace negotiations. One of those children, Harry Finkleman, now a real-estate agent in Middletown in his late 70s, told me: 'The great thing about the tin-panning was that Mr Simon came out and gave us all a nickel. We went away after that.'

There was perhaps just one disappointment for Frank as far as having his own wife and home were concerned. 'When I stayed in hotels,' he told Mary, haltingly, 'they'd give me clean sheets every night. I liked that.' Mary got her point home quickly enough. 'If you think you're going to get them here, I think you had better think again,' she told him. He accepted the *fait accompli* as just another of the concessions he had to make for living in Middletown, along with hearing what he still frequently thought of as a cat's chorus which called itself the Armco Band.

He continued to audition, continued to suffer the noises being made by musicians who were anything but and just occasionally found one who blew into his instrument without making it sound like a bicycle pump. And then, even more occasionally, there was a machine operator who showed more promise with a bassoon than he did with the bellows or a typist who was an even better trombonist. When he did so, the twinkle in his eye which the Sousa musicians had known so well appeared for all to see. All in all, however, it was a hard, uphill fight.

Yet Armco stayed delighted. It was all very good public relations. The band was being spoken of about town. The *Middletown Journal* reported its various appearances with the avidity that the Cincinnati press used to cover the performances of the city symphony. Even Frank had to admit that when the music press started reporting the activities of Bandmaster Simon, he was not a little pleased. It was proof that he was making a go of something that could just turn out to be fairly big. What Sousa thought about it when he read the reports Frank could only guess: Foolish man? Really down on his luck? Going downmarket? He could only guess because for the moment, they were not talking – or at least, were not in communication.

What Frank was facing, however, was a familiar phenomenon. Edwin Franko Goldman went on record saying he was 'amazed and shocked by the difference in standards between the summer bands and the orchestras'. As he said: 'The orchestras were rehearsed carefully and each man was expected to perform his part to perfection, but in the bands there were no rehearsals at all and the most slipshod performances were permitted. There [is] no finesse, no exactness, no artistry.' For the time, that was the problem that Frank Simon faced – and it hurt. It did him no good at all to hear other bandsmen like Goldman rubbing in the same salt, saying that bands of the era were not realizing half of their potential. The difficulty for Frank was that he was not sure whether he was not getting *all* the potential his amateur musicians did have at their disposal.

He was a generous man, but he could not have felt happy reading about the success of Goldman's summer concerts on the Green of Columbia University, an unprecedented success that seemed to hail a new factor in band music, a new generation playing a new kind of music with the old instruments. Sousa may not have totally approved, but it was keeping his kind of music alive. What was Frank doing? All he could really point to was keeping the vanity of his players alive.

Nevertheless, thanks to Simon, the musical ambitions of Armco expanded. Sunday-afternoon concerts would include performances by visiting orchestras. But the Armco Band was the mainstay. In a matter of months there were 55 members of the band. On 21 November there was a different kind of concert, still with Frank Simon on the podium – the first performance by the Armco Symphony, made up of employees and some of their wives and children. It offered no competition to the nearby Cincinnati orchestra and certainly no one in Boston or New York was perturbed, but Armco felt it was establishing the cultural capital of Middle America.

The first symphony concert was held at the First Baptist Church's remodeled auditorium, sponsored by the Stiles Bible class. They played Schubert's 'Serenade', the 'Poet and Peasant' overture and Frank soloed with 'Robyn's Answer' – which brought so much applause he gave an encore. Plainly, it was the only professional performance of the evening. The *Middletown Journal* recorded that the public was pleased with the initial concert in which the orchestra was strongest in the woodwinds.

In his heart Frank was able to counter the continuing frustrations with growing satisfaction, except that it seemed all so relative. The orchestra was not going to make much of an impact, but were the members of the band perhaps really getting good? Or were they just so much better than when they had first started?

It was hard work, made all the more so because it was his own reputation still very much on the line. If the band failed, Frank Simon would have failed, too – gone on record as a failed bandmaster. He knew that he had no choice but to make it big. He would never have been satisfied going back as a soloist in someone else's band and, short of finding an existing star band waiting for him to take over, building up his own organization was the only thing now open to him.

By the time the first anniversary of Frank's Armco contract came up for discussion there was really nothing to talk about. Both he and Armco wanted it renewed on a permanent basis. Already Frank Simon was as essential a part of Armco as the buckets pouring the molten steel.

11 · 'One of the Greatest Woodwind Ensembles'

But still the frustrations grew. In fact, they got worse as the Armco Band became better known. The more melodic the men became, the more Frank Simon was aware of their inadequacies – and worse still, real or imaginary, he was convinced that his colleagues were, too. They may have admired his business acumen, but were they laughing up their sleeves at this ragtaggle operation he was now fronting?

Armco may have set up a very nice bandstand at Melody Meadows, the appropriately named section of Armco Park where the ensemble played on Sunday afternoons, as well as at Armco Field, and employees and their families flocked to the winter concerts held in Middletown, but Frank knew that he was not playing in the top league. It hurt as only a man so professionally concerned for the fostering of musical talent could be hurt.

Before long, changes were necessary. 'I tried hard and I kept increasing [improving] the quality of the music, but some of the men couldn't negotiate it,' he remembered shortly before his death. As he said, 'They weren't musicians. Musicians are born, they are not made.'

They were weeded out. Some quit of their own volition. Others accepted the gentle hints that Frank passed their way. He had the gift of tact and at moments like this, the gift was not to let him down.

If he was going to stay with Armco – and there was no doubt that the appointment had been more than confirmed on both sides – he had to have serious changes. As he said, even he could not make a silk purse out of the proverbial sow's ear. He was more tactful in his discussions with the company board. The existing set-up, he told them, was not going to work other than as a fairly competent amateur band which occasionally doubled as an equally amateur symphony orchestra.

It was a surprising statement for the Armco men to hear. Hook and the company president, George Verity, were happy enough, in the same way they would have been delighted had the firm's team won the amateur baseball pennant or if the Armco amateur dramatic society had been awarded first prize in the regional finals. Except that in this case, they had an amateur baseball team led by Babe Ruth and a part-time dramatic group with John Barrymore prompting from the wings.

To Frank Simon, the serious changes he demanded amounted to one thing: the band made up of steelworkers who might be able to play music had to be changed into an outfit of musicians who might also be able to work in a steelworks. The board gave its agreement – except that there was no question of there being any 'might' in the new equation. Frank was given the company's authority to find musicians who definitely *could* and would be expected to work in a steelworks.

He scoured other plants to see if these men existed in workforces up and down the country. Then he went to the colleges and universities, the chief nursery at the time for future band personnel. He wanted to know of band virtuosi who had studied metallurgy or similar subjects. Again, he would also go to the white-collar people, or at least potential white-collar people – musicians who could get away with holding down a job in an office. Of course, there had to be vacancies on the shopfloor, in the laboratories or the offices of Armco, but not surprisingly, by some weird coincidence when Frank Simon had found a musician he wanted, there just happened to be room in an Armco department for which the man was suited.

Eventually – and it certainly did not happen overnight – Simon had about 60 musicians who individually could stand the test and be considered professional. Before long, he had an ensemble that was as professional as any on the circuit. Now he wanted to make it the *most* professional band in the country.

Whatever happened, the company was well suited. They knew the potential value of what Frank Simon was bringing them. In

Middletown and the whole Cincinnati area, the name Armco was standing for something – not least as a caring employer of labor.

They knew everything was going well the day that Frank said that he wanted to take the band further afield. And he did. The Armco Band went traveling – to the Canadian National Exposition, a sensational experience except that the entire band was seasick on the way home. They also went to the Ohio State Fair. In 1923 the Armco Band made its first recordings for the Genett label, based in Richmond, Indiana. The company had sent talent scouts to the concerts at Armco Park and these strange 'spies' were glad they went. They immediately wired the home office of what they thought they had at their disposal.

One of the first recorded sides was Fillmore's 'Men of Ohio'. Frank was taking advantage of old friendships in a way that both appreciated most. Other early recordings included 'The Whistler and his Dog', 'The 136th Field Artillery March', 'Three O'clock In the Morning', 'O Sole Mio' (Frank on solo cornet), 'Smilin' Through', 'Just A-Wearyin' For You', 'Drink To Me Only With Thine Eyes' and 'I Love You Truly'.

Meanwhile, the name of Frank Simon was being burnished again and Armco was not doing badly out of it either. For every dose of publicity it received, hand in hand with it went a huge amount of goodwill. An editorial in the *Middletown Journal* on 25 July 1921 commented:

> The concert given every Friday evening by the new Armco band has become a community event. These open-air affairs fill a niche in the activities of Middletown that has been empty, although probably the people were not aware of that something which was lacking. Now the weary populace can turn from the workaday world and in the cool of the day assemble at Armco field, lounge upon the greensward of the natural amphitheatre and in relaxation listen to the soothing, soul-inspiring symphony of worthwhile music under the direction of the nation's premier cornetist – our own Frank Simon.

The paper went on: 'These weekly concerts are appealing to the people of the entire Miami valley and they are looking to Middletown as the center of wholesome, unselfish community intercourse where the intermingling of community life is making for the development of a happy and contented citizenship.'

Frank's family was equally happy, providing Frank himself with plenty of goodwill, too. Previously they had depended on his visits home while 'resting' between Sousa seasons and at other rare moments like the band's visit to Middletown and Cincinnati in 1919. Now, though, they could take him for granted – and enjoyed doing so.

For her part, Mary was nothing less than delighted. She liked her small Middletown home and loved basking in her husband's glory. She also loved the fact that, the odd touring engagement apart, he came home every day – even though she was still not prepared to change the sheets each night.

But there were changes afoot for the Simon family. In July 1923 the family increased. Mary gave birth to her first child, a son whom they called David Leo. Solomon and Bertha could only have been thrilled. Calling the baby Leo was following the Jewish tradition of naming a baby after a much-loved deceased relative. It must have made the elder Simons feel that *their* Leo had, in a way, been reincarnated. The following year, the family rejoiced again – with the arrival of the second Simon son; this one was called Joseph.

Frank was a proud man as well as a loving one. Now the sort of pride he was beginning to show for his own band he was able to take in his family. The devoted son and loving husband was an even more doting father.

Now, when he went to band rehearsals, he could tell stories about the doings of the younger members of the Simon family. But what pleased him just as much was the way people were talking about the Armco Band. No longer was he having to be ashamed of the kind of outfit he was fronting. His men were dignified as well as talented. One man saw them arriving for a winter concert, all dressed in long coats, and asked where the morticians' meeting was being held.

Frank was now able to hold his head up high. People were going to have a chance to hear the band – to an extent he could never have imagined. Armco was proud of having the first industrial band in Middletown – and already knew it was the best in the country.

The opportunity for real change and advancement came on 26 January 1925. The Armco Band made its first broadcast, on the Cincinnati station, WSAI, in a program sponsored jointly by the station and the *Cincinnati Enquirer*. 'Middletown Triumphant,' declared the paper the next day – as well it might, bearing in mind it was its own show. Its critics explained the opening of its review:

> We failed to catch the prophecy in those words as they appeared on the WSAI-*Cincinnati Enquirer* radio program last night, but their significance was clear after the Armco Concert Band of Middletown had played its first number . . . Armco, the American Rolling Mill Company's band, has been a familiar name, but it is more than that today. Cincinnati knows it now as something worth bringing into its musical family circles more often and the band's conductor as an artist who has won to heights off the beaten path and more difficult of achievement than the straightaway road to instrumental accomplishment.

And, the paper added:

> From the throbbing industrial hive that is Middletown, Mr Simon has welded an organization of musicians that is destined to take a unique place hereabouts and perhaps in cities out beyond and give to Middletown and the flaming hearths that have made the Armco Band possible a brighter luster.

The people of Middletown were not slow in coming to the conclusion that Frank was benefiting their city as much as he was helping his company and his own career. In March 1925 they presented him with a gold medal in recognition of what he had achieved. Quite clearly, the band was perceived as a success back home.

On 26 November that year, it was broadcasting again – from the Dayton Radio Show. Across a telephone link-up from Dayton to the Cincinnati studios of the WLW station, the Armco Band played and were picked up across the ether, between the static, by enthusiasts – every new invention needed its enthusiasts to get started – hearing it quite clearly one moment and then hardly at all the next. But it made an amazing impact on those first listeners. Two months later, on 4 January 1926, the same enthusiasts put on their earphones, manipulated onto the crystal the piece of wire which instantly was dubbed the cat's whisker, and heard a second Armco show.

There were always soloists and not just Frank himself. If he could, he fostered local talent – like using Paul Katz, who came from Dayton, as a violin soloist.

Now there was prestige attached to the Armco Band's name. The transmissions received on crystal sets in the area were extensively reported in the trade press. Quite suddenly, the enthusiasm which had been in danger of being dismissed as a toy – just as the band itself had been dubbed until so very recently – was being taken seriously by Frank's professional colleagues. He could not have been more happy. Alongside his adoring family, he now felt fully vindicated in the profession – even if it did at first take a little persuasion to make the Armco executive share his excitement for what the British persisted in calling 'the wireless'.

They could, however, see how the band had shed its amateur status and was now being spoken of with . . . respect. It was not another Sousa's Band yet, but in its own neck of the Mid-West it was certainly as important as Goldman's was in New York, and Simon could ask for little more. Especially since it was now being billed as 'Frank Simon's Armco Band'.

There was now something of a paternalistic attitude to his band from the man who so enjoyed being a father at home. He showed an interest in what its members did and when newcomers applied for jobs he did his best to find them factory places. One of these was a young man called Corwin H. Taylor, later to become supervisor of instrumental music for the Baltimore Public Schools, whose only previous experience of the Simon technique had been watching him at the 1919 Sorg concert for which he had cycled nine miles before chaining his bike to the opera house railings. Years later, Taylor wrote to Frank to remind him of the time he had been offered a job with Armco: 'My principal recollection of that interview is of your kindness,' he wrote.

Other names were becoming important, and if Frank had previously blamed the personnel of his band for its failure, now he was doing the only right thing and thanking his musicians for its success. On that second Armo broadcast Frank had been joined on cornet by Paul Blagg. On trombone were Ernest Glover and William McFee – two names with which Frank would be associated, professionally and socially, for the rest of his life.

They were not just colleagues, not just friends. They were also an audience – for Frank's jokes. They instantly formed the nucleus of the coterie whom Frank would entertain with stories about the bands in which he had worked as a youngster. They were even more receptive to those jokes which he now began writing down on cards that he would bring out on what were judged to be the appropriate occasions.

People liked him for that. A great many people also liked him for a lot of other equally sound reasons. The radio audience was growing as well – occasional forays into broadcasting that were being picked up via WLW's ever more powerful transmitter into new parts of the United States and even into Canada.

New members of the band were joining the Simon outfit, although he would insist he had never actually forced anyone to leave. By now, there were thousands of applications to join the Armco Band. He told all of them that he was now looking for qualities in addition to pure musicianship – 'character, skill, reliability [all] of vital and equal importance, for without these requisites he was of no value to me or to the company'. And there was a requirement from the company, despite the ease with which he had previously hired people: 'To stay in the band it was necessary for [a member] to make good on his job.'

Once the staff had been recruited they were expected to put in an eight-hour day – frequently on shift work, which played havoc with rehearsal schedules. In return, Frank himself was now reaping the benefit of the promises that the Armco executives had given him. He had an office with the fire-proof cabinets he decided were necessary for his personal library, and there was a full-time librarian on salary, a man who also occupied one of the band's first chairs. Eventually, he would have a full-time staff of seven working in his own office – the first flute, clarinet, oboe, horn, bassoon and trombone players.

In case other band members balked at this (why should these staff not have to slave over a flood of hot steel?) Frank had a ready answer: they were not there because they were players but because their jobs were to arrange, copy, file and look after correspondence as well as publicity and promotion – the last was William McFee's job. Ernest Glover, the first trombone, was band manager and assistant conductor. All the musicians were union members – 95 per cent of them of the American Federation of Musicians.

By now, they were part of an institution, the kind that was recognized by the company and its employees as something they could no longer do without. In fact, it was the kind that made people wonder what they had done before it all came into existence – if there ever was such a time.

Every summer there were twelve concerts at Armco Field alongside Curtis Avenue, with the band working in a magnificent new bandshell specially built by the company for their own band, which now performed for an average of 10,000 people each Thursday evening. Attendance at the summer concerts was so high that the field was proving not to be big enough and the venue for these was changed to the much larger Armco Park, although they continued there on Friday evenings. The band even played for dancing.

'It was like a reunion,' Lynn Mendenhall, a saxophonist with the band, remembered. 'All the families of Armco would come, have a picnic and have a good time.' Sometimes 12,000 people would attend the concerts, all of them having that good time. If they were critical of the band's performance, they kept that criticism to themselves. Judging by reactions to the band, the only real critic was Frank himself, still occasionally smarting from having gone from the big time to the tiny time – at least as far as his fellow-professionals were concerned.

Every now and again he would give his musicians a pep talk – although what he was doing as much as anything was giving himself one. 'What you lack in musical ability,' he told them once, 'you more than make up for in enthusiasm. If you will remain enthusiastic, I promise you that together, we will, by golly, forge Armco a band.' By golly, he was going to do so.

In 1922 Frank had presented the great Middletown May Festival that involved 1000 local children. The bandsmen were expected to take part in two weekly rehearsals. There were now fees for playing in the band, provided by the association – the amount varied from a usual $4 minimum to an exceptional $7 – in addition to the members' Armco salaries. In the winter the concerts were held in the local high-school auditorium. Season tickets were sold for the eight winter concerts from which the musicians were paid and professional first-rank soloists were engaged.

Before long, however, the Middletown municipality decided it had a civic duty to help foster this local cultural endeavor, and underwrote the cost of the winter concerts, which meant that the people of the city could attend them completely free. They spent $6000 in 1928, a huge sum in those days. It was the first time those concerts had been given without an admission charge. At the same time, the local community chest, the Civic Association, paid for Sunday-afternoon concerts in Melody Meadow, the company's own beautiful woodland park just outside Middletown. Every week, thousands of people took out their cars to drive to the free concerts from all over the valley. Frank later estimated that about $4000 was spent every year for Armco's musical activities, including sums that went on buying the larger, more expensive instruments like tympani, tubas and chimes.

In part, some of the money the band spent was recouped from its tours, including one of the entire home state as well as of Pennsylvania, West Virginia and Indiana, where there were guarantees of $1200 a day. They earned $6500 from the Canadian Exposition and another $7000 from playing at the Ohio State fair.

The *Armco Bulletin* of July/August 1925, published for the benefit of the company employees, reported:

> The Armco Band is now in the midst of its busiest and most successful season of its history. The previous years have laid a foundation upon which the band is now reaping and if the present attendance at their concerts is maintained, it looks as though the total season's attendance would approach the hundred thousand mark. That is some little crowd of people, if you could get that many together at one time . . . Conductor Simon has spent much time in the preparation of his programs, alternating light stuff with the classics, soloists with instrumental selections; in short he has worked out programs of such variety that they should be appealing to everyone.

Meanwhile, the Armco Symphony seemed to prosper. The *Middletown Journal* noted:

> How Middletown came to have these magnificent musical organizations is an inspiring story of a gifted musician who had reaped all the laurels that were to be gained in his chosen profession in distant lands and the great theatres of the world who had a vision of giving his own home town the benefit of his wide experience and who gave up his great career in the wide world to come back here and undertake to teach youngsters and amateurs how to make music. The man with the vision was Frank Simon.

It was a much-repeated kind of plaudit. The *Middletown News-Signal* reported on 10 December 1926:

> Middletown music-lovers thoroughly enjoyed last evening's concert of the Armco band at the high school auditorium . . . and the organization under the inspired baton of Conductor Frank Simon, never played with more verve, with finer feeling for bringing out the hidden beauties of the compositions they essayed to interpret or with greater beauty of instrumental tone . . . Conductor Simon is deserving of great congratulation for the constant improvement which the organization has shown in the last five years until now it deserves to be ranked with the greatest military bands in the United States if not the world.

The competing *Middletown Journal* was equally ecstatic about a concert in February 1927. 'Letting the imagination wander, one could easily vision the atmosphere for a Persian garden when the band next presented "Scene Oriental", which was considered one of the most delightful numbers of the evening.'

Thanks to his Armco position, there were also a dozen spin-offs for both Frank and for musicians outside his now-normal orbit. He was beginning a series of undertakings that would become a part of his professional agenda – judging music festivals all over the country. In those early years he went to Pennsylvania and then to Oklahoma for the national band finals at Tulsa, where he adjudicated – and awarded the prize to the Mason City High School Band, recalling memories for local people of his discovery of Meredith Willson. 'I want to say that you have a very fine organization and more than that a real find in a leader,' he wrote to the band after the contest. 'Don't ever let that man get away from you as he has a great ability.'

Meanwhile, the local papers were doing their best to keep *their* man at home. 'Frank Simon', wrote Stella Weller Taylor in the *Hamilton Daily News* reviewing a concert in her town, 'paramount cornet soloist of America, conducted with a grace that rivaled the hitherto unrivaled grace of Sousa with whom he was so brilliantly associated for years.'

As George Crout remembered for me: 'The great thing about Frank Simon in those days was that he tended to make Middletown a kind of cultural center by cultivating the musicians whom we had in this area.' He even started a community choir – which, in addition to the 70-member symphony orchestra, was beginning to take up a great deal of his time. Before long, however, Frank had to decide upon which of the enterprises to concentrate. He could not do them all. He chose the band and the others faded away.

There was a considerable degree of truth in that statement about making Middletown a cultural center. But there was something else that Crout said which seemed to say much more of his contribution to local life. 'Frank Simon was the key to Middletown's entertainment in the 1920s.' Somehow, he had awakened an interest in talents available in this small Ohio town which most of the inhabitants had hitherto hardly known to have existed.

As Frank himself had written in what was now becoming something of a Simon Bible, the *Armco Bulletin* of September/October, 1922: 'Music in our country has had no easy row to hoe for its development. It hasn't been so long ago that the majority of our businessmen couldn't discern, even with the spy glass, any real reason for encouraging the best music performed as it should be.' Good music had meant classical music in the past. Now, though, he continued:

> We no longer have to attend the opera, the symphony or theater to hear good music. Industry has recognized its immeasurable value as a forcible element in the intellectual, spiritual and social upbuilding of any community and is now maintaining bands, orchestras and choral societies within its organization. These activities not only provide the employees with clean, educational diversion, but they render service in their respective communities, the influence of which resolves into a more cultured place in which to live.

His own band had increased to nearly 60 men. 'Due to constant practice and extended effort . . . the players have developed to a degree of proficiency which has [been] proved by their work and the class of their performances, given that they can now be classed with the best industrial organizations in the country'. He played all the old Sousa repertoire and widened it, too. He played Broadway show scores and revelled in the title of 'Symphony in Brass'. But he was never happier than when he had something really exciting to offer – like the first band version of Gershwin's 'Rhapsody in Blue'. He would play it in concert after concert, almost as often as the man he was said to resemble so closely, Paul Whiteman, who had first introduced the rhapsody. Frank also became a close friend of its arranger, Ferde Grofe, who played a large part in the Armco Band story in the coming decade.

He continued to play a part in the life of the community. At one concert he devoted a whole section to the Middletown firefighters. They needed a boost, he thought, and there was no better way for him to give it.

It was good news, the sort that a teacher likes telling his school principal or a parent enjoys when talking to a friend. He was not boasting, but bearing in mind all the problems of the band's start, 'gratifying' was hardly a suitable word to describe his emotions now. The Armco Band seemed finally on the map and he rejoiced.

And now it was not just Middletown that was celebrating the Armco name. There were other Armco plants in Ohio and Frank took the band there to play for its workers and their families just as he did in Middletown. There were plants in Kentucky and Pennsylvania, too. The band played at these just as frequently.

The press continued to sing his praises as loudly as the vocal soloists at his concerts sang their party pieces. When the band was about to launch its ninth series in June 1929, the Middletown *Sunday News Journal* declared: 'As the band enters its ninth season with the finest personnel and the best playing conditions in its history, it finds Middletown more receptive than ever before.' And the *News Signal* reported: 'The field, the bandshell, the band's personnel, parking arrangements and policing arrangements for the crowd of thousands expected to be there have all been perfected.'

What the Armco position allowed Frank to do was to celebrate a kind of freedom. For the first time, he was able during the year – and not just in lay-off periods – to take on other work which not only stimulated his income but also gave him opportunities to spread his wings, to let other audiences hear him – and sometimes to let his contemporaries in the music business hear and work with him, too.

He was elected a brother of the Alpha Theta Chapter of the Sinfonia Fraternity of America. He was also a Rotarian and frequently led concerts for good causes sponsored by Rotary. He was a Mason, too, and was also a great follower of the Shrine movement, which made it all the more appropriate for him now to conduct Shrine bands. He regularly played the solo spot at concerts of the Syrian Shrine Band in Cincinnati, which was more a labor of love than practically anything he was currently doing, if only because it was conducted by his old friend and former Sousa colleague, Henry Fillmore. For the Antioch Shrine Band in Dayton, an important group which would regularly tour other parts of the United States, he was himself the conductor.

Frank corresponded with other bandmasters all over the world. With the Band of the Royal Air Force at Uxbridge, England, he swapped music. They copied specially for him the manuscript of Waldteufel's 'Toujours ou Jamais' waltz, which he had heard the RAF ensemble play and, in return, he sent them examples of American band music.

He also wrote to bandmasters of the past – including his old teacher, the now ageing Herman Bellstedt. From Los Angeles in 1925, Bellstedt told him of the band he himself was now conducting. He had been ill, but on 9 September, he could write: 'Feel much improved and hope to continue so, but always a bit nervous.' Quite a confession from teacher to pupil, even all those years after that relationship had changed.

Bellstedt had been arranging music for Frank's band as he had once done for Sousa. 'Now, here's a good one,' he wrote. 'I do not remember what happened with the check you sent me in payment for William Tell burlesque. Did I cash it or loose [*sic*] it? See if you can find canceled check – issued about July 7, 8 or 9, or 10th or 11th. Of course, if you have that I cashed it but if you have it not.' That sort of confession of age and absentmindedness could not have given Frank much pleasure.

But plenty of other things did. When the Pittsburgh Railways Company Executives heard Armco's band play, they invited Frank to advise them on setting up a band of their own. He did so without wondering whether they were going to offer him a job or being afraid that he was helping foster a rival organization.

He played for the foremen's club at Armco and the concert went down so well that the Frigidaire firm asked him to play for their foremen. There was nothing in his Armco contract to prevent his doing so.

He took the Armco Concert Band, as he now enjoyed calling it, to play at the Osiris Temple at Wheeling, West Virginia. Afterwards the manager of its own band, a certain W. G. Yates, wrote to Ernest Glover: 'I want to frankly state that our committee was a bit skeptical about "Factory Bands" but we now feel that this is a misnomer and all doubts were immediately removed after hearing your afternoon performance.' Plainly, the Temple took a risk that they were not letting on about to their audiences. 'Frank Simon,' declared the program, 'may well be termed the "genius of the cornet", for no cornetist of this or any other age has shown the remarkable talent that Mr Simon has in mastering the technic [*sic*] of the cornet . . . He uses the Holton Clarke cornet exclusively.'

That was a fact not lost on the Holton Company, which continued to be grateful for his patronage. In a letter to Frank on 20 September 1928 Frank Holton himself wrote:

> As I know you are deserving in every way, it gives me much pleasure to see you coming to the front the way you are with your band and your solo work and I can see a splendid future for you and it looks to me as though there is good prospect of you being at the head of America's leading band, a few years hence. I can assure you that Frank Holton and Co. are very proud to have your band sponsoring our instruments.

The letters poured in from all the organizations for which he played: from the Business and Professional Women's Club of Mansfield, Ohio – 'Mr Simon's conducting seemed to have developed in each member of the band a sincere desire for artistic rendering of each composition'; the Tadmore Temple at Akron – 'Your band cannot be too highly complimented . . . The Finlandia and the Festival at Baghdad were outstanding numbers'; the Akron Oddfellows – 'Of course, Mr Simon is recognized as one of America's foremost cornetists and we are fully satisfied that he deserves the title which he has acquired.' The letters piled up, from Oddfellows clubs and from exhibition organizers. When he appeared at the Toronto Canadian Exhibition in March 1929, the manager of the Department of Attractions, Mr C. W. Ross, wrote: 'We wish to take this opportunity of stating that the Armco Band made a tremendous hit with our patrons and was a success from every angle.' Later that year, the band played at the Ohio State Fair. 'Having now had time to analyse causes and effects entering into our recent record breaking Ohio State Fair,' wrote Oliver Hartley, Director of Publicity for the Department of Agriculture, 'I am constrained to say that the Armco Concert Band was one of the leading contributing factors of success.' Probably no letter was received with greater pleasure than the one that came from Roy Hornikel, manager of Frank's alma mater, the Cincinnati Symphony, now under the direction of the eminent Fritz Reiner.

> I have been following with pleasure the activities of the Armco Concert Band both in your city and on tour. In my opinion, your artistic endeavors in the industrial field are most unique. I have known of industrial bands in the past and do not recall music being perpetuated in such an extensive way as by your organization. It is fit and proper to congratulate the officials of the American Rolling Mills Company on their very high ideals in engaging a man in the band field so renowned as your present conductor, Mr Frank Simon . . . I feel positive that you have earned the reputation that many critics have given you in placing this band as one of the greatest woodwind ensembles

Simon would always say that his greatest inspiration in life came from 'helping others get somewhere'. He was not sorry to see that he was going a fair distance himself.

The only trouble he was experiencing was in the Armco Band itself. Or rather the trouble was in Armco. Nobody in 1929 was yet singing 'Brother, can you spare a dime', but they certainly were saying it. The Depression was eating into American industry and it was hitting Armco as much as any other branch. In a way, it was affecting it more than many. The company was providing the raw material for all those automobile firms who were now shutting down production – and the automobile had been at the very root of the economic problems of a nation that suddenly woke up to the fact that it had thousands of cars sitting in lots with no one to buy them. Because there were no cars being made, there were no jobs for the car workers who could not spend anything on all the other luxuries and necessities of life. So the people who made those were also put on the breadline, a word that came horrifically to life.

If there were no new cars, there was no need for the basic material used in its construction – the steel turned out by Armco. If Armco could not sell its steel, it could not afford to employ so many workers. It if did not have the workers, it did not have musicians either.

The car chain was complete. Quite suddenly, when finally something worthwhile was finally being achieved, it all looked like coming to an end. To use Frank's own words, the band was wrecked. Or was it? The conductor of the band looked at the ashes and hoped that just somehow a phoenix could be found. It was.

Perhaps Frank Simon's greatest success of all was in knowing what new trends were on the way. Quite fortuitously, this extended beyond his music. Just before Wall Street crashed and executives went searching for skyscraper windows from which they could throw themselves, Frank sold most of his holdings. Personally, he was untouched by the crash – except that, for a song, he *bought* stock in the Kroger grocery chain when everyone else was selling. It turned into a nest egg that hatched very satisfactorily indeed in the years that followed.

Meanwhile Armco itself was providing as much a steal as steel. Its own stock went down to $3 a share. Frank wanted to mortgage everything to put all his money into Armco. 'Don't do it, Frank,' advised his mother. He took her advice and regretted it for the rest of his life. The few stocks he held in the company multiplied like rabbits in the Middletown hedgerows.

Of course, he also had his finger on what his public wanted to hear. And not just just what they wanted to listen to today, but what they would be enjoying in the months and years to come. That was why he was convinced he was onto a good thing when he asked for a meeting with the president of the company, the same George M. Verity he had first seen all those years before.

The radio broadcasts, he told him, had been an amazing success. People were listening to the Armco Band who had never before even heard the name Armco. Armco, he suggested, should book a season of weekly programs of its own. He would provide the music if Armco provided the money. Verity dithered and then decided. It might just be a good idea.

1 Simon's store: Solomon and Bertha with Leo (left) and Frank

2 The young bandmaster: at 14 Frank Simon was already proudly leading the Middletown Band

3 Simon's Band, Middletown; Frank is fifth from right in second row

4 Solomon and Bertha in 1915

5 Kopp's Band at the Fort Lexington Fair, Kentucky, 1909. William Kopp holding the baton; Frank Simon fifth from right in the second row; Henry Fillmore with trombone third from right in the third row

6 Herbert Clarke, the best cornet player in America and Frank Simon's mentor in the Sousa Band

7 With Weber's band, Oakland, California, Christmas 1910. (Frank is second from right in front row.) Twenty years later Frank used this picture for a Christmas card

8 One of the few occasions when the March King went marching. Sousa leading his band during the First World War

9 Frank Simon resplendent in his Sousa Band uniform

10a–e Conductor and cornet soloist with his own Armco Band

11 Rehearsing with the Sousa Band at the New York Hippodrome in 1919. Frank Simon is on the front row, to the conductor's right, wearing a derby hat and with his cornet to his lips

12 The Sousa Band traveled everywhere by train. Frank Simon is first left

13 His beloved 'Maryla' in 1919

14 WLW called itself 'The Nation's Station'. Frank Simon was the nation's star

15 The Armco Band in all its glory, Frank Simon at the head

16 Frank hoped that his sons David (left) and Joseph might follow in his footsteps, but musically they didn't get much further than posing for this picture issued by the Armco publicity department

17 With Ferde Grofe, who after working with Gershwin and Paul Whiteman, spent three years as Frank Simon's arranger

18 One of Frank Simon's proudest achievements was helping to set up the American Bandmasters' Association. Frank poses (right – note his trademark spats) with founding president Edwin Franko Goldman and the first life president, the 'Governor', John Philip Sousa. Frank saw to it that the ABA's first convention in March 1930 was held in Middletown

19 Al Hirt, the jazz trumpeter. Frank never told him he didn't care for his music.
This feeling wasn't mutual: Hirt paid tribute to Frank on his 75th birthday

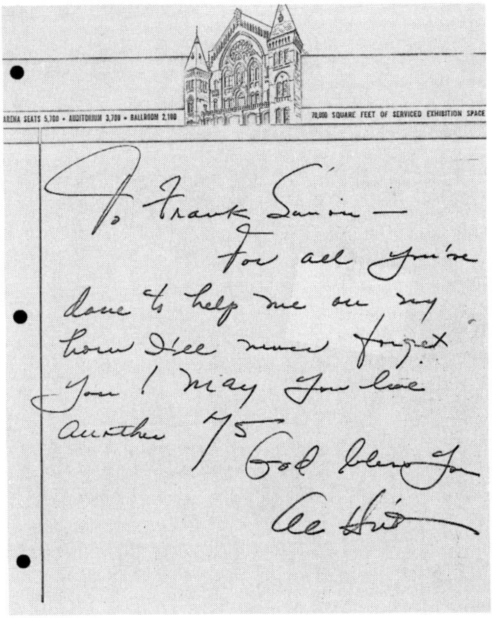

ARENA SEATS 5,700 • AUDITORIUM 3,700 • BALLROOM 2,100

70,000 SQUARE FEET OF SERVICED EXHIBITION SPACE

To Frank Sarin —
For all you've
done to help me on my
horn I'll never forget
you! May you live
another 75
God bless you
Al Hirt

20 Give Frank a good cigar, the company of good friends and a good catch of fish and he was a happy man. He is seen here with his friend Richard 'Witchie' Dowling and Mr Shively, the proprietor of the Canadian resort where the walleye pike were biting

21 Congratulations at Tucson; Frank shakes the hand of his friend Jack Lee

22 With baton raised – the way musicians knew Frank best

23 Frank and Mary, happy in old age together

24 In 1964 the ABA annual banquet was at the Langley air base, San Antonio, Texas. *Left to right*: Major Samuel Kurtz, bandmaster, Air Force Band of the West; Dr Paul Yoder, ABA president; Frank Simon, life president; General Prescott M. Spicer, commanding officer of the base. The picture shows Frank conducting, surrounded by Sousa, Edwin Franko Goldman and Austin Harding

25 One of the last pictures of Frank

26 The final tribute: receiving the honorary degree of Doctor of Music of the University of Cincinnati from the president, Walter Langsam

27 Visiting Sousa's grave

12 · *Radio Days, the American Bandmasters' Association and the Cincinnati Conservatory*

Frank had had his taste of radio and liked the flavor. His job was to convince Armco that they might like it too. Clearly, it was a move of some kind of desperation. He had to think quickly of salvaging something of what was now a highly successful operation at just the point when the firm could not stand it, financially.

Armco estimated it was losing $2 million in 1929, a phenomenal figure at that time. The only way to recoup some of it was to lay people off. The first out had to be the last in – which accounted for most of the band personnel. Frank's genius idea of making jobs for musicians had turned triumph into disaster. As he later remembered: 'My band went out like the tide. Just went out, my fine musicians just went out.'

The idea of a commercial radio program at a time like that was either brilliant or the epitome of stupidity. It was a gamble, but one that had to have a calculation or two behind it. What made the calculation worth while was a senior executive at Armco named Bennett Chapple.

Of all the bosses at the steelworks, Chapple had been the most supportive. He loved the band. He loved band music. Both facts were relics of the days when as a boy he had played in a band himself at home in Iowa. So it was to him that Frank took what looked to most people to be his crazy idea.

It will be great public relations, he said, at just the moment the company needed it most – no doubt thinking that Chapple would either agree it needed public relations seriously or like a hole in the head. 'Radio,' Frank told him in a conversation he never forgot, 'is coming into the picture as one of the greatest means of advertising that the world has ever known. Why don't you put us on the air with what we have, and what we do not have we will engage in Cincinnati – and we'll put us on WLW.'

He had made some inquiries and he knew that WLW – by then a 500,000-watt station which took its programs miles outside the Ohio area and earned it the right to the slogan 'the nation's station' – had been pleased with the occasional Armco shows it had already broadcast. Yes, it was interested. Was Armco?

Chapple was. After talking to Verity, so was the corporate entity that was Armco. The very scenario that nobody could have predicted at a disastrous moment like this was finally happening.

In truth, Frank immediately knew this was the greatest opportunity he had ever had. The bandmaster who had been forced to employ second-rate musicians was now being given *carte blanche* to get the best there was. The band was to be an advertisement for Armco as a company, not for the employees. Now nobody expected the men in the band to have anything to do with Armco at all, although some of the former instrumentalists might be retained. Now Frank was free to bring in, if he wanted to, brass and wind players from the Cincinnati Symphony or any other orchestra he chose, and he did.

He would also now be able to give more opportunities to youngsters – girl singers, boy violinists who would appear on the shows and get a gold medal for their trouble and a chaperone for their parents' comfort. Every time he featured a youngster, he imagined, the newspaper in their locality would publicize the fact – and publicize the band and the program at the same time. He could not have been more right.

Soon after WLW broadcast the first shows, NBC agreed to network them. It was justification indeed for all that had gone before. Both their Blue and Red networks were running Armco from the WLW Cincinnati studios and Armco was appearing in one of the most successful radio shows in America. For the first time, people who knew nothing about steel, nothing about Cincinnati or Middletown, Ohio, and even nothing about band music were tuning in on Sunday afternoons, 26 weeks a year. Armco's name was a household word – and the people who listened allowed a word or two from the company, too. The show became known as 'The Ironmaster' program and Bennett Chapple was the Ironmaster himself, providing a three- or four-minute homily about the new steel table on which housewives could now prepare their Thanksgiving dinners, or what went into the automobile that was going to take the family to the beach for Easter. And the band was still playing its concerts, all over the country but, most important to them, still in Cincinnati and Middletown. Frank Simon would never have permitted himself to be seen to forget his roots.

There were all the names that were now so familiar to people who listened to the radio shows, names like Ernie Glover (nobody now called him Ernest) and Bill McFee. But occasionally one of them went sick and Frank had to call on the stock of understudies who were always waiting in the wings.

Just occasionally, however, the wings were bare. Frank's solution or attempted solution was to call on one of his old teachers. Herman Kopp was still around in 1929. Did the old wizard know of a youngster who could play the French horn for a concert at Middletown's Sunset Park? Kopp suggested a local high-school boy called Luther Morrison, who today remembers it as one of the great moments of his life, although he never played the instrument professionally and, coincidentally, went on to work at Armco. But he remembers the occasion as being 'quite an honor for me'.

People at Armco were beginning to feel much the same about having the band associated with their company and their name. Steel was on the map and so was Frank Simon's Armco Concert Band. But in a way, the spread of his work was much, much wider. Quite suddenly at a time when all the indications should have pointed to the final demise of such an old, even antiquated, entertainment, bands and band listening were more popular than ever before.

It should not have been. By all the indicators, its day had come and gone. Radio was so popular now, so much a part of everyone's everyday life that there was little reason for people to go out looking for entertainment. And there were other ways to hear music.

If people were not listening to the Ironmaster program in 1929 they could well have been going to see Al Jolson's second film *The Singing Fool*, which was making the rounds a year after its opening and was still drawing wide audiences from the unemployed who had the price of a movie ticket when they could afford nothing else. Those who could not afford it would go to see a film just to have somewhere to go even when they were pretending they were at work. And yet people did still want to go to hear the band – even though things were definitely changing.

By now, Sousa, the March King, was almost a sovereign-in-exile. If he had not actually abdicated, Frank Simon was all but holding his scepter if not quite sitting on his throne. Sousa's was not a name on everyone's lips the way it had used to be, but Frank Simon's was.

Radio was the main home entertainment medium of the age and was enjoying its spin-offs even in the times of the Depression. The people who had bought phonograph records for years might now be feeling the pinch and cutting down, but because of the things they heard on their radio sets a whole swathe of others who had never spun a disc in their lives were now contemplating doing so. Millions of 78s were being bought, mainly by a section of these newcomers to the world of music. Had there been no Depression, the numbers would have increased a hundredfold, but there were still more than enough to keep the manufacturers in business.

The same went for the instrument makers, people like Holton, who were boosted every time Armco went on the air, but every other firm producing a trumpet, trombone or set of drums, too. The influence of a prime-time radio show was immense, which was proved every time Frank took his band to a bandstand and played to his standing-room-only audiences. By every definition, now he was a star.

Fans wrote him letters. One man sent Frank a poem – one he liked so much, he pasted it in the front of his scrapbook, although whether Mr Barton Rees Pogue of Upland, Indiana, ever knew that he had done so is a matter for conjecture:

> Band! Band! Band!
> My Land but ain't you grand!
> With a tootle, tootle, tootle
> And a wootle, wootle, wootle,
> You take command!
> You make a fellow stand!
> At the fife note and the drums
> There's a surge of spirit comes
> Lifts a fellow off his feet,
> Heaves his chest and lights his eye
> Makes him hold his head up high.

It went on for two more verses and then ended:

> To the cornets and the drums
> And the tubas, big old bums
> To the clarinets and saxes
> No I haven't paid my taxes
> But I'll yell my bloomin' head off
> For the band! Band! Band!

The poetry may not have been all that wonderful but the sentiment was and Frank loved every barely scanning line of it.

It was not just the Simon ensemble that was so well received and admired. Because it was so much *the* thing, youngsters were playing and listening to bands all over the country. The Goldman Band, which did its own share of broadcasting in the New York area, was reaping the benefit, too. All over America, bandmasters were figures of respect and great importance.

That was why they thought that they needed to get organized – to talk through the various problems they all had, to discuss ways of promoting band music even more, to work with the unions, to see fair play and fair pay among their musicians and to be sure that they were not competing unnecessarily against each other. It was Edwin Franko Goldman's idea to set up an American Bandmasters' Association and Frank was one of his first supporters.

Remarkably for any new group, it all happened very quickly. The association was formed not only by the 'new boys' in the business but with the blessing of John Philip Sousa himself – and with his name at the top of the notepaper. But the real guiding forces were the other two names on the sheets – Frank Simon and Edwin Franko Goldman.

People who knew something of the Sousa–Simon relationship were thrilled to see that the tales of animosity between them now were either patently untrue or exaggerated. In fact, as we have seen, they were true enough, but by the time the men got round to setting up the association – for ever after to be known simply as the ABA – they had settled their differences. Sousa made a point of telling Simon that he knew he had been wrong in blaming his old assistant conductor for the strike. Somehow or other, he had been told of the mistake and he regretted it. Frank no doubt burst into tears as he thanked the master for his vote of confidence. Certainly, leaving the Sousa Band to take over Armco had, in retrospect, been the best thing Frank had ever done in his life.

The first ABA meeting was held in New York City under their joint chairmanship. It declared its objectives officially to be:

1. Mutual helpfulness and the promotion of better music through the instrumentality [*sic*] of the school.
2. To secure the adoption of a universal band instrumentation, so that band publications of all countries will be interchangeable. [A big problem, that, hitherto. It was not always easy for an American band to follow and perform the music played by bands, say, in England or Germany.]
3. To induce prominent composers of all countries to write for the band.
4. To establish for the concert band a higher standard of artistic excellence than has generally been maintained.
5. And to do all possible to raise the standards of bands and band music.

Frank Simon was, before long, recognized as the real force behind getting the association under way. Because of that role and, most of all, because of what his Armco shows were doing for the band movement, he was getting the kind of recognition he had previously not even considered.

Early in 1930, the man who had always stressed the value he, and his mother in particular, had put on education, was awarded his first honorary degree. The Capitol College of Oratory and Music at Columbus, Ohio, almost on his own doorstep, awarded him its doctorate of music. Unlike so many other *honoris causa* honors, this one was well deserved. When he put on his cap and gown for the ceremony, Frank was not walking with professionals and academics who knew so much more than he did. There were indeed few people who knew more about his kind of music than he did. As both he and his former 'Governor' had said so many times, there was no one alive who could say that one kind of music was better than any other. From that moment on, Frank was happy to be addressed as 'Doctor Simon'.

He was a doctor who was now as busy with bureaucracy as he was with his music. The ABA was formally incorporated as the American Bandmasters' Association under the laws of New York, with Frank as one of the incorporators. But there was also no doubt where the first meeting of the Association should be held. It was scheduled for 13 March 1930 – in Middletown, Ohio.

It was an obvious tribute both to Dr Simon and to the town which had not only seen his own development as a musician but which had given birth to the band that was making all the headway now that a new decade was under way. It was perhaps the greatest day Middletown had had in its corporate life. There is also a very strong argument to say that it has never had a greater one since. The *Middletown Journal* – 'Full leased wire telegraph news service' – featured the event as the lead story on its front page: 'Bandmasters Open Convention Here Today' screamed the banner headline – above the much less important news: 'Murder Indictments Returned In Melvin Horst Case.' It was almost as if the editor of the paper wondered if he himself would have been murdered had he chosen to lead with anything but the event all Middletown was talking about.

John Philip Sousa arrived at the Middletown train station on a dismal gray day, wearing a long gray coat and carrying a homburg hat. There was no longer any need for him to have on his uniform. The 'Governor' was frail and hoping to give every indication that his days as a tough operator were over.

He was greeted by Frank and Edwin Goldman, each paying the tribute of young disciples to their musical messiah. There was also a band at the station – there had to be a band. As the instrumentalists made up of Middletown high-school pupils were about to strike up 'The Stars and Stripes Forever' for a beaming John Philip Sousa to appreciate, the conductor handed his baton over to its composer.

Standing on a chair hurriedly provided for him, it was the first time John Philip Sousa had conducted the number in Ohio since the 1919 concerts. Now he was there again – with all the enthusiasm of a baseball coach seeing his team carrying off yet another pennant. The band played loudly, but the applause at the end – from the musicians as well as from the audience who packed into the environs of the open-air depot on that drizzly day – was louder than anything the drums or the brass could produce.

That done, the three eminent bandsmen posed for photographs with each other – Frank looking fatter and more prosperous than ever, even if his trousers seemed more than a little too long over his crisp gray spats, and carrying his derby hat in one hand and a cigar in the other – smiled and waved to the adoring masses and moved off in gleaming cars for the start of business at the Manchester Hotel, a place that was on many subsequent occasions to feature in the Frank Simon story.

The local and musical press were full of the events of the convention for days afterwards, and there are still to this day Middletonians who tell of it when recalling old times for grand- and great-grandchildren. It still features in histories of the area, the days when bandsmen came to town.

Middletown was really in its glory. Throughout the proceedings, there were concerts, dinners, luncheons – all to celebrate both the occasion and the great men in the world of bands who had descended on this little spot of Ohio. Most important of all, it was the greatest gathering of bandsmen America had ever known. The students at the local junior high school who were allowed to leave their desks to see the parade from behind the classrooms' large first-story windows were left in no doubt as to its significance. Naturally enough, Frank Simon had never been happier. More than 30 years later, he wrote: 'You may well imagine how proud I am of this distinguished organization which was born and had its beginning in Middletown.'

Armco, who were the official sponsors of the event – Bennett Chapple was particularly excited about it – had gathered other firms from Middletown to enlist their co-operation. As Chapple said: '[We] set up a display of hometown products in the basement of the hotel as a sort of welcome mat.' Printed digests of short talks on different aspects of Middletown's industrial life were prepared for the participants.

It all also betrayed a strong sense of what Frank himself, as the guiding light behind the whole thing, wanted. It was no coincidence that when Sousa was welcomed at the station, standing in a place of honor ('beneath the Sousaphone' noted a local newspaper) was Herman Kopp, who had been conducting the high-school band in readiness for the veteran's arrival. But it was Sousa's presence which thrilled everyone most, it seemed. For Frank, there was one task he set his heart upon more than any other. It was his first and last real opportunity to lay the ghost of the strike. He kept bringing up the subject whenever he and the March King were together. 'I want you to know, Mr Sousa, that I had nothing to do with that,' he told him. 'I was not the ringleader.'

'I know that now,' the 'Governor' repeated, 'but look what you have accomplished.' Years later, Frank told Paul Bierley: 'I swear to you on my mother's grave, I was not responsible for that strike.' The charge that he was still lay on his chest like some heavy undigested meal, and he had a few of those, too.

Sousa was not slow in settling into the routine of the occasion. When he heard that Ernie Glover had to go off to Dayton with two of the visiting bandmasters, he offered to take Glover's fiancée Loucille Kimbel to the movies. With Victor Grabel, one of the leading bandsmen of the day acting as chaperone, they saw the current heartthrob Charles Farrell in *The River*, the movie playing at the Sorg.

Soon afterward, he spent a few hours at the Armco mill. Bennett Chapple recalled taking him round and noticing how the sound of the machinery registered with him. It was, he recalled, 'as though he had been inspired by a new theme'. Sousa stopped and said, 'Listen. That's rhythm.' Chapple went on: 'As we washed up after the trip, I watched the great Sousa squeeze the soap through his fingers after he rolled up his sleeves like any other workman who had finished his job.'

Perhaps the most notable feature of the ABA convention was the ability Frank showed in staying in the background and not *appearing* to mind. It was Edwin Franko Goldman who was in the limelight most of the time and who was about to be made the ABA's first President. He told the people there:

> We must influence composers of this generation and generations to come to write seriously for the concert band ensemble. Second, we must collectively raise the playing standards of the concert band. Third, we must make every attempt to govern the ethics of our profession. Fourth, we must convince the public everywhere that the concert band by the educational, entertainment value and uplifting effects of its programs is entitled to their enthusiastic support.

But everyone there knew that the whole thing was Frank's doing and so made it Frank's week. His friend R. C. Dowling, a highly influential figure in Ohio politics who was both the local postmaster and chairman of what was known as 'Municipal Music of Middletown' gave his greetings. And as if to demonstrate that his firm had had something to do with it – Armco paid many of the bills – Bennett Chapple said he was grateful for the fact that Middletown had been 'honored' by its role as the ABA's first meeting center. The local press was beside itself, with the *Middletown Journal* ('Middletown's Popular Newspaper') giving pages of editorial and advertising space to the convention and featuring photographs of the bandleaders coming to town. But none was displayed more prominently than Frank's own.

The convention dealt with the problems of securing financial municipal support. Karl King, the former circus bandmaster who was now Director of the Municipal Band of Fort Dodge, Iowa, and who was regarded as the greatest composer of marches after Sousa himself, gave the paper, and Victor J. Grabel, the ABA secretary, read another on 'Revising Published Band Arrangements'. Bad band arrangements, he said, had done as much harm as bad bands. Herbert Clarke's influence was felt, too. By now he was Director of the Long Beach Municipal Band. He could not get to Middletown, but his paper on 'The Proper Use of the Cornet and Trumpet in the Concert Band' was read for him by Victor Grabel.

Then there was the contribution from Sousa himself. 'The Orchestra and Band as they Originally Existed' may not have been the most inspiring or controversial subject for discussion, but he was listened to with all the deference of a gathering of maharajas at an Indian durbar hearing their emperor. 'Our object,' Sousa declared, 'is to bring about a uniformity for a band. We lead in a great number of things in this country and if we can lead in presenting the world with instrumentations we know are the proper kind it will be worth while. Publishers will have to help us in this respect.'

Fritz Reiner – not normally a man to join in the fun of an occasion – conducted a special concert of the Cincinnati Symphony for the delegates and invited Sousa to conduct two of his marches, 'El Capitan' and the inevitable 'Stars and Stripes Forever'. Then there was the whole succession of banquets, given by a women's group one day and the local musicians' federation the next.

Helen Gerber Ramsdell, who was just beginning her career as a vocalist with the Armco Band, recalled it for me as 'the biggest event of all time'. Frank was put on his mettle and sometimes the pressure showed. 'Frank had the quality, the ability to put people at ease immediately,' she said. 'But on occasion, he'd lose his temper. When a certain section kept repeating the same mistake, he flew off the handle a little bit, but he never swore. He just pounded on the music stand a little bit.'

But perhaps nothing that went before it matched the convention's finale – probably the greatest band concert America had ever heard, given by the Armco Band under more than a dozen conductors, the leading participants of the convention.

The nation heard the concert on the Armco program – all two hours of it. For days there had been advertisements in the papers. 'Tune in this Sunday to any of the following stations: WLW, WOR, WMAQ, WTAM, WIL, KMBC. Hear our own Armco Band under the baton of John Philip Sousa.' The advertisement said that the concert could be heard best of all on a Majestic Electric radio. But it sounded pretty good on any set, even then.

The 60 members of the band were never in better form and neither had Frank been better either, genially playing host to his colleagues and offering them something which they could never offer themselves. None of them, though, had his own pulling power. Now their concert was being transmitted by the six radio stations. It had never happened before, but then there had never been a band concert like this before.

It could, of course, all have seemed like a wonderful way of Frank's showing off, but he made it seem as though it were he doing *them* a favor. And he was. 'It is now my pleasure to hand over my baton to . . .,' Frank announced time after time and visiting bandmasters like Victor Grabel or Captain R. B. Hayward of the Toronto Concert Band found difficulty reading scripts that had them saying no more than, 'Thank you Frank Simon, it's my pleasure to play . . .'

In Grabel's case it was playing the overture *La Princesse Juane* by Saint-Saens – a tribute to the maestro's love of band music – before Captain Hayward conducted 'The Khaki Review'. Goldman played an extract from Sibelius's *Finlandia*, and other conductors like Captain Charles O'Neill of the Canadian Army played their own specialties. Peter Buys, of the Hagerstown Municipal Band, wrote a piece specially for the occasion, 'The Iron Master'. But the star was, of course, John Philip Sousa, conducting his epic 'Dwellers of the Western World'.

Listeners did not even wait for the show to be over before they were phoning in and sending telegrams of congratulation. George M. Verity, President of Armco, sent a wire to Bennett Chapple:

> ARE OUT IN COUNTRY HERE WITH NO RADIO FACILITIES SO COULD NOT HEAR CONCERT STOP IT WAS CERTAINLY A WONDERFUL AND MEMORABLE OCCASION WHICH DID GREAT CREDIT TO FRANK AND TO THE BAND AND TO MIDDLETOWN GIVE THEM ALL MY WARMEST CONGRATULATIONS STOP THE ARMCO BAND IS UNQUESTIONABLY GROWING IN POWER IN EXPERIENCE AND IN LOCAL AND NATIONAL REPUTATION.

Some people were happy to admit they had been wrong. Frank probably was happiest of all to receive this telegram: 'HEARD YOUR ARMCO BAND OVER RADIO YESTERDAY CONGRATULATIONS BEST WISHES COUSIN JULIUS.' It was as though he had been presented with the most valuable item out of the complete stock of Noah's Ark. The town felt much the same way. At a banquet on the last night, attorney Ben Harwitz told the diners: 'We hope your future will be as sweet as the music you bring.'

When it was all over, the echoes were a long time fading – like the reverberations from a Frank Simon solo. 'I am home again and during the long trip from Middletown I had plenty of time to reflect upon what I saw and heard in your wonderful city,' wrote Edwin Franko Goldman from New York:

> The more I think about what you have achieved during the last few years, the more impressed I become. I repeat what I said at the concert on Sunday afternoon, ie: that you have built up one of the outstanding organizations of the country and in doing this you had many obstacles to overcome. You have proven yourself not only a fine musician, an excellent conductor and a remarkable cornetist, but a wonderful organizer. Due to your great leadership, the Armco Band occupies a unique position in the world of music today. To say that I was amazed at its performances is putting it mildly. I was inspired and thrilled . . . As for

> the convention itself, it was an accomplishment that will live in the memories of our members forever. I believe that the convention, together with the concert, was the greatest event of its kind ever held in the history of the world and the largest part of the credit for its success is due to you.

Frank was equally generous in his reply. 'It was a distinct pleasure to have you here,' he wrote, 'and you have made a deep and lasting impression on all of the people of our city, especially the ladies are all singing the praises of our handsome President.'

The convention was not without its politics. A row appears to have blown up between Goldman and Sousa, who had for some time been refusing to take any letters or calls from the New York bandmaster at the behest of the 'Governor's' manager, Harry Askins. It was up to Frank to act as peacemaker. He wrote to his colleague:

> In a private conversation with Mr Sousa I told him what your treatment by his office was and he was much put out over it. I gave him to understand, notwithstanding anything that Askins might think, that you are his friend and he replied that Harry makes many mistakes. I know that he feels kindly toward you and it was only the jealousy of his manager which caused him not to receive your mail, etc.

To cement his own relationship with Goldman – they were writing to each other on 'Mr' terms – Frank promised to feature his 'On The Mall' march on a future program.

But Goldman's appreciation of the Simon convention style was genuine enough and was replicated a hundredfold. The head of the York Band Instrument Company, Karl B. Shinkman, wrote: 'I have never attended a convention that was so beautifully handled as the ABA Convention and I do not see how one could express his appreciation with mere words.' And not just appreciation for the way the convention itself was organized. Mr Shinkman added:

> I think I owe you an expression of thanks for a great improvement in my general health. Prior to going to Middletown my appetite was shot – for several weeks I couldn't eat a full meal – the sight of food actually nauseated me. Well, I got over that quickly after reaching Middletown and by Sunday noon I was eating like a horse and incidentally feeling much better.

Captain Hayward was happy enough to remember the privilege of conducting the Armco Band for the broadcast concert:

> I find it very hard to get back to the hum-drum way of life after the wonderful time that you gave us last week and am living it all over again in my memory daily . . . You made band history and it will be very difficult for anybody to follow you.

Simon himself knew it had all been a huge success, but he was not relieved of the frustrations himself. In reply to Captain Hayward, he wrote:

> It was a terrible let-down after you all left and really I had to go to bed for a day to rest up. Every night I had a genuine nightmare, heard music, saw all the conductors, the various banquets were before me and I paced the floor a good portion of the time.

But there was a good taste, too:

> If you men were pleased with the program that we had it is nothing compared to the pleasure it gave us to have you here. The hotel manager remarked that it was the finest and cleanest convention that he ever handled. It is still the talk of the town. I have never seen our people so enthusiastic over anything since the Armistice.

Afterward, a resolution in illuminated Gothic script was presented by the delegates to their host, offering

> grateful thanks and appreciation to its illustrious associate, Mr Frank Simon, Director of the Armco Band, for his gracious kindness, his consummate skill and his ceaseless and untiring effort without which, this Convention could not have achieved the success with which it has been crowned. And it is further resolved that this resolution shall be suitably inscribed and copies thereof formally presented to the City of Middletown and to our beloved member and colleague, Mr Frank Simon.

It was signed: 'Edwin Franko Goldman, President; Charles O'Neill, Vice President; Victor J. Grabel, Secretary; A. Austin Harding, Treasurer; John Philip Sousa, Life President.' The last position had been decided upon as much as anything to recall Sousa's visit to the convention. He was not going to have any duties to perform. But no band organization could expect to get anywhere without Sousa's obvious and official blessing.

If Frank's place in the band movement had ever been in doubt, now it was assured. The hardest audience of all, his own peers, had shown the status they accorded him. The dog with two tails had now seemingly grown a third and was wagging them all – in unison of course.

Sousa was as happy as anyone else. He was presented with a gold baton by his colleagues, former players and fellow bandmasters. It was a demonstration of the fact that they still felt he was the March King to whom they owed so much.

Ask Frank Simon, however, what the real high point of 1930 was for him and he would have left no room for doubt. It was the year he was invited to join the faculty of the Cincinnati Conservatory of Music. Even the doctorate he had received earlier in the year paled in significance compared with this honor. It was total recognition not just for him and for his band but also for his kind of music. Respectability had been conferred on him finally in these two gestures by the people who previously had been seen to look down on his kind of material. There could be no doubt that band music had arrived and was recognized as having done so.

In years to come he pointed to the Conservatory even more than the Armco Band as being the place where he himself achieved most. 'I could name you three or four hundred young artists I brought to the Conservatory,' he said. And it was no more than the truth. The young artists were brought to the Conservatory and, via that establishment, brought to band music. Some of them were to make their names in other kinds of music, too. But had they just become celebrated bandsmen and soloists – even if they had done no more than celebrate their art to themselves – he had reason to be satisfied.

Quite suddenly, there was a new string to his bow, or mouth-piece to his cornet. Youngsters who had never heard of a steel mill or who were far from ready to join his band were benefiting from the instructions he formerly had to limit to his own instrumentalists. Previously, he could have said – with justification – that the finest music lessons of all are the rehearsals a band or orchestra has to have. Now, though, he was extending his field of vision and a whole new 'audience' was benefiting from what he had to say and do.

The dapper Frank Simon was in business. He walked down the corridors of the establishment looking more like an industrialist than a musician, but the youngest and poorest scholarship kid could rely on a smile from him. Sometimes more. It was the start of perhaps the happiest period in Frank Simon's life. He had discovered a national audience for both his band and for himself and he had made an even more significant find – that he loved teaching.

Frank had, of course, always done the odd bit of coaching. It went hand in hand with being a bandmaster. In Chicago, he had tried his hand at it on a temporary fill-in basis and it had been no more than frustrating. Then in those early, depressing Armco days he had been forced to be as much teacher as conductor. It was his only option. He either gave rudimentary lessons or he did not have even a rudimentary band.

What he needed was an opportunity to be able to make teaching an adjunct to his real profession. Now, with the Armco Band so well established, he did not have to worry about not being able to spend enough time on doing what he considered to be his 'real' profession. Now there were no worries on that score – or on any other score from which he worked, for that matter. He spent hours in his own studio planning his radio broadcasts, choosing his music and, with a stopwatch in hand, timing what they were going to play. He would hum or whistle a piece to himself, making each chord last precisely the length it would take to play with his full 'concert band'. Sometimes he did it with records. But nothing was left to chance. The hour-long programs (later, they would be half-hour slots) would last precisely that, no more, no less, but with just the right intervals for commercials, then as now the backbone of American radio – although most of these referred to Armco and the steel it produced.

He was the star, so he could decide the format the shows would take and precisely the time he wanted to make his broadcasts. He was the star, so young musicians lined up for the chance to say that Dr Frank Simon was their teacher. That was why he enjoyed it so much. He wanted to teach. But he also wanted to be the star. Now the Cincinnati Conservatory was giving him the opportunity to be both. It was the perfect arrangement.

There were a number of institutions and a great many individuals teaching music in Cincinnati in the early 1930s, but there were principally two to which keen young musicians aspired: the College of Music and the Conservatory, an older establishment housed in a three-story ornate Victorian mansion in Mount Auburn, then the most fashionable area of Cincinnati, where former President William Howard Taft had once lived. The mansion, formerly the home of the Shillito department store-owning family, at the corner of Oak and Burnet Avenues, replete with beautifully carved wood paneling, had an adjoining dormitory and concert hall block.

The rivalry between the two houses of learning was intense – not helped by the fact that the College was Catholic-sponsored and the Conservatory had been set up by Protestants and ne'er the twain would meet. The rivalry, in fact, was so strong that both places sometimes seemed to lose touch with all reality. But it was to the Conservatory that Frank went.

It was based on the German Hochschule. For all his joy at being accepted by the Conservatory, going there in the first place had been Frank's own idea. He had suggested it to Bertha Bauer, a white-haired lady whose family had run the Conservatory for 50 years. The founder was her German-born aunt, Clara Bauer. She loved Frank's suggestion that it might not be a bad idea to have a band department – and if she needed someone to run it, there just happened to be a few spare moments in his calendar. 'Miss Bauer,' he loved to recall telling the matriarch of music, 'you're missing the boat. Other fine schools are training people to go out and teach band music.' She took the bait and Frank walked out of her office with the promise of a contract.

It was not altogether surprising. Miss Bertha, as everyone there knew her, had done her best to put her hands up to the Depression and was not interested in the problems it brought. It was not wholly realistic, of course, for students were finding it difficult to pay the bills and she was finding it difficult to pay her salaries, but she did – and expanded the Conservatory in the process. She set up a dance program at a time when most people did not think there was very much to dance about. But she had benefactors who were happy to get out their checkbooks at fairly regular intervals.

In truth, this was a woman with a reputation for being in touch with most developments in the field of music – a remarkable quality among lovers of classical music and the orchestras which played it. So, once having been given the suggestion by Frank Simon, she needed no persuasion. Only a few years earlier, she had gone out of her way to find means of expanding her operation (like going to Moscow to bring in an expert to run an opera department – and, before long, full stage productions of Russian operas). As much as a maiden lady in charge of young students of the arts could be imagined to do so, she jumped at the opportunity.

Almost immediately afterward, Dr Frank Simon became a member of the faculty of the Conservatory. What he was doing was setting a new trend. He was establishing not just the first band department there but also its first orchestral and instrumental departments. Until then and before the Russian dance classes started, the Conservatory had specialized mainly in voice training and individual violin lessons. Young girls went there almost as a finishing school.

Frank changed all that. There had been a marked reluctance, a snobbery about it in fact, from a mainly European faculty who regarded anything outside of a symphony as inferior. To get involved with band music was close to heresy.

But the heresy worked. More than a decade later, when Bertha Bauer was on her deathbed, she threw her arms around Frank's shoulders and said, 'Thank God for sending you to me.' (For years before, she had been admitting to friends that by agreeing to Frank's proposal, she had saved the Conservatory from bankruptcy.) Philip Wyman, Chairman of the Fine Arts Association of Cincinnati which partially funded the Conservatory of Music as well as the Symphony and Art Museums, and Minna and John Hoffman, both former Deans of the Conservatory during Frank's days there, all echoed Mrs Bauer. Frank had attracted many students from throughout the United States during those dark days of the Depression, and this had saved the school.

It was obvious from the outset that he was different from most of the other teachers at the Conservatory. Not for him the untidy hair or the corduroy jackets that seemed to some to be as vital a part of the makeup of the professional musician as their knowledge of the great composers. In winter Frank Simon walked into the Conservatory in the kind of overcoat with its velvet collar and white silk scarf in which he had greeted John Philip Sousa at the Middletown station. When the coat was off, there was a smart single-breasted suit, sometimes with a flower in the buttonhole to impress the earnest youngsters, who had rarely been exposed to such sophistication. If they had never seen spats before, Frank Simon walking through the college corridors provided them with the opportunity to do just that.

His classes left a lasting impression. Even in the 1990s, there are veteran bandsmen who recall at the slightest opportunity what it was like to stand in front of Dr Simon, listening to his instructions on the best way to form an embouchure. He worked in a big room – standing in a corner, listening to his pupils blowing their own horns. The students knew how they had done simply by watching the expression on Frank's face. A badly formed note would produce an equally badly formed expression on the master's face. But if he was happy, he was a concerto in contentment, a symphony in satisfaction.

By now Frank was an expert and regular card player. But away from the card table, keeping a poker face was for other people. He knew no way of concealing his emotions. It was a fact of life which his students had to appreciate. Every lesson from Frank Simon received an instant report card. They never had to ask how they were doing. And he never had to tell them.

He was friendly with his students – even with the ones like Jack Watson who were not actually taking lessons with him. Watson used to play with the band at his home in Dillon, South Carolina – after having taught himself to play. But he had problems with his embouchure, until seeing an advertisement for a new kind of mouthpiece manufactured by Holton, a spring that helped the sound. Frank was noticeably interested and invited Jack to play for him. 'I didn't,' he told me. 'At that time, I hadn't played the trumpet for about four years, but Frank had heard from my own teacher about it and wanted to discuss it with me.' As Watson now recalls: 'Students tended to follow him around and to take advantage of his being there – to just talk to him.' But he was never *too* familiar. He would ask about their health or smile if he passed them in the

Conservatory, but he would rarely involve himself in more than that. On the other hand, he knew a great deal about the people who faced him in the music room.

It became common knowledge that waiting in line in front of Dr Simon in the Conservatory's dining room was like wearing one's soul on one's sleeve. Many former students tell how Frank waited behind a youngster in less than pristine clothes who took no more than perhaps a glass of milk and a slice of bread. As the boy or girl was ready to pay, Frank would step in. 'Oh, this student is having lunch with me today,' he would say to the cashier and then suggest that that young man or woman join him at his table – once, that is, he had fillled their tray with something more substantial. 'He was an enormously friendly guy – very stylish gentleman,' recalled Watson, who, a generation later, became Dean of the Conservatory. 'He had quite a few students.' But that was not surprising. As Watson said: 'He could bring students to study with him and then get them employment in the band.'

There was a double edge to his teaching – the work he did at the Conservatory and the private lessons he was now giving on Saturday mornings at home. A private lesson with Frank Simon was no tea party. He insisted on hard work and wanted results. But it was something of an entertainment – students who came to the house had a chance to hear Frank himself play his cornet as well as to enjoy the plaudits he handed them.

But he was not going to teach at home young people who had no talent. Those who came to him were students who had something to offer. He enjoyed their work the way a gourmet (and he was that, too) enjoyed a good meal prepared by a young new chef. If that were so, Frank's Conservatory classes were a veritable catering academy. But there was always a supervisory eye on what he did. Even the young Jack Watson knew that if there was one other star at the Conservatory besides Frank Simon it was Bertha Bauer: 'She must have been in her late 60s at the time and enjoyed being the reigning queen, which she was. We'd see her coming, we'd fight to hold the door open for her and flatter her.'

It was the peculiar chemistry which existed between Bauer and Frank Simon that made the idea of a band department at the Conservatory work so well. 'He thought even then,' Frank's son David now remembers, 'that Armco and even the broadcasts wouldn't last for ever and he believed that teaching would give him opportunities for expansion.' Certainly, those opportunities were appreciated by his students. As the now Dr Jack Watson recalled for me:

> He had the same thing that Sousa had, of being able to make these subtle changes in the tempo of marches, which you don't always see. It was like the way that it took a Von Karajan to get the real beauty out of a Viennese waltz. You knew that he was making those subtle changes when he came back to make a repeat. It would be a little slower, a little more rhythmic.

It all became very infectious. His students were going out into the professional world – if the Depression allowed them opportunities to get jobs – and were conveying the message that band music was not the inferior commodity a lot of them believed and as they had sometimes been taught by their other teachers. Even more important, the Armco radio broadcasts were influencing a number of conductors to include band pieces, particularly Sousa marches, in their symphony programs. Rarely did a pops concert omit the band touch.

What was more, the classical musicians knew they were embarking on something significant. Armco was now a national institution. People canceled social engagements so as not to miss the shows. And when they knew there was an Armco show coming their way, they lined up at the box office for tickets.

It was *mostly* Frank's doing, but not completely so. Ernie Glover, the ever-faithful Ernie, the band's manager, organized all the tours and set up all the outside engagements. He also clarified the problems which inevitably occurred from time to time between band and sponsor and sometimes with management. He got to know Frank almost as closely as did his own family. He went fishing with him – now the Simon idea of the perfect vacation – along with other friends like Bill McFee, by then the sales director of Armco who had joined the company as a bandsman, and sometimes with Frank's sons David and Joe. They fished in a number of rivers, but one of their favorite spots was in Ernie's native Canada. It was there that he himself had learned to play the trombone – in the local Salvation Army band. His father was a senior officer in those days and later became the head of the army in Australia.

From his home in Canada, he had heard early on that Armco was recruiting new musicians and immediately applied for the post. What he did not realize at the time was that his real position at Armco was as Frank Simon's best friend.

But it was very much a two-way relationship. Running the radio band was a full-time job. Few who had been in at the birth of the band could have realized just how true that would be.

13 · *A National Institution*

Frank Simon was now a national institution, but he did not forget his roots. He was as much of Middletown as he had been in his childhood and as his parents still were. Or rather, as his mother now was. In 1932, Solomon died.

His son, to nobody's surprise, took it all very badly. Frank's emotions were never far from the surface. Now he was overcome by sadness, the tears never far from his eyes. Solomon had suffered an attack of hiccoughs that totally exhausted him. As the *Middletown Journal* said, reporting that the death had 'left the city in sadness over the loss of a well-loved citizen', Solomon had 'failed to respond to every known remedy to conquer the stubborn malady'. Solomon was 77 years old.

It left Frank more convinced than ever that he had to take full responsibility for his mother, reversing the roles of the past. For the woman who had done everything in her power to launch her son on his career he was now doing all he could to keep her in comfort. He was constantly at her house and she at his. Before long, the store was closed and Bertha, as active as ever in her women's clubs and the Eastern Star organization (a kind of women's masons), converted it into a new home for herself.

There was now in fact a new Frank and Mary Simon home at 2804 Central Avenue, a magnificent red-brick detached house east of where Bertha lived, and what was, to all intents and purposes, an Armco executive belt. Many of the senior managers of the company lived in the area and, before, long had streets named after them.

The house standing on a raised, terraced bank had two verandas either side of the front door and looked as imposing as its owner.

There was a beautiful small garden complete with lily pond and enough fish to keep the children entertained. One of the most important rooms in the house was the basement. There, Frank kept his music library and planned his broadcasts, stopwatch in hand, listening to recordings on what would now be called state-of-the-art equipment. It was long before the days of demo records, so much of his planning was still done in his head. He knew he had 21½ minutes of radio time now that the show was on the air for a half hour and he still planned it all in his mind as he had always done, knowing when to add and when to cut. By the time he went to rehearsal, he knew exactly what he was going to do. He told his musicians and when they went on air on Sunday afternoons, he had his 21½ minutes, no more, no less.

He gave lessons in the solarium of the house on Saturday mornings. Everyone knew about those instruction sessions – having a child taught by Frank Simon was every mother's dream in Middletown. But he would not waste either his own or a child's time. If he did not detect a nascent talent in a student he would kindly suggest that the youngster take up some other kind of pastime.

But there was another feature of the house and of the Simon family's activities that was not quite so well known. Frank Simon now had his own publishing company, dealing with all his own work as well as that of some of his colleagues. It was never going to be a huge operation, but it would expand – other composers who trusted Frank wanted him to look after their material.

It was especially so after 1932. There was another significant death for Frank that year. The 'Governor', John Philip Sousa, died. It was as if in the space of a few months Frank's two fathers had gone – his real father and the man who had overseen his leap to professional triumph.

When a Sousa memorial was dedicated Frank was in the forefront of the bandsmen who came to pay him tribute. But the real memorial that he dedicated was his determination to play Sousa's music – the way that Sousa wanted it played. By now, he did so with what was close to a religious fervor, as if any wrongly played note, or any note played in a way that the 'Governor' would not have recognized, was a breach of orthodoxy, another heresy.

Other musicians who felt the same way would dedicate themselves to similar ideals, and the meetings of the ABA were replete with stories of the terrible things done to Sousa's music. Herbert Clarke certainly shared Frank's feelings on the subject. He also published the works of his old mentor Herman Bellstedt.

No one, however, asked the not-irrelevant question when they saw the Simon Music Company advertising in the trade press, or in the occasional mail shots (the advertising industry had its own degree of sophistication in the early 1930s), or when Frank, by some strange coincidence, managed to mention that he had added to the Simon industry: how did he find time to do it?

The answer is that Mary did it. She earned enough pin money to keep her happy by rolling up the sheets of music and sending them off to new clients. Frank certainly had enough to occupy himself, playing his music and conducting his band – the one that broadcast and the orchestra which now sometimes gave concerts with the musicians in white ties and tails. He was also his own secretary, typing the letters that he either sent to colleagues or in reply to firms and organizations to which he had played. That, too, was part of being a son of Middletown. The commercial classes he had taken at school were, in their way, as important a part of the legacy of being educated in this corner of Ohio as his first cornet lessons.

Publishing was never the most important thing that Frank did, but the business expanded almost in spite of itself. It was as though he was doing a service to all those who had come before him. When he had a request to publish the work of Herman Bellstedt it was all he could do to accept and happily to propagate the work of the man who was largely responsible for it all by making the introduction to Sousa.

He was also writing his own works. There would never be another 'Willow Echoes', but other bands were asking for copies of his 'Cincinnati Post' (shades of Sousa again) and 'Four Square' marches, both published by Frank Simon himself, of course. He played his own works, but that was never the principal intention. He wrote them for publication and he made money from them all.

By now, he was beginning to build up one of the finest personal libraries of band music in the world, estimated in the early 1930s to be worth $50,000, a phenomenal sum at the time. But nothing could replace the sheer exuberance, the utter joy that he felt fronting his band. One critic about this time called Frank Simon 'the Toscanini of brass' and it was true. He did not hanker after fronting a 'real' symphony. It was not that he did not have the ambition. He was involved in what was an entirely different art form and he had reached its pinnacle.

To add to the delight of it all was that ever-present feeling of being the local boy made good. His mother always thought of him like that; she went to his concerts – frequently clapping at the wrong time.

People were still telling him how grateful they had been a couple of years earlier for the pleasure they had been given during the driest summer on record. No rain fell in the area during the longest and most arid summer in the history of Miami Valley. As one friend wrote to Frank 34 years later: 'There were no air-conditioners, no drive-in theaters, the highways uninviting for pleasure driving. What a relief, what a pleasure, to go to Sunset Park and listen to the music of Frank Simon and his Armco Band.'

His students flocked there, too, wearing their striped blazers and straw hats just like those in the days before the First World War but with their girls in the new 1930s styles which quite suddenly allowed them to show that their bodies had a shape. It was a tribute to Frank Simon that when he was on the bandstand, the shape with which these earnest students were principally concerned was that of the music he played.

It was a perfect practical demonstration of what they were being taught in the Conservatory. Frank did not always realize they were there or how important it was for them to be in his audience. As one of those students told me: 'He had no idea of the effect he had on people.'

But what was really exciting was the reaction he received from listeners thousands of miles away from what was normally thought of as Simon territory. Even before the show was taken by NBC, the WLW network was being beamed virtually from coast to coast – and further. The purser, chief engineer and steward on the S.S.*Chargas* wrote a warm letter of appreciation from Chile.

> Your selections from old-time songs was very good and the newest one, 'I Wish I Had A Talking Picture of You' . . . all were much appreciated.

> Your program played by the Armco Concert Band . . . came through loud and clear with classical music, including the 'Merry Wives of Windsor' and was greatly enjoyed . . . This is the worst place in the West Coast for reception on account of static and interference from a large power plant about 100 yards from the ship, but your music came in through so loud that the other noises were hardly noticed.

This sort of response did not go unnoticed. George M. Verity wrote appreciatively from the President's office at Armco:

> I read your writeup in last evening's *Time Star* with a great deal of interest. You have certainly succeeded in getting good publicity all round the circle. It will, of course, help very greatly in securing the outside work which you so very much want. The band has made marvelous progress during the past five years and its position in the musical world is quite unique.

Verity enjoyed Simon's company to the point of being in the group to whom Frank would tell jokes at the slightest opportunity. This letter from the company president ended: 'Will be glad to have you stop in at some time mutually convenient and tell me the balance of the story you were giving me yesterday when we were interrupted.' And in another letter he wrote: 'There is no question . . . you are going to do a very great work in behalf of your art and an equally good job in the interest of our company. Verity was a great fan, and even when he was on vacation at Pasadena, California, he still wrote to his bandmaster – by hand on the notepaper of the Huntington Hotel:

> The world knows of the character of the Armco organization and when a group of High Grade Artists go out carrying the Armco flag and make such an impression, it is proof conclusive as to the character of the organization to all those who have only heard of it . . . Give my congratulations, regards and best wishes to all the Boys of the Band.

His son-in-law and vice-president, Charles R. Hook (nepotism held perfect sway in those days), wrote his letters, too. 'You and your association have done a fine piece of work,' he wrote adding that he wanted to be present at a banquet being given for them at the Elks Temple, 'so that I could talk to them personally and express my pride in their accomplishment and the appreciation of the spirit which made this accomplishment possible.'

It had taken Frank some time to get used to radio, even though he had been the one to press the idea of the shows. He missed the communication he enjoyed with a live audience. But before long he adjusted and live audiences formed part of the shows he broadcast from the WLW studios on the eighth floor of the large white Crosley Building, named after the founder of the station, Powell Crosley.

Part of his success was the *way* he played his music. He continued to play Sousa in the manner that the 'Governor' had played it. By the same token, he played Tchaikovsky just as he thought the composer had written his work – he still cherished the soubriquet 'Symphony in Brass'. It was not the function of any orchestra, even a band, he believed, to embellish other people's work.

He was never a flashy conductor. In fact, he was critical of those conductors who did move around a lot. As his son Joe told me: 'He regarded what he did as playing serious music, not light entertainment.'

There were frequently problems over this attitude with the advertising agencies involved with the Armco show. All they really wanted him to play were Sousa-type marches – and for almost a year to fairly disastrous public reponse he did so. But Frank's idea was that his shows and concerts were opportunities for the public to hear classical music.

Certainly, his audiences appreciated that philosophy. Things were moving ahead with all the speed of one of Armco's steel processors, even though the times of the shows would change. Sometimes they were broadcast on Sunday afternoons, sometimes on Thursday evenings, but always at prime time. There were now what would today be called band 'groupies' – fans who followed the group's progress and went wherever they played. They wrote asking for pictures of the band – and they stayed loyal. One man wrote from Westwood, Ohio: 'I go to work at 3 a.m. but never fail to stay up and hear the "Armco Program".' Other musicians expressed similar appreciation. From Angola, Indiana, the Pokagon State Park Band joined in a letter to Armco saying: 'This organization is superb and one of which you, as its sponsors, may justly be proud.' When Clark Miller of the Tadnor Temple Band in Akron, Ohio, wrote to his fellow-mason expressing his appreciation of the 'wonderful band', Frank replied: 'It certainly was kind of you to write such a splendid letter to Armco. It proves beyond doubt that the Armco concerts of last season were greatly appreciated not only by laymen but by real musicians as well.'

He had requests too. The Ringling Brothers and Barnum and Bailey combined circus asked him to play Sousa's 'Riders of the Flag'. No sooner said than done, as if decreed by the crack of the ringmaster's whip. 'I have ordered the march 'Riders of the Flag' by Sousa and will include it in [the] next program,' Frank replied, typing his own letter.

A. J. Williams, the bandmaster of the Army and Navy Veterans Prize Band, made a point echoed by others: 'It is quite a treat to listen to a good band over the air once in a while as most of the time all that one can get is jazz.'

Armco took advantage of the advertising possibilities the programs allowed them. 'Rain causes rust,' ran one slogan. 'Rust causes leaks. Leaks cause trouble and expense. Avoid this by using Armco ingot iron.'

Frank was mostly concerned with boosting his own image and that of the band which provided it. The theme of a letter he had written in May 1931 to Dr C. F. Sexauer of Newcastle, Indiana, was constanly being repeated: 'For ten years, I have labored unceasingly to bring to our city the finest instrumentalists from the four corners of the world and develop them into the finest band in the continent and judgeing [*sic*] from the thousands of letters we have received not only from our country but from many Latin American nations, we are on the road to our goal.'

Frank liked to quote the radio executive who told him his show rivaled Amos 'n Andy in popularity. Certainly, there were thousands of people who recognized the program's signature opening, the Ironmaster's opening welcome, 'Good Evening, Friends', Frank announcing, 'Hello everyone – and now the famous Armco Band' and then the opening bars of 'The Entry of the Gladiators'.

If these were gladiators, the only competition in combat was from themselves – keeping up with their own reputation. Every program was like a child's report card, which always had to be better than the one that went before it. The nation's station, let alone its audiences, would have accepted no less.

Of course, it was all run in a highly professional way. Frank never bothered himself with publicity – he had Ernie Glover and William McFee (whose father had been Governor of Massachusetts and whom Frank had introduced to Bennett Chapple with the intention of getting him a job) to do that but he was always conscious of the image he was projecting.

Every week, there was a youngster giving his solo broadcast debut on Armco – to the accompaniment of suitable press notices. 'Boy Genius Is To Be Heard with Armco Band Sunday', declared the Hamilton *Evening Journal* over a photograph of an Eton-collared Louis Kohnop, aged ten, at the piano, and the practice was repeated all over the country. Sometimes it was a young singer. Sometimes 'Three Prodigies Will Appear With Armco Band Next', and the event was always recorded and repeated in every area of the country where the news might remotely hold some interest. 'Youthful Baritone Will Be Featured At Armco Concert' seemed to appear in the headlines month after month – if with a different 'youthful baritone's' picture and caption underneath. By doing this Frank Simon's band was not only benefiting from young talent, it was also scoring a great deal of much-needed publicity.

The American Bandmasters Association knew the value of what he was doing for them. In 1932, the ABA convention was held in Washington DC. Frank posed with colleagues on the White House lawn – with President Herbert Hoover in the center of the group.

In a way, he felt he had a mission in life – to improve band music. For that reason, he began the band 'clinics' he was to run for the rest of his life, a sort of masterclass, writ large, at which bands would play and he would criticize and try to cure their problems. It was extraordinarily remunerative, but one had the feeling that he would just as easily have done it for nothing.

As always there were great opportunities to socialize. In 1964 his colleague Mac E. Carr wrote to Frank:

> I will never forget the first time I met you: a period of time when I do not believe you knew I existed. It was at the national band clinic at the University of Illinois with our dear friend, Austin A. Harding in 1932 when you were a guest director. I think I sat for two hours, at least, until the wee hours of the morning, at this restaurant in downtown Urbana, listening to you spin yarns and tell stories.

It was an inevitable outcome of having Frank Simon around. He visited people's houses and regaled them with jokes and anecdotes. He made them laugh without opening his mouth. His gestures, a shrug of the shoulders, a movement of his arms, a wide grin, were enough. The press told the people who were not able to enjoy these personal encounters about the celebrity Frank Simon, although the jokes and the gestures were strictly for private consumption.

Seemingly, everything about the Armco show brought what two or three generations later was called media reaction. Columnists wrote things about him the way they wrote about film stars. 'It might interest you to know', reported the critic Pat Dennis, 'that when Frank Simon, the band leader, wields the half-ounce baton for half an hour, he loses five pounds at least. It would be tough on him if he had to take care of his own furnace.'

Frank only had the best musicians working for him, although he was frequently augmenting the full-time professionals (most of whom were now also members of the Cincinnati Symphony) with students. The band played for conventions or church gatherings at which he was introduced to a young student who lost no opportunity in informing the master that he did not always play the organ or the piano and that he was also a deft performer on the trombone. Frank always found the time to hear him. If he was impressed, there was the usual rejoinder: 'I think I can fix it for you to play on the radio this summer.' If he said it, the youngster inevitably found his way before long to the Cincinnati radio station. Many of them spent the rest of their lives telling how Frank had not just influenced their careers but had actually *made* them. William McFee, who was not to achieve his success as a musician, said about Frank: 'He not only took me out of the decaying roadshow business but he, with his wisdom and insight, discovered an innate writing talent in me. Thanks to Frank Simon, I went on to a successful 42-year career with Armco as a writer and teacher and counselor to writers. I still pursued my love of good music.'

He was much like that at home. The perfect father, David and Joe Simon now recall: 'I never had a better friend,' says David of the man who in those early years was always 'Daddy'. (When they grew a little older, he became 'Dad' and always with the same degree of affection.) Frank built a basketball court in the backyard for the children.

'We could have whatever we wanted – just as long as it wasn't a bike,' recalled Joe Simon. 'That was because of what had happened to his brother. We could never have a two-wheeled bike, although we just rode everyone else's. But we had everything else, although we didn't overdo it. There was a natural instinct which told us how far we could go. I didn't go out and get the best tennis racquet, for instance. We wouldn't have dreamed of buying one for $25 because we knew we could get one for $8.50.' Neither was Frank a disciplinarian – he left that sort of thing to Mary. He was as good a father as he was a son. But Bertha and he still had a warm close relationship – 'which was very difficult,' Joe remembered, 'because she and my mother didn't get on very well.'

He was also an extremely good and generous friend. When he heard of someone in trouble, Frank's recourse was to his checkbook. 'He would keep those things to himself,' David remembered for me. 'And that annoyed my mother immensely. Years later, we found old checkbooks with stubs showing the money he had given away. No one ever knew about it.' Mary kept an immaculate, well-stocked home, just the same. 'Everything was top drawer,' said Joe. 'First rate, very nice.'

Frank could have afforded the best for himself by now. 'But he was frugal about money, sensibly frugal,' Joe told me. 'He didn't have much interest in things mechanical. He had no great interest in possessions. My mother did though, paintings and things – no originals, but paintings to put over the mantel. Her china was of the best – $150 a piece. That was tremendous money in those days. She had service plates which had gold on them. She liked all that stuff. Dad could have paid for a Cadillac, but we had Buicks, Oldsmobiles, Plymouths. He was a very good driver.' On the other hand, Mary was not. As Joe told me: 'She was a terrible driver. I remember the insurance man telling my father that if she had any more accidents, he couldn't sell her any insurance.' In which case, Frank would have had to foot her bills as well as those of his friends.

The band was doing wonderfully well and he wanted to be able to share his bounty. Meanwhile, Armco, a company whose factories were belching smoke all over that part of Ohio and Indiana (no one talked about pollution in those days; smoke was prosperity), was achieving the seemingly impossble. Here was a product which the general public, the listeners to the program, could not actually buy and yet because of the broadcasts, in the face of the worst depression the world had known, its manufacturer was achieving bigger sales than ever before.

George M. Verity continued to appreciate what the band and the programs were doing for his company. When the show had an additional outlet on shortwave – on station W8XAL – Verity himself gave the Ironmaster's talk. He called it 'There can be no end to progress'.

The shows were being reported everywhere. Even the nation's undertakers were encouraged to put up their feet in their highly polished black shoes, take off their top hats and listen. It was the business end of the operation that appeared to appeal to this profession. As the *Embalmer's Monthly* noted in October 1931, it was all a tribute to George Verity who, 'during [his] long and interesting career as an industrial executive . . . has always been a student of business economies and human affairs and he has studied intently the hills and valleys through which the tide of business has flowed'.

Perhaps they were hoping to encourage the band to play a funeral march, which was not, however, the Simon style. Nevertheless, Frank always gave his programs a seasonal touch – with somber melodies for Armistice Day and always special emphasis on Christmas and Easter. The company tried to match the musical content of the shows with their Ironmaster chats. One Thanksgiving Day, Bennett Chapple began his 'spiel': 'The subject of my talk is mighty timely. Thanksgiving, the time to talk about the kitchen range. I almost have to loosen my belt to think of it.' He contrasted the way the ironmaster's art was used to produce a kitchen range in the 1890s with how the modern stove of the 1930s was made. 'It's a good thing those days are gone – for it's progress.' (He had no idea what the microwave would bring half a century later.) 'On Thanksgiving Day add to the things for which we give thanks, the kitchen range.'

America continued to give thanks to and for Frank Simon. He was so busy now that he needed help, and not just managerial assistance. Now he brought the eminent modern American composer and brilliant arranger, Ferde Grofe, into the operation. Before coming to Cincinnati to arrange music for Frank's program he was the arranger in New York for George Gershwin and Paul Whiteman. It was Grofe who claimed he gave Gershwin the main theme for 'Rhapsody in Blue'. It was Grofe who had just produced between 1929 and 1931 his seminal work, *The Grand Canyon Suite* and the *Mississippi Suite*. He wrote and arranged a special work for the Armco Band called 'Christmas Eve'.

Grofe lived six weeks at the Simons' Middletown house and at the sponsors' mill. Every day, starting at four o'clock in the morning, he watched the great buckets of molten substances turned into sheets of white-hot metal. The result was his composition dedicated to Armco, 'Rhapsody in Steel', which hit the music headlines in 1935 and was one of the most imaginative pieces of its kind – complete with its array of clangs, splutters and hisses. He was Simon's arranger for three years. He said the music was intended 'to portray man's conquest over the forces of nature and the sweat and toil of men in the mills who transform ore into things of beauty and use'.

But Grofe's work extended beyond that – and so did Frank's. The visiting composer arranged music which could, as a result, be adapted for bands. But he fitted it in between bouts of depression, out of which it was up to Frank to try to bring him. Grofe's wife had just left him and before the Simon treatment could be brought into play he locked himself for days in his room at the Netherland Plaza Hotel in Cincinnati.

It was much easier for Frank simply to run a band – which was strictly his own domain. He was the first band broadcaster to realize that it was not enough to copy the concert hall line-up for radio. There had to be changes to suit the microphone and, more important, to sound good on the radio speakers. Now there was just one main band microphone suspended from the ceiling of the giant WLW studio, about 10 feet away from the closest instruments, the woodwind, which inevitably were the least powerful in the ensemble. The trombones, cornets and trumpets were at the back, French horns and euphonium sections in the middle and the saxophones in front of them. The clarinets, piccolos, harps and flutes were always just in front of the conductor. There was also a solo mike (frequently used by Frank himself and always by the young soloists who were still regularly part of the shows) and a third for special effects. Both were turned off when not in use. It was the highest fi available, but very different from the stereo broadcasting 60 years later, when perhaps a dozen microphones are in regular use, each concentrating on different parts of the orchestra.

But clearly for the 1930s, the Simon arrangement was just about the best sound that could be captured on radio. Frank would have accepted nothing less. It was certainly good enough to boost the image of Frank Simon, which in turn only served to help his other activities.

Now more than ever before, he was involved in judging other people's bands, particularly those of the ever-expanding school band movement. In May 1934, for instance, he was one of the judges at the National School Band contest at Des Moines, Iowa, along with people like Edwin Franko Goldman, Arthur Pryor, Captain Charles O'Neill and a 32-year-old named William D. Revelli. Fifty-eight years later, still active at the University of Michigan where he had conducted the band for a generation, Revelli remembered judge Simon in 1934.

> He was one of the kindest men I ever knew. He had a wonderful knowledge of band literature and could spot a talent the moment he heard it. After Sousa's band, his was the most profound educational experience in band music I know.

During those Des Moines contests an exhausted Frank Simon – judging one performance after the other, giving each one total concentration, was very hard work indeed – was approached by a young soloist who clearly was not happy with his own performance. Frank agreed to start early next morning and then spent hours listening to the youngster and coaching him. 'But he knew how to enjoy himself. There were always those wonderful stories which he kept in a little black book. And he knew how to eat, too.' Frank loved Italian food – which suited a man called Revelli very well indeed.

On another occasion in 1934, Corwin Taylor, the youngster who had cycled to the Sorg Sousa concert and had later become a member of the Armco Band, asked Frank – with 'incredible presumption' – to conduct a county festival for him without fee. He accepted immediately. 'You did it with wonderful spirit and grace and I still blush when I think of the things you said about me to that audience,' he wrote to Frank years later.

Frank's reputation had extended beyond the band world. Corwin remembered another incident:

> I think a sidewalk loafer in front of the old US Hotel in Middletown summed it up for me and for all of us many years ago. I remember it so well. It was a summer evening and you were walking from the post office to the hotel for rehearsal. After what must have been a good dinner you were striding along, cigar cocked to the southwest, exuding good humor, artistic intentions and purposes to be accomplished. As you passed, the loafer turned to me and said, 'There goes a man'.

Those walks to the post office were part of the Simon ritual and also part of the Simon mystique which Mary, his beloved Maryla as he loved to call her, never really understood. He would disappear to the post office at the strangest times, always saying that he was going to pick up his mail (he had a post office box there). The post office was, as Corwin remembered, next door to the hotel.

Behind the hotel was the Elks Club, to which only an honored few were ever allowed access. Frank was there to preside over the most prestigious poker game in town. Other members of the game included two local doctors, George Lummis, the Middletown Health Commissioner, and Walter Reese; Walter Weber, a lumber merchant – who died after suffering a cerebral hemorrhage during a game – Tony Walberg, very big in Middletown's paper business, and the local undertaker, Joe Baker.

The Saturday afternoon games were only for small stakes, but also only for the invited few. The conversation and the camaraderie – to say nothing of the jokes – were even better than the cards. Frank liked to succeed at cards, but not quite as much as he wanted the Armco Band to succeed. As he said, the band 'repaid our company at least in added prestige, goodwill and advertising which could hardly be contained through any other medium.'

Every year at the ABA convention it was Frank who held court. It was never again held at Middletown, but the city's favorite son again hosted a radio program on which once more he was able to 'hand over my baton' to respected contemporaries. In March 1935 the ABA convention was just about as close as it could be to its original 'home' – at Cincinnati. Herbert Clarke was the retiring President and on Frank's show his old mentor was extended all the courtesies that had been Sousa's on the original program. So indeed were the other nine conductors featured on the Armco broadcast, including Dr J. J. Gagnier, described as 'one of Canada's greatest composers' who was conductor of the Montreal Symphony Orchestra, leader of his country's Grenadier Guards band and Director of the Canadian Broadcasting Commission. Also on the bill, as before, was Captain Charles O'Neill of the Royal 32nd Regiment Band of Quebec. As before, too, Edwin Franko Goldman could not be left out. Nor could Karl King, Captain Taylor Branson, of the US Marines Band, and Lieutenant Charles Benter, Director of the US Navy Band.

Again there was a scripted introduction and response with every conductor. Herbert Clarke was warmly welcomed and equally warmly accepted the invitation to conduct the Armco Band. 'We'll do our best, Herb,' said Simon as Herbert took the baton and conducted his two old friends in his brilliant duet, 'Side Partners', which he and Frank played many times while in Sousa's band. Following the duet Frank introduced Mr Goldman and gave him the baton. 'Thank you, Frank,' said Goldman, stumbling over the words, 'I know there's magic in this wand of yours.' The concert lasted for four hours and featured, altogether, 30 conductors. Three years later, in a letter to Herbert Clarke, Frank confided it had been 'entirely too long, not only for the musicians but the audience as well'. Nevertheless, Frank was fêted and, once more, he was in his element. He was in the company of people he liked and was again able to demonstrate that in the world of broadcast band music he was king. It was a recipe for contentment.

Certainly it was an opportunity to plug Armco's products. The Ironmaster decided that the time had come to stress the great advantages of a steel casket next time there was a funeral to organize, but nobody appeared to take that amiss or let it dampen the proceedings. It was also once more an opportunity for the other Simon recipe – how to make a bandmaster happy by letting the world know he is as good as the best classical musician.

Frank presented a certificate to Eugene Goossens, by then following Reiner as conductor of the Cincinnati Symphony, making him an honorary member of the ABA. He also took part in the Armco show.

Frank had been elected Vice President of the ABA the previous year. Ever since the first meeting of the association his colleagues had asked why he had not yet been elected to the principal post, a question never satisfactorily answered. There is one possibility: a single member of the association's board of directors, Cliff Bainam from North-Western University, had taken a dislike to him. But at the 1935 convention the neglect was put to rights. Frank Simon was elected President – and once more the tears rolled down his cheeks. He said he had never been happier and there was no reason to doubt his claim. He served as President for two years.

His colleagues smiled as they posed for pictures with him, among them his old friend Henry Fillmore, an ABA director, who a couple of years earlier had written a march he called 'Gifted Leadership' in honor of Frank, and rejoiced in his success which vicariously was also his own as it was that of every other member of the Association.

'At ABA conventions,' recalled Dr Al Wright, later to be ABA president himself as well as a professor of bands at an Indiana university, 'he and other people like Henry Fillmore would sit up all night telling stories. He was the most immaculately dressed man I remember – whether he went to concerts or meetings. He was also a very positive person. If he said the sun wasn't going to come up tomorrow you knew it wouldn't.' The immaculate Frank Simon shirtfront suffered from the ebullience of his friendship with Fillmore, Al Wright remembered for me:

> It was a time when they were competing for the same job in Cincinnati. Frank had had a couple of beers and went to sleep in a hotel lobby. Henry Fillmore took out a pen, drew a staff and wrote four bars of music [on Frank's shirtfront]. Later on, Frank was showing it to everybody: 'That was a good tune,' he said, 'I'm going to publish it.' And he did – he wrote a march based on it.

There was a lot of politics at ABA meetings, Wright recalled. It was very easy to keep people out of the organization.

As well as conducting the Armco Band, Frank Simon was a frequent guest conductor for school bands

In 1932 the ABA held its convention in Washington, D.C. All the bandmasters present signed this commemorative document. Frank Simon's signature is close to the right-hand corner, alongside his Sousa Band predecessor Herbert Clarke's, and above those of his own two sons, who went along for the ride

> I remember Frank adamantly refusing to allow one man to join. He said that he wasn't a full-time bandmaster and that was it. He had convinced himself that this man didn't have any musical ability – because he didn't like the work he did on the radio.

Nobody drew that conclusion from Frank's participation in broadcasting.

There was no question that, thanks largely to Frank Simon's introduction, the Association was now internationally recognized as the principal representative body of America's bandsmen. Major H. E. Atkins, who had begun his military life fighting in South Africa in the Boer War and was now director of Neller Hall, the Royal Military School of Music in London, was a guest at the convention and also conducted the Armco Band. He paid tribute to the influence of the American bands, particularly in schools where there was no comparable British movement. But he also had a barb for his US colleagues. 'I think you can also learn something from us,' he said. 'That something is versatility. Our bands, I believe, are trained to be more versatile than yours.' It did not faze Frank. He and Atkins became lifelong friends.

Frank was a man to be courted. 'Flashing across the continent,' ran a full-page advertisement in the trade papers, 'listen to the thrilling strains of Frank Simon and his famous Armco Band. NBC Every Sunday' – and then came an endorsement by Frank for instruments produced by the King company. Everyone wanted to get into the act. When the new terminal for the Louisville and Nashville railroad was opened in Cincinnati (with all the traditional pomp; speeches by the Governor of Ohio, the Mayor and everyone else who seemed important) it was the Armco Band who played for the occasion. The proceedings were broadcast live (the only way they could be relayed in those days) and there was no competition as to which was the most popular part of the program.

Frank was at the stage in life when honors came to him from seemingly every direction. After Herman Bellstedt's death his son Erwin chose an Armco show in which to present Frank with what had been one of his father's own medals, an award which had been given to the veteran musician by the Omaha Elks. Once again, the tears flowed down Frank's cheeks as he heard the younger Bellstedt declare: 'I know of no better way to perpetuate the memory of my loved one [Herman] than to present to my dear friend Frank Simon this same token of esteem in recognition of his talents which in my mind are the personification of the qualities with which my father was endowed.' Frank was so moved, it was almost incredible that he was able to continue the broadcast.

The Simon 'groupies' continued to please – and sometimes to amaze – him. They were not just simple fans. Frank McGran, a bank president, loved band music in general and Frank's music in particular so much that he had his own recording studio – a rare thing indeed in the 1930s. He even had outdoor recording equipment and followed the ABA around from convention to convention, putting the bandmasters' work onto disc. He was never happier than when he could invite Frank to the studio to 'talk shop'. Sometimes he would merely send his friend a letter in sound. 'Dear Frank, I'm in my studio. I thought you'd like to hear what Herbert L. Clarke said at the ABA convention . . .' Or he would say, 'I heard a band play this . . .' and then add the recording to the 'letter' he was sending. He would end up 'How did you like that, Frank?'

In Washington, DC, there was Dorothy Dixon, who 50 years later still had a syndicated 'I'll-tell-your-fortune' newspaper column. She loved Frank's music. But her husband, a wealthy real-estate man, loved it even more. He used to go to ABA conventions and follow the band when it went on tour. Whenever Frank went to Washington DC for a concert the man always had a car ready for his use in the city.

There were other people in his life who were not so influential. As Chris Christensen, who was later to lead a Cincinnati band of his own before becoming a theatrical agent, recalled, Frank gave 'free lessons, overcoats, rent money, instruments and kind words to musicians who had more talent than money'.

Christensen knew what he was talking about. When he had turned up for his own Armco audition, he did not even have a saxophone to play. Frank found him an old one to demonstrate – and when he liked what he heard presented the youngster with a new baritone sax which cost him $350. His contract signed by Ernie Glover said:

> I hereby engage you to perform for me, to my satisfaction and under the following terms and conditions, in a rehearsal and radio broadcast known as 'The Armco Ironmaster Radio Program', consisting of band music and other entertaining features . . . A compensation of $20 shall be paid to you within one week after completion of this broadcast. In event any broadcast is prevented by recapture of the alloted time or any cause beyond our control we shall not be liable for compensation to you for the broadcast thereby omitted.

Of course, Frank never 'welshed' on a fee in his life. There were scores of similar stories of Simon generosity in the years to come.

The Armco show still was not Frank's only interest. He constantly played and conducted benefits like the Gilmore Memorial Concert in the Mechanics Hall, Boston, held under the auspices of the ABA for the benefit of the Boston Musicians Relief Fund. Nothing gave him greater pleasure in 1935 than when he was invited to guest conduct the newly formed Dayton Philharmonic Orchestra. He no longer conducted the city's Antioch Shrine Band, but he always appeared with the Syrian Shrine Band in Cincinnati as a cornet soloist. He played with the Salvation Army and, above all, there was the work at the Conservatory. This was now, thanks to the fame of Armco, turning away students while almost every other Depression-hit academic institution was desperate for people to pay their fees. There was also now a Conservatory band – conducted by Frank, of course – and that could have had something to do with the popularity of the course. He always said 'My greatest inspiration is helping others to get somewhere.' In the Conservatory band they always got somewhere. If they did not, it was not Frank Simon's fault. Certainly, the Conservatory was a unique bright spot in a pretty bleak world.

There was another – the group known as Frank Simon and His Band, made up of some Armco players and a number from the Conservatory who played at private functions which the Armco Band, for contractual reasons, could not attend. It was a little more than hair splitting, but it was that, too.

The nation's economy was not being quite so easily sorted out. Franklin Delano Roosevelt was into his third year of office, the New Deal was in full swing, but unemployment and the other symptoms of that Depression were still all too evident. Frank wanted to do his bit to help. The opportunity came with a concert held at Cincinnati's Music Hall in aid of unemployed musicians, which he conducted along with two other distinguished colleagues – Eugene Goossens and his own look-alike Paul Whiteman. Each of the conductors, when he wasn't 'on' himself, sat in a box listening to the others. Young David Simon talked for weeks how he had shared a box with Whiteman during his father's show.

As the *Cincinnati Enquirer*'s George A. Leighton wrote:

> Simon, showman de luxe and excellent musician, put on a real entertainment as well as a worthwhile musical presentation. His ensemble was a band – a concert band – and what a band! Four Sousa horns and a dozen trombones with the remaining instrumentation to balance. So Simon alternated 'heavy' music with martial, the latter including a march by Reuben Lawson, personnel manager of the Cincinnati Symphony; one by Elgar and a third by . . . Sousa, his 'Stars and Stripes Forever'. The audience responded nobly, even applauding the opening bars . . .

Leighton described how the band moved to the centre of the stage, the six piccolo players, followed by a dozen trombones, and then the same number of trumpets and cornets:

> the 30 blowing with full-lunged power into the ears of the 4000. Was there cause for enthusiasm? Most surely! The word for it is showmanship – but after all, we all are poor, emotional humans and we like to be thrilled, even if afterward we see it was done with aforethought. And we thank the thriller deeply.

In a way, that was Frank Simon's real business. Providing the thrills in music.

14 · The Educationist

Frank Simon was never just a cornet player or just a bandmaster. As the middle 1930s gave way to the second half of the decade he was a one-man band *industry*. Spanish-language newspapers in Latin America were giving him the same headlines as the ones to which he had become accustomed in his own country. As the crew of that ship had indicated with their fan letter a few years before, the Armco show was jumping to top the ratings in South America. Being aired on both NBC networks was just about the best exposure any entertainer could possibly wish for.

Yet still there was the teaching at his beloved Conservatory – later to boast a string of distinguished alumni, not least among them the conductor James Levine – still the private lessons, still the publishing, still the meetings and still the band clinics. At those remarkable clinical sessions where no one wore a white coat and where the only medicine dispensed was in the form of a blow of a cornet or the tootle of a clarinet (and always a word of advice), the sight of Frank Simon's cigar on one of the music stands was as familiar as his jokes.

But jokes were never allowed to take over from his music. Frank went into the minutest detail when discussing playing techniques. And his students had to know what he was talking about. It was not a place for beginners. A degree of expertise was required to deal with this typical note of sagacity from the Simon lips: 'In a piece of music on a cornet where an E on the fourth space comes in between two Fs on the fifth line, the E is always made one and two valve rather than open. It is the natural fingering for this note. It is a good thing to know because all cornets do it, you know.'

But he did not keep his advice solely for the benefit of the younger students. He thought the teachers had to be taught too – taught how to teach. 'I want to say', he declared at one clinic about this time, 'that every bandmaster before he plays a march should make suitable explanations to the students concerning this work even if he has to use the blackboard to demonstrate his points.'

Frank had the most elaborate posters advertising his clinics put up in school bandrooms all over the nation. One of his students, Bob Hornyak, recalled for me: 'If you walked into the bandroom of any high school, the focus was on Frank Simon because of the Armco Band. Sousa had died and the reality was that there wasn't a band of national stature which so influenced school bands as the Armco one.'

The instrument makers knew that as well. Simon no longer appeared in advertisements praising the merits of the Holton cornet. Now he was a 'King' man, with his photograph appearing all over the country above a shot of a whole range of King instruments. It was a vein of gold for a leading musician – Horowitz was constantly singing the virtues of Steinway pianos in the quality press – and Frank was astute enough to mine it.

In addition to his school work and clinics there were now the band camps – six or seven weeks away in the country where young musicians would blow and puff between fishing expeditions, playing tennis or ping-pong or riding the trails. Looking at Frank's diary was an edifying experience, akin to probing a haystack for the mythical needle. But there was nothing mythical about Simon's activities. As, above all, his students appreciated, he could generally be relied upon to find the time which anyone else would be sure to say just did not exist.

It was the same with his money. He may not have been fabulously wealthy but he was extremely prosperous. The Armco Band took in $25,000 a week, from which he had to pay wages and other expenses. But for half the year he was personally banking about $15,000 a week. It was money to put by for a rainy day – and, so soon after the start of the Depression, that kind of rain was a very familiar memory for millions in America. Unlike many others in his income bracket, he used what was needed from the sums he had at his disposal as a reason to be generous. A whole generation and a world later, Robert T. Braunagel, by then Associate Professor of Music at Florida State University, remembered how Frank was treating students at the Cincinnati Conservatory:

> I fondly remember the excitement of playing for you, studying trumpet with you and the time Bob Scott and I wrecked his old jalopy and we needed $30 to fix it. Neither of our parents had $30, for this was like $300 today [and perhaps $3000 nearly 30 years later] and you were so wonderful to lend us the money and told us to pay it back when we could.

It was a not unfamiliar tribute to a man described by Robert Braunagel as 'much more than a teacher or director – you have been one of the kindest and finest persons I have known'.

People from all backgrounds came to him and said similar things. One was the brother of the maid working in the house next door. She told him her brother was talented and wanted to learn to play the trumpet properly. 'Send him to me,' Frank told the young woman, as much as anything impressed by the devotion she showed to her brother. 'I'll see if he really does have any talent.'

The youngster's name was Gerald Morgan. He was a boy who Frank did decide was worth an investment. He gave him a horn to blow and lessons to learn – all free of charge. Morgan went on to play in a highschool band, to get a scholarship to Wilberforce, a black college, and then to become a music instructor. But it was still not enough for him. He did not like the idea of getting his own lessons free of charge and raised money to pay for them by cleaning cars. Frank refused to accept the fees. Eventually, this student reduced the amount of time he spent on his music. He became a doctor instead, but he always said that it was Frank Simon who put him on the road to his profession.

Frank had his own techniques in teaching, most of them based on what had become the established Sousa practice but owing more than a little to Bellstedt, Kopp *et al*. 'Never sneak in on entries,' he told his students. But he could be cutting, too. A squeaky clarinet, he said, made a player sound as if he were using an 'Armco ingot iron reed', which, if nothing else, enabled him to publicize his sponsors off air as well as on.

Perhaps his greatest – and kindest – forte was the ability to be able to finish an important concert, and then while the sweat was still covering his brow and soaking his shirtfront, spot a student in the audience and go over to talk to him – not a rudimentary courtesy even if it was sometimes just to ask how he or she was, but because he was genuinely pleased to note the interest of a youngster whom he rarely saw outside the classroom. Sometimes he would go into the most considerable detail to discuss the evening's playing and then compare his soloist's achievements with the boy's or girl's own efforts or, at the other extreme, with the way someone like Herbert Clarke would have played it.

On the other hand, some of the students were content enough just to hear the performance – and to see it. A concert ending with 'The Stars and Stripes Forever' also climaxed with a scene that usually could be relied upon to set an audience cheering with excitement. Toward the end of the march the instrumentalists, first the trombones then the trumpets and cornets, would file out and form a line across the front of the stage. They would turn and face the audience. The people in the seats in front of them went wild.

In a way Middletown went wild too. Despite the Depression, the town had an element of prosperity. 'Parking was tail to tail on Saturday,' George Crout remembered for me. Even so, as he further recalled, they were 'mostly Fords. They were the cheapest.'

The star attraction on the Armco outdoor concerts, particularly on the Fourth of July, was usually the *1812 Overture*, complete with cannon and fireworks. (Not that a Simon Armco concert was not a kind of fireworks display in itself.) Frank Simon was *always* drawing in the crowds. If he played at Soldiers Field in Chicago (a popular outdoor showbiz setting that Al Jolson had made his own) there could be 100,000 people in the crowd. They came to the concert in broad daylight. They stayed till after dark – which was usually the time for Frank to suggest that everyone there light a match. It was a spectacular sight, but how this regular routine always managed to proceed without at least one match setting light to the parched grass underfoot is perhaps a miracle that went along with Frank's playing.

The broadcasts were, naturally enough, the activities which occupied his attention most of all. They were family occasions. Sometimes the Simon clan went to the Netherland Plaza Hotel in Cincinnati after a program. On one occasion Frank's mother, who had been cheering the show, joined him and Mary for dinner there. She did not know what to order, so Frank chose crab for her, a delicacy forbidden by the Jewish dietary laws which in this one solitary respect she had always followed. She was auditor to the Council of Jewish Women but that in itself would not have inhibited her. It was just something that she did not do. 'She didn't know what it was and thought it tasted wonderful,' her grandson Joe recalled. 'When he told her it was crab, she wasn't happy.'

Frank was less religious and certainly a lot less traditionally observant than his parents. In a letter sent to Simon on his 75th birthday a former student, Josef Marx, wrote from his home in New York City, 'You were very important to me in my youth for two reasons. At your home in Middletown I ate shrimps for the first time. Out went all my kosher upbringing.' Isaac Nemiroff, another musician present on the occasion, recalled Frank telling his friend: 'Go ahead, Joe, try it. It won't hurt you.' Marx added, almost by the way: 'You also gave me my first job in music.'

One of his favorite stories was of the Orthodox synagogue in the area which suddenly found itself in credit to the tune of $2000. What to do with the money? 'I know,' said one of the board members, 'we should have an organ.' He was shouted down. An organ in an Orthodox synagogue! Impossible. 'We should . . .' said another man in a wonderfully familiar East European accent, 'we should buy a chandelier.' 'No,' shouted the President. 'For one thing it's wrong. For another, we haven't got anyone to play it.'

Mary may not have enjoyed his jokes as much as he or his friends did, but she would go to all the broadcasts – and, now that they were getting older, their two sons would too. After the programs, if they fancied a change from the Netherland Plaza they went to Loretta's, a popular sandwich shop of the day. Frank loved tongue sandwiches. He liked to say that he had only three meals a day, but enjoyed a snack here and there, particularly before bed – when he would make himself a cheese sandwich. 'Always of the kind that smelled the worst, which is why I hate cheese today,' says David Simon. 'He would always be hungry', David recalled. 'He never drank, although many drinks were offered at parties. Just a little wine with dinner occasionally, but that was it, apart from an occasional cold beer on a hot day. But he did love food.'

Meanwhile, Ohio continued to boast how much it loved Frank Simon, who, reported the Dayton *Daily News*,

> proved himself as much of an artist as a band leader as Walter Damrosch is as a symphony conductor. The playing of the band was like that of a great orchestra. In the 'Andante Cantabile' from Tchaikovsky's Fifth Symphony (Op. 64), Mr Simon gave a superb reading of the number; and the response showed the remarkable virtuosity, the delicacy and shading of the highest order of musical performance.

This illustrates an important contribution which Frank Simon made to the band world. He introduced the kind of music which no other band had ever played before – and proved it worked. He also continued to write his own kind of music. One march he called 'Camp Hook', after the Boy Scout camp named for the man who by now had succeeded his father-in-law George Verity as President of Armco. A little later, he and Hook had a falling out – so Frank changed the name of his march.

The band paid for advertising space, too – not necessarily, it has to be stressed, always in the journals that found him so praiseworthy. 'Outstanding,' read one of the ads, 'in recent sensational achievements in the music world is the astounding development of the Armco Concert Band from a small body of musicians gathered from the employees of a great industry to what is today a magnificent organization of sixty highly trained musicians, known throughout the country as "America's greatest industrial band".'

His sons meanwhile still considered he was America's greatest father. Providing they did not ask for bicycles, they still got almost everything they wanted. They asked for roller skates and got them. They wanted to see the country, so Frank paid for them to go on a trip West under the care of their junior high-school principal. They went to the Grand Canyon, visited all the national parks. 'It was an expensive trip,' Joe remembers. 'If things were worthwhile, he happily spent the money.'

The happiest holidays *with* Frank were the fishing expeditions, particularly to Canada. 'My mother only went on one,' says Joe. 'She found out there was no indoor toilet and wouldn't go again.'

Mary was not the easiest person to get along with, as Bertha and others were to discover, partly because she was constantly eclipsed by his fame. But she and Frank remained very much in love and she revelled in his obvious stardom. She was happier running the publishing business, sometimes earning $200 or $300 a month, not an inconsiderable sum in those days but never likely to take their 'firm' into the big time. She happily pocketed the takings. Frank paid the expenses. The best-seller was undoubtedly 'Willow Echoes'. 'There was not a cornet player in the world who hadn't played the number,' remembered David Simon, who used to love eavesdropping on those of Frank's pupils who met in the Middletown house's solarium and were trying to master it. He did not shout when they failed the 'Willow Echoes' test and if he thought that even in failure they showed promise, he persevered. Frank acted the same way with his Armco musicians. Once he took people into the band, he worked with them. It was a kind of act of faith. If he had done anything less, it would have been an indictment of his own instincts in appointing someone unable to make the grade. One old Armco hand, G. D. Tranter, remembered how nervously he played a saxophone solo with the band for the first time. Frank told him: 'Don't worry, Dave. We have 60 [men] behind you and they will take up wherever you leave off.'

It was inevitable that both the Simon boys should pick up a cornet and *try* to play it. They never did more than try. 'Don't depend on music for a living,' Frank advised David after his second lesson, which he was eager to have. 'David, make music an avocation, not a profession.' He advised the mothers of some of his students to think on the same lines. They were frequently the same breed of stage parents who expected daughters to become Shirley Temples and sons to turn into Mickey Rooneys. They wanted *their* youngsters, who would rather have been outside playing baseball, to become stars.

But there were others who, through Armco, succeeded beyond their dreams. Not all instrumentalists. Not all men. Helen Gerber Ramsdell, for instance, still loves to talk about the way Frank had plucked her as a 15-year-old from a junior high school and encouraged her to sing with his band on the radio shows. 'It was a small town, so he had to hear of me.' He also was an old friend of the young mezzo-soprano's family. 'He was very kind, gave me very many opportunities to sing,' she recalled for me. 'And he was always very protective.'

Not for Frank Simon to risk the security of a young girl singing with his band. Always, he collected her from her home before a broadcast or concert and then took her back again. But he was equally protective of her professional position. 'I had a strong voice, but he still didn't allow the band to play too loudly while I was singing. He was a very good accompanist.' As for Helen herself, she was also very popular. Frank's mailbag continued to weigh heavily enough to bring not a few problems for the local postmen. Helen was mentioned in hundreds of the letters – which convinced him to use her in more concerts than many of his solo singers normally were allowed.

Through Frank, she got a scholarship to Miami University. But it did not affect her participation with the band – rehearsing three times a week and once before every broadcast, too. The rehearsals were always at the top of a large building at the corner of Central Avenue and Verity Parkway in Middletown, above Robertsons' sporting goods store. When they had a concert at one of the neighborhood or Armco parks, the rehearsals would be on-site at the park itself. Nothing was left to chance. Every rehearsal was scheduled to last 45 minutes and last 45 minutes it did. There was never any doubt that Frank was in charge. As Helen remembered:

> Dr Simon wouldn't tolerate any bad language. He was a real gentleman – and so were the others. My family wouldn't have allowed me to sing with any other orchestra. Dr Simon would put me at ease simply by the tone of his voice.

He encouraged other young girls to develop their musical talents with Armco. Like Helen Dowling, daughter of Frank's friend Richard Dowling, the local postmaster – known as 'Witchie' because that was the way his wife pronounced the name 'Richard'. Dowling was the main reason (of course) for Frank's numerous visits to the post office to pick up his mail from box 208 and then to join in the card game. It was during their joint fishing expeditions that Frank regaled him with stories of John Philip Sousa and Dowling recalled the days he was the local party 'boss' Mark Hannah's lieutenant at the Republican National Conventions.

Helen Dowling, on the other hand, knew nothing of such things.

She was a highly competent pianist who was given lessons by Frank before playing with the band, and was David's piano teacher. The soloists were as vital an ingredient of the shows as ever before. There were violinists as well as other vocalists like Lulu McLellen, another highly popular and regular feature of the Armco shows. These people grew into old age remembering Frank and his work for them. He enjoyed their success, but would claim little credit for it. Their talent had been responsible, nothing else. He could also say that recognizing that talent and moulding it was as much a benefit for his band – and, indirectly, for his audiences – as it was for the soloists themselves.

He liked to talk about his students to his own contemporaries. It made a change from the jokes. There was still nothing like a good conversation after a good meal to the accompaniment of a good cigar to make him a very happy man indeed. If he was really content, he fell asleep, although nobody else managed to copy Henry Fillmore and pen a tune on Frank's shirtfront. But when he awoke he was the contented center of attraction. To him, that was the companionship of music and he said he was its most contented recipient.

Others were, too – in a different but equally professional way. Morton Gould, now the doyen of American composers, was asked by William Revelli to write some band music. He balked at the idea. His first thought was that he was, as he put it, 'writing down'. He told me, 'I thought it wasn't a good idea. After all, what could I write for the fireman's band?' Yet he now adds: 'That was until I heard it. I was instantly converted. Frank Simon and people like Revelli and Goldman had made it respectable.'

The band was also respectable from a purely commercial point of view. There were comparatively so few orchestras in the country – and each of those with such a wide variety of instrumentalists but not enough wanting individual parts – that it was difficult for new orchestral works to be made worthwhile for a publisher. The bands, however, were a different matter. As Gould said:

> In the '30s, people were writing 'practical' things – so that publishers could make money – things of a not very high standard like children's music. Orchestras were getting their music through rental departments. After all, how many clarinets in an orchestra? Perhaps four. But bands would have, say, 20 clarinets. And there were so many more bands.

So suddenly, band music became attractive to composers – or, at least, to composers' agents. Mills Music were the publishers who were the pioneers in this field. They had a huge catalog of popular numbers. But in 1936 they got involved for the first time in non-popular music. 'Deficit publishing' they called it. 'Music Not to Make a Profit with.' The head of that department, Mike Stahl, suggested that Gould should add to the catalog and write for bands. His immediate reaction was: 'Are you crazy?' And he added for good measure: 'I've got enough trouble writing for orchestras.' The problem – and it was this which worried Gould most – was the image that bands could not shake off as far as 'serious' composers were concerned. As he explained: 'What I remembered were those firemen's bands, the police bands, the American Legion – cockamamie bands who just about hung together with a march.'

But, as he had said, he was instantly converted – at an ABA convention in Michigan. For the first time he heard really good bands playing really good music. Among them was Frank Simon – although to be fair, it was not *his* music which immediately registered:

> All I can remember about him at that time were his jokes. He was a great storyteller. He had cue cards and I remember him saying, 'I won't use this one. I'll try this.' They were his own reference files which he carried around with him all the time.

But there were more important reasons for him to remember that convention – like writing his first piece of band music. He had to admit that those commerical reasons were the main impetus he had for taking up the idea brought to him by his manager Max Stark – and then agreeing to write a piece for Revelli called 'Cowboy Rhapsody'. As a result, he came to a series of conclusions. Band music could sound marvelous. It could be highly commercial. And it offered as much and as wide a scope for the composer as it did for the band.

Al Wright knew exactly what Gould meant, particularly with reference to Frank Simon:

> He would have made a great symphony orchestra conductor, a fine symphonic musician. He certainly wasn't the kind of conductor who could just beat time. But he wasn't flamboyant like Fillmore (who was

> known to change into red underwear to illustrate a story) but he was Business.

The business angle was what appealed to the publishers – once, that is, they were sure that the sound could be made right. 'It's a different kind of sound,' Morton Gould told me.

> But you can do things with a band you can't do with an orchestra. You have much more sound at your disposal. A great band has a homogenous sound and a charisma that sometimes a symphony orchestra doesn't have. The band has a wide range of subtle colors. So the bands, the good bands, had to be capable of the big musical sound and more subtle sounds, too.

Frank Simon was a huge influence.

> The village bands were all over the country and were not very good. If you could play an instrument, you could join a band. But people like Simon and Goldman established quality control. They set standards. This was the fastest conversion. I knew *of* Frank Simon at this time, but suddenly I was with him and with the pantheon of band people. And it was important to remember that people like Frank Simon were involved in educational work. 'I saw it at the conventions – an interesting exchange between the professional band leaders and those involved solely in educational work. There wasn't the same wall between them that existed in the orchestra world. That impressed me.

The mechanics of the convention had their own fascinations for a stranger to its world: the band clinics; the demonstrations by instrument makers all were an introduction to a life outside of anything else. Gould himself went on to become an important feature of the band world. His most famous band work, 'Pavanne', had one of its first airings on one of Frank's broadcasts.

The Armco show, meanwhile, continued to top the audience ratings, although there were more disputes with the management now that Hook was in charge. The new president continued to say that Frank's music was too good for the men on the shopfloor and Frank continued to say that if he persisted in that notion, he had to recognize he had the wrong man in Dr Simon – and Simon was not going to change for anyone. Richard Dowling, sometimes now called 'the major' and a friend and confidant of both the adversaries, raised the point on Hook's behalf on one of Frank's regular trips to the post office. Later he made a point to the Armco boss that Simon would have appreciated: manufacturers of the best steel needed to be represented by the best music. As Frank later recalled: 'Now, I never played over anybody's head. I was too smart for that. Nevertheless, I was trying very hard to present the image of a great company and the humanity that's connected to them and the humaneness of the people who operate the company who were the officers and founders of this company.' The ratings spoke for themselves.

There was plenty of support from other Armco officials, however – particularly the Ironmaster. 'Friends,' Bennett Chapple said in one of his talks, 'I have just finished a fine breakfast of ham and eggs. Now, you ask, what in the world has that to do with the great steel industry? Well, I'll tell you. The farmer could not do his work without steel implements . . .' Any more perhaps than Frank could do without his 24-cent Lord Beaconsfield cigar ('not the most expensive,' recalls David Simon, 'but better than moderate'). He still bought them from Mary O'Connor, the crippled woman who worked at George Schrafenberger's stand at the Manchester Hotel.

Most people were just as convinced that they could not do without the Armco show. To the bandsmen, the oldest tradition of all, that the show must go on, was no more than an obvious fact of life. Never was it put into play more perfectly than in the winter of 1937, when Cincinnati had one of its worst floods in history. People were traveling through the streets on rowboats. That, too, was the only way Frank and a few of his musicians managed to get to the Crosley Building. Although built on a hill, it was already partly engulfed. The studios were on the eighth floor. Somehow, the music men managed to get past the third floor, which was by then at flood level. From there they were able to climb up the water-sodden stairs to the broadcasting studios five floors further up. There was no power for the elevators, but the engineers who, as they did every week, had come from Chicago for the broadcast, had managed the trek to the eighth floor, too, and had installed a generator.

But there was still the problem of getting all the musicians into the building. There were not enough boats to bring them, but there was a spot behind the Crosley Building that had not been affected – yet. A factory next door was built on a higher point of the hill. It had a flat roof, which was only two feet away from a window on the fifth floor of the Crosley Building.

Frank found a working telephone and gave his orders. Every first-chair player was to call every other man in his section; the men were to get to the flat roof and then climb through a window. No labor union worth its dues would have countenanced such a move and clearly it was highly dangerous, but, equally clearly, the power and authority of Frank Simon extended beyond his baton.

Even so, things were so bad that nothing could happen until the band had actually voted on whether or not to proceed with the show. 'We wondered if we ought to get out of the building because they were frightened it would cave in or something,' Frank was to recall. 'But we decided to go on with the show. I even had gloves on – although the clarinet players had to take their gloves off.' There was no heat, so the men played in their overcoats and broadcast with the assistance of the temporary generator. WLW now had a new 500,000-watt transmitter to justify its role as the nation's station although eventually the government would insist that the transmitter should be downgraded to a mere 50,000 – it did not want any national stations in America. The show was constantly interrupted by flood news.

This was not an event to be easily forgotten. As Frank later laughed: 'I recall that Ernest [Glover] here, playing trombone, was blowing steam out of his horn. The listeners were none the wiser.' As Frank said, 'It was a terrific show.'

This was the kind of thing that went toward enhancing Frank's reputation as a supreme professional – and made him more than ever sought after as a judge at band concerts. William Revelli remembered those occasions. 'Just to know he was the judge was something,' he said. Once Frank judged Revelli himself:

> He was one of the few adjudicators who took time to come round and tell you about your strengths and weaknesses, which was 100 times better than having a written adjudication, which you would never just get from Frank Simon, who could himself produce that sweet, docile, liquid, Mozart-like sound. He could enchant you – like a singer. In fact, he made his cornet sing. You had the feeling that the music started in his

> head, moved to his heart, then to his feet and then to his instrument. I always think that tone is more important than technique and he had both – and more: tone, intonation, rhythm and technique.

If that was the view of a fellow-professional, any number of people outside the band movement could give their own testimonials.

'He was a very good, genial man of great dignity,' Rabbi Albert Goldman remembered. He had his own reasons for liking Frank, who frequently gave him lifts in his car when he was a young student, and later performed the 'Kol Nidre' on his cornet at Goldman's synagogue.

At this time the large, influential Jewish community of Cincinnati – the home of American Reform Judaism – was especially worried about the power of Hitlerism in Germany, to say nothing of the spread of anti-Semitism in America. Matters were not helped by the extent of pro-German feeling in Cincinnati, a city that still harbored huge German influences. The immigrants, on the whole, were still alive and still active in the commercial life of the area.

Rabbi Goldman, of the Isaac M. Wise Temple in Cincinnati, told me: 'Cincinnati was a somewhat assimilated community. When Hitlerism broke out, there was a terrible problem for German Jews, a great setback for them. But we, on the other hand, were bringing in Jews from Germany.' In fact, in 1937, together with Leo Yassenoff, a cousin living in Columbus, Ohio (an All-American football player who had become a successful architect and builder), Frank made arrangements to bring over from Germany their mutual cousins Jacob and Henrietta Felsenthal Hertz and their relatives and another family, too. Said Rabbi Goldman: 'Frank wasn't like those assimilated Jews. He felt the same way we did about needing to help the victims of Nazism.' He wrote his checks for the cause, generous as ever.

As a teacher, he was never in better form than at the Gunnison, Colorado, band camp, which had an international reputation and was roughly the band equivalent of Tanglewood, the Boston Symphony's summer home at which promising students were taught by eminent conductors like Kussevitsky, Bernstein or Previn.

Frank loved the camps himself, but he took them seriously. His jokes were reserved for the after-lesson sessions. Just about the most serious thing he could say to a group of young musicians was

'I've never heard anything so awful in my life' – but he kept his cool just the same.

He had just one problem with one of the camps – the food was terrible, which to him was a crime much more serious than playing the wrong notes in 'El Capitan'. It was not what he had been promised – and breaking promises was a sin he tried never to commit himself and would never tolerate in others. So he walked out, taking the entire music faculty (and his own children) with him. There had never been a band camp strike before.

But there was no question now that most of the young people who contemplated going into the band had rid themselves of all the prejudices that existed against their kind of music. William Revelli thinks he knows why. As he told me: 'The orchestra is the Queen but the band is the King. Anyone who knows anything about cards will know that the King takes the Queen.'

Frank himself was the king of the bands, which was why he was so keenly sought out by prospective students. The impression he made on them was so profound that they took the memories of those first lessons with them into middle and old age.

Maurice Callahan had his first euphonium lessons from Frank Simon at the age of 20 during his 1937 Christmas vacation. He recalls vividly how his teacher came to meet him at the railroad depot before going on to a cousin's house in his large black Packard. 'I remember him wearing a little derby hat and smoking a cigar. He was very outgoing, telling little anecdotes about his early days.'

They got to be fast friends, teacher and student, two totally committed musicians. He even experienced some of Frank's more intimate moments. 'I remember being with him when David came in – he was just a teenager – and told him he'd had a fender bender with his car. He was not pleased.' Callahan recalled Mary trying to pacify her husband. 'What a lovely person she was.' It was, though, Frank's teaching that was the most effective and most enthralling part of all the times that they spent together:

> He was very effective and could teach by showing, rather than just talking about it. I would play and he would play along with me. I would start playing and he would pick it up. A very patient man, he was not just a good teacher, he was a great teacher.

Most people knew that. What they did not always know was how he helped them financially – a loan here, a gift there. Callahan recalled: 'He often said to me, the most talented kids were the poor kids.' Those who could pay were charged $15 for a 30-minute lesson. 'Those 30 minutes always became an hour or so. Frank Simon was always very, very generous.' Generous enough to offer him a chance to play with the Armco Band. 'I couldn't do it because I couldn't afford to give up a full-time job for 13 30-minute programs on a Sunday afternoon.' So Callahan had to content himself with playing with Simon in the Cincinnati Conservatory band.

When the lessons were over he kept in touch with his ex-students, wrote to them, met them when they were in the same town at the same time – just as he himself had maintained his contact with Herman Bellstedt and Kopp and Clarke. Once, he now admitted, Bellstedt had chastised him in a note in which he said 'Out of sight, out of mind'. He determined never to do that again, either with Bellstedt or, now that the boot was on the other foot, with his own students. Years later, Bob McSpadden wrote to Frank about his own experience of being one of his students:

> . . . My family moved to Cincinnati so that I could study at the Conservatory . . . This would never have happened if you had not arranged for me to audition for a scholarship (while I was still a high school sophomore) after hearing me sing at the Indiana State Fair. Because of this chance the whole direction of my life changed – the years of professional singing, choir direction, dance band work and teaching that have been my life would not have been without the initial impetus you supplied.

At about the same time, another student who had suffered a serious injury and then been unable to work for a year came to Frank's attention. When the youngster had to get home to Kansas City, Frank paid for his sleeper train ticket – and gave him enough to buy breakfast the next morning.

He invited home favorite students and newcomers to his band to have dinner with him and the family. Isaac Nemiroff played a violin solo with the Armco Band at the Cincinnati Zoo. He said he never forgot how Frank steered the band to blend with his playing. 'Half a step up,' Frank whispered as he began to play 'Valse Bluette' by

Drigo. He remembered just as fondly the conversation, 'Not the least of which was the best joke I ever heard . . . about the rabbi's serving girl'. Alas, details of his concerts are better remembered than this tale.

The strength of Frank Simon the educationist was demonstrated time and again by the references to him in the *School Musician*, the journal of school band teaching. When 7000 music lovers crowded into the Milwaukee Auditorium in March 1937 for that year's ABA convention – 'the largest crowd for a purely musical event that the building had ever had' – the magazine reported the scene when Frank, in white tie and tails, mounted the rostrum. The crowd were 'enraptured as Frank Simon, retiring president, directed the band through "Mardi Gras" from Ferde Grofe's *Mississippi Suite*'.

Bennett Chapple was to use similar language talking about the Armco shows. 'Oftentimes,' he said in 1937, 'in the midst of an Armco broadcast as I listen to the superb musicianship of the Armco band under co-worker Frank Simon, I became so enraptured that I almost forgot the chat of the Ironmaster is next on the program. I had become a bandsman again.'

A freemasonry was developing around membership of the band quite as strong as that in the organizations to which Frank belonged, which required him to wear a fez and go through secret rituals. The relationship with his musicians was, as has already been shown, much more of an open secret.

The octogenarian Emil Schmachtenberg, a clarinet player with Armco who went on to study at the Curtis Institute and play with the orchestra of the Philadelphia Grand Opera, told me how he had joined Frank as a teenager in 1928 at the Ohio State Fair at Columbus and then begun an association that continued throughout the 1930s. 'He was a very fine conductor, and a very correct player,' he told me. 'Immediately I joined the band I was accepted as one of the bandsmen.' He contrasted the life of an orchestral player with that of a bandsman:

> It was not quite so serious, I have to say. You couldn't get it quite so serious, especially since I had to play violin parts. So it was a little more blatant. There were limitations for a band conductor. On the other hand, a symphony conductor would have limitations with band music.

Frank never pretended his music was easy to play or that his work was simple. Writing in *Billboard* in April 1938, he noted:

> The activities necessary to the perfection of a half-hour broadcast are greater than may be apparent. Good radio programs, unlike Topsy, are not 'just growed'. They are born of many hours of arduous thought and preparation. For example, it is easier for me to prepare a week's program with its split-second timing of about six numbers crowded into a short half-hour period. I have in my music library well over 20,000 compositions of every description imaginable, yet I am always bewildered as to how to start selecting a short radio program from this abundance of material.

Even so, he was now planning programs much further in advance than once he had. In a series of full-page advertisements – paid for by King band instruments ('Frank Simon and his famous Armco Band again spotlight King superiority') the entire programs for the months ahead were published, the title of the pieces he was going to play in the following four weeks and descriptions of them:

> January 9 1938: 'Calinerie' (Flattery) . . . Here is a short and dainty piece by Henry Ravina, quite suggestive, as its title implies, of clever flattery. The oboe has a very important part with its suave, soft and impelling tone.
> January 30: March: 'Espagnole' . . . This march is typical Spanish music, full of the beautiful color, melody and life of the gay Spain of old.

Those who did not read about the programs in newspapers got them in letters. Via the King company again, there was a mailing list of 100,000 people who were sent regular details. Numbers were important. Frank knew that millions listened to the weekly broadcasts. His live concerts also drew huge attendances – like the Episcopal rally at Nippert Stadium in Cincinnati which brought in 30,000 delegates, all of whom attended the concert.

Frank was nothing if not ecumenical. He played 'Eli Eli' at temples and tried never to turn down invitations to conduct 'Onward Christian Soldiers' for the Salvation Army.

But the radio program continued to be his most important activity – and not just his. Top soloists, not just gifted amateurs, were now a major feature in the broadcasts, like Dan Beddoe, the Welsh American tenor. It was also why the show received so many commendations. Eugene Goossens put his views firmly on the line. 'It is a very sterling band, plays excellent music in splendid fashion,' he wrote. 'The band numbers about 40 or 50 and offers in every way an artistic and brilliant entertainment of good music, splendidly performed.'

When he chose young unknown soloists the civic authorities from their home towns took it as much as a tribute to their communities as to the musician himself. In April 1938, after hearing a broadcast, Joseph Gannon wrote to Frank:

> As Mayor of Chicago Heights (Ill), I am very proud that you selected George W. Gass, Junior, of our city for your guest soloist . . . To appear as a guest soloist of the noted Dr Simon and his famous Armco Band on a nationwide broadcast is indeed an outstanding honor which this young man and the people of our community should never forget.

The tributes that Frank appreciated most were those from his contemporaries and colleagues. When he heard that Herbert Clarke was going to be a guest conductor at the clinic he was organizing at Urbana, Illinois, he was beside himself with excitement. 'What a thrill when I learned [about it]', he wrote his old partner and mentor. Clarke was going to be chairman of the panel of instructors at the clinic. 'My heart dictates that everyone should have a chance, but after all we are in the show business and must always put our best to the front,' Frank wrote to his old colleague.

When details like that could be ironed out and the radio show was having its seasonal rest, Frank could concentrate on the really important things in life – like fishing. Bennett Chapple, newly recovered from a serious illness, told him about his own success in angling. 'You certainly made me nervous when I read about the sail fish. What a thrill it would be to hook into one of those and I really intend to do that when I come down [to Florida] in May,' he wrote in March 1938.

But Frank was mostly concerned that Chapple would be well enough to resume his Ironmaster talks next season. He had not liked a certain Mr Prosser who had taken over during Chapple's illness:

> We are all 'fed up' with the importance of Mr Prosser, who has now had to find a hat two sizes larger than the one he had prior to the opening of

> the season. He makes a hit with me and when he criticizes the intent of the composer! You would think that he was some super Toscanini by the way he acts, but we all know it is part of the racket that the agency people have to justify.

Another of the guest speakers had been Father Bernard R. Hubbard, a Jesuit missionary known as 'The Glacier Priest' who talked about his recent trip to the Arctic. To be fair to Frank Simon and his band, the talks were usually the time that people chose to make the coffee. Frank, nevertheless, had good news to give to the company vice president:

> You have no idea how popular the program is this year. It seems as if everyone is most enthused and now I have some real good news to give you: It is generally conceded, by the radio world, that when *Variety* magazine issues a statement, it really means something and they have selected what in their opinion are the ten most outstanding broadcasts on the air today and we have crashed the gate and are now among the tops in radio. Of all the radio shows which Ayer [the advertising agency] puts on the air, only two received this distinction, the Ford Sunday evening program and ours. I know you are as elated over this triumph and vindication as I am and everyone at the office is all 'het up'. Today at noon, I ran into Mr Hook and he was most interested in the report.

The musicians were pleased too. Charles Payne, who played in the band at the time, told me: 'I never considered it hard work because I enjoyed it.' Payne was one of the 19-year-old Conservatory students whom Frank brought into the Armco organization.

He enjoyed the work, as he said, but there were certain strains. 'We'd rehearse on Sunday mornings for two hours, break and then work for another two hours. Then we'd have a dress rehearsal for half an hour. But we wouldn't know what we were playing until Sunday mornings.' That was when Frank had whistled and hummed his way through the week's program, timing every piece on his stopwatch. 'I often thought about it as desperation time,' Payne recalls now. 'But there was very good camaraderie. We got on very well together. Frank Simon was responsible for that.'

Frank continued to be responsible for other people's careers. In January 1938 the Mayor of Oklahoma City presented the Armco Certificate of Merit to a 13-year-old cornetist called Billy Snyder who had appeared as a soloist on an Armco broadcast. The same ceremony was repeated two days later in front of 3500 Shriners gathered for their convention at Guthrie, Oklahoma. Meanwhile, every soloist featured in the previous year was presented with a gold medal with the words 'For Distinguished Musicianship' on one side and a picture of a microphone on the other.

Frank would tell anyone at the slightest encouragement that band education was good for a youngster. 'The great educational movement is sweeping the country by storm and among the leading women's clubs throughout the United States they are using educational music as an antidote to juvenile crime.'

Everything seemed wonderful in Frank Simon's life – until May 1938. That was when his mother died. He had driven Bertha in his car earlier that day and had taken her to dinner in the evening. The following morning, Frank called to see her and found her unconscious. She had had a stroke. As the *Middletown Journal* noted, 'She had been in declining health for months but had refused to admit her condition or accept the terms of ill health. Because of her courage, the seriousness of her condition was not generally known.' Frank wrote to Herbert Clarke about his feelings. 'After lingering for 17 days, she passed on. You can imagine what a terrible ordeal it was for me, since mother and I were so close.'

Suddenly, one of the great anchors of his life was gone. Bertha had been his inspiration. More than that, she had been the reason he had become a musician, the reason he had done so well, the reason indeed for Armco topping the pops on American radio. It was a blow harder even than his father's death six years earlier.

He could not work, so he and Mary took off for a three-week break to Texas. He returned in time to undertake his prescheduled engagements in the East, ending up at Des Moines, Iowa. The organization was now *formally* known as Frank Simon and His Armco Band, which in truth was what a lot of people had been calling it for years. What a lot of people did not know was that its days were now numbered.

15 · *Close Down*

If Frank Simon was a showman (and that was very much what he was) he had to recognize he was part of showbusiness, a situation with which he was sometimes not totally happy. He would have preferred to be compared with Toscanini and say that the music was everything. Just occasionally, however, he had to play the showbiz game and agree to do things for the sake of publicity – like playing basketball in the backyard with his two sons, David and Joe.

The kids normally had to be content with their fishing expeditions during vacations, going to concerts and watching their father eat, although occasionally they were allowed to amuse themselves with his typewriter and checkwriter (under careful supervision, it has to be said). But basketball? He *could* be persuaded, the boys soon discovered.

The Armco PR department thought it would be a good idea for Frank to play the game and invite photographers down to the house in Middletown to record it for a magazine layout. Now, apart from waving his arms around – and that was an athletic pursuit known to exhaust professional footballers – Frank was not interested in playing sports and would claim never to do anything more athletic than picking up a playing card and snapping it down on a green baize table. But for the sake of the game – the game of promoting the Armco Band – he agreed to play. But minutes after starting, he pulled a tendon and spent six weeks on his back.

But still he was the star of Middletown. He was also very much the star of radio, the kind of star who is there not simply because he was better than anyone else but for what he had created – something that had not been there before. People still appreciated that he had started from scratch the whole notion of the radio band – not just a band that played on radio but one that was tailored exclusively for the microphone at one end and the radio loudspeaker at the other.

His programs were not the sort he would play in the parks or on bandstands but were sharp and concise, enough to whet the appetites of listeners at home, not to allow their attentions to wander and perhaps to leave them gasping for more. At the same time, the instrumentation was precisely what sounded best within the limitations of a studio and across the airwaves in those pre-FM, pre-hi-fi days when 'The Entry of the Gladiators' and everything else had to fight through a sea of static. As Bob Hornyak told me: 'In his day, he took the symphony band to the next level because of what he had done on radio.' But it was enough to develop a following that was phenomenal. More people heard a single Simon radio program than had heard half, perhaps more than half, of all the Sousa concerts put together, almost a quarter of a century's worth. You went anywhere in the United States and talked of bands and before long you were talking about the Frank Simon Armco Band. And that was still the case outside of the country too.

In August 1938 he had what was perhaps the supreme tribute of his entire career. He was invited to Canada – to conduct the Toronto Symphony at a series of promenade concerts. He was taking the place of the orchestra's own regular conductor, Reginald Stewart. It was a hot summer and the attendance suffered as a result, but the trip was a triumph. He had some celebrated soloists with him, including the Chilean-born pianist Alberto Guerrero, who had lived in Canada for 20 years and who played the Grieg piano concerto, and Maurice Solway, who played the Wieniawski violin concerto. The first concert opened with Goldmark's 'Sakuntala' and included 'A Carnival In Paris' by Svendsen and the funeral march from Rimsky-Korsakov's *Mlada*. Eric Coates's *London Suite* was also featured. The audience, said the magazine *Saturday Night*, was 'one of the most enthusiastic of the summer'. Reported Hector Charleworth in his review, 'absentees missed a very good time'. More pointedly, he went on: 'It is musical snobbery to make a caste distinction between an orchestral conductor and a band conductor; something like saying that a fine violinist is a better musician than a first-rate oboist or French horn expert.'

His sons certainly thought it worth while. David was photographed in the *Star Weekly* magazine, holding a camera himself and 'shooting' his father at work. He and Joe had a marvelous time exploring the best hotel in town, the Royal York, where Frank and his ensemble had been booked. At the end of the tour they were each given a fishing box by one of the orchestra's board of directors who manufactured them.

As for Frank himself, he was not only given a more than useful fee – which he doubtless would have forgone had he had to do so in exchange for the opportunity of fronting this important orchestra, the first band conductor ever to do so – but he was also feted as though he really were Toscanini. Civic receptions were held in his honor. Music critics and local dignitaries made speeches paying tribute to his work.

When he returned to Middletown, he felt like more than merely the king of the band world and director of the most successful operation of its kind. He was a respected musician. He could ask for nothing more. Or so he thought. The new year of 1939 dawned full of plans. He was working on a splendid program of activity. But he was going to concentrate now on conducting. Herbert Clarke had stopped playing at 50. Now Frank was going to follow his example. He knew he would not be able to keep up his standard for very much longer and he was determined to be remembered only for what he could do – not what he could once manage.

It was a momentous decision, a turning point in the Simon career. For the boy who had dreamed of being a professional cornetist to the exclusion of practically everything else in life who became the man whose very appearance at a concert anywhere in the United States guaranteed record turnouts, who had just had that remarkable triumph in Canada, it was an amazing turn of events. He was not to know that there would be others, more momentous and more startling.

He went to Armco, dressed as always in his immaculate suit and the ever-present spats on his shoes and derby hat on his head, ready to talk plans for the coming season and everything seemed perfect. He was always warmly welcomed into the office, given a big cigar and an enthusiastic reception to his jokes. He did not then know what was being planned for him. Indeed, if he had heard about the state of the American steel industry in general and Armco in particular, he might very well have thrown that derby into the air and given a rousing cheer.

Armco was doing well, better than ever. Just months after the Munich Agreement, which sold out the people of Czechoslovakia – 'In a far-away country . . . of which we know nothing,' said Britain's Prime Minister, Neville Chamberlain – and allowed the Nazis to take over, the nations of the world were finally awakening to the possibility of war.

Rearmament was now a commitment. And to rearm, all the forces of the world needed one basic ingredient: steel. Armco and the other steel companies of America had their work cut out. The one thing they did not need was advertising. The Armco Band full-filled no obvious purpose. So Charles Hook made his decision: he was axing the band and canceling the radio show.

Frank had first wind of what was about to happen at the New York Ayer office, Armco's advertising agents, where he was planning his eleventh year of programs. For the first time, he told them – and to their evident enthusiasm – he was going to feature a male quartet and was actually beginning the long-drawn-out process of auditioning quartets when there was a phone call from Armco's advertising manager in Middletown. 'Frank come home,' the man said. 'We're off the air.'

To Frank Simon, it was a betrayal not just of him but of his musicians and his audiences, who were as big and as loyal as ever. There was also an understanding between Simon and the steel company. He made it very clear that this was a breach of contract. No discussions had been held before the axing was revealed. Hook, backed by the Armco lawyers, was perfectly sanguine about it all. Where was the contract? There was nothing in writing between them was there? Frank was drawn to admit that there was not.

When he got home after his meeting, Frank collapsed – and spent days in bed. He vowed to do two things: fight the closure and change the name of the 'Camp Hook March'. He did both (the tune became 'The March of the Majorettes').

It was a long, exhausting battle. He was fighting for his professional life and the efforts he put into it were those of a general with his army at his rear caught in a pincer movement. The only big guns were on the Armco lines – and, as the Ironmaster had said every week, there was nothing like steel for strength. There was no way that Armco could lose if they had it in mind to stay the course.

Frankly, the company saw no reason to give in. The show was popular and so was the band, but Charles Hook himself no longer needed it to boost morale. His workers were putting in all the overtime their constitutions could stand. Unemployment in their industry was a thing of the past. And everyone needed steel. Everyone. Why waste not only the money that the show took up but also the effort and the office space it occupied? Quite rightly, Hook concluded that the Kaiser shipbuilding empire was not going to choose its steel suppliers on the basis that its band played 'The Stars and Stripes Forever' better than any other group of musicians in the country. And if Frank wanted to be difficult, there still was no piece of paper to say they ever had any further plans.

Probably what hurt most was the ingratitude of it all. Despite what the company now believed, he had done a tremendous amount to boost their image. The facts now known showed that he had needed the Armco connection as much as they did themselves, but they had gone to great lengths to persuade him to join them. Was this gratitude? Plainly, it was not.

If there had never been a written contract, it was always because he took the view that gentlemen did not need such formalities. Now he was advised to sue. He would not do so, but he was having to fight for what he could get – and not just himself. He fought, too, to get Ernie Glover a year's fees. Eventually, the company agreed to keep the show running for the 1939 season. But there would be no more.

The publicity continued as though nothing had happened. Station KTOK in Oklahoma City advertised with a letter to 'Mr and Mrs Oklahoma, 0000 Main Street, Oklahoma City':

> Dear Mr and Mrs Oklahoma, I am happy to announce that beginning Sunday, January 15 at 2pm, Radio Station KTOK will present the Armco Band directed by Dr Frank Simon. The program will be heard over the NBC network, with which KTOK is affiliated. As you probably know, the 52-piece Armco Band is recognized as one of the greatest concert bands in the country. Twelve members formerly played in the famed band conducted by John Philip Sousa . . . May I suggest that you listen

> in Sunday at 2pm over KTOK and join with me in the enthusiasm of a finer and better show for 1939.

It was signed by Kenyon M. Douglass, General Manager KTOK.

The last show went out on 9 April. The *Middletown Journal* recorded the event in much the same way as it recorded the other broadcasts – the conductor Frank Simon was 'genial' and the soloist Robert Pfaitzgraff, son of a Dumont, Iowa, hardware dealer, was 'youthful'. Strangely – but perhaps not so strange since the paper knew where a lot of its money was coming from – it concentrated on 'the well-known ironmaster' who was to 'discuss the famous Armco continuous rolling process for manufacturing iron and steel sheets. This process, as many Middletown residents will recall, was invented by a local man, John B. Tytus, now vice president in charge of operations for Armco.' NBC would probably have wanted to keep the broadcasts going, but without a sponsor, there was little chance of that happening. N. W. Ayer were trying to organize something but even a leading advertising agency was having no luck. In the end, the network – who decided there was room for only one band on the air – replaced Armco with the City Service Band, a group formed by the New York City musicians' union.

The advertising agency was not pleased. They even put a damper on the one thing that Frank was determined to carry through – the band's appearance at the New York World Fair. A letter to Simon from the company on 22 February 1939 read:

> You probably have read in the newspapers or music journals of the general collapse of plans for music programs at the New York Fair this summer. The difficulty behind all this is that no financial provision has been made for music of any kind. The whole affair has been somewhat clumsily handled and I am not sure that we should advise anyone to become involved in it unless some new angles develop.

There *was* a band at the New York World Fair – the Middletown high-school band in which Frank's son Joe played. Frank gave a concert to raise money for the youngsters to go to the fair and financed the venture. When David heard he was going to New York, he made his way into the band, too. Today, David remembers sneaking out during the evening when everybody thought he was asleep to go on an exploration of the city with a fellow Middletown bandsman.

Meanwhile, Frank continued to put his all into the Armco shows as if there were no ax hanging over his head. The same letter from N. W. Ayer, warning of the difficulties with the New York World Fair, pointed out that the previous week's program 'was not only the best of your current series but unquestionably the best band music we have ever heard on a broadcast'. The letter was signed 'Harry', who wrote 'In my estimation, the Moussorgsky composition was the best band selection I have ever heard in my life. I am sure that any listener cutting in as that piece began would have believed he was listening to a full symphony orchestra.'

In normal times that would have been, literally, music to his ears. Frank himself might have got over his disappointment over the cancellation of the programs had it not affected his health in the way that it did, an effect that was to last for years. He developed hay-fever which turned into asthma. He was allergic to the Ohio air – it was in the heart of what was known as the ragweed belt – and so took the advice of doctors and looked to a new invention. He installed one of the first domestic air conditioners. He used to say (it could have been a good excuse, but the results spoke for themselves) that was another reason why he used to go to Canada fishing. But really, it was much too serious to joke about.

The irritating thing was that people continued to say how much they loved his music. An internal memo from Armco's office in Detroit soon after the firing in February 1939 commented on an appearance Frank made at a local Salvation Army dinner which was followed by an Armco concert in the city:

> I am writing to advise what a fine job Dr Frank Simon did last week when he made a talk and presented Miss Kellogg with the new cornet. [Miss Kellogg was a Detroit employee and Salvation Army lass whom Frank had featured on a recent broadcast he called 'Parade of the Prodigies'.] He made a very fine talk there, also and at the end of the talk the applause lasted quite some time. Attendance was approximately 2500.

The newspapers were all headlining Nazi actions in Germany, Austria and Czechoslovakia, but Frank's appearances comfortably made the second lead in most of them. 'Last night's concert given at the Junior High Auditorium,' recorded the *Clearfield Progress* in Pennsylvania, 'was acclaimed by veteran musicians as "Sensational".'

Everywhere it was the same. The same headlines that had greeted Sousa's appearances in past year, now referred to Frank Simon. 'Famous Conductor Returns to Lead Central High School Band Friday.' 'Frank Simon Coming In Concert Friday.' He was photographed in white flannels and sports jacket, in white tie and tails, in a vest conducting students. He was pictured on top of makeshift rostrums in the open air, among the potted palms of municipal auditoria stages. He was shown in his kitchen, making spaghetti.

He was leading student bands and lodge bands and conducting clinics. But for the moment it was not enough. The big problem was coming to terms with the reality of the situation. Frank could not understand it. What the magazine *Radio Dial* wrote in February 1939 seemed no more than both justice and what people expected: 'A band program of the Simon caliber, three or four evenings a week, would do a lot to compensate for the punishment of "Tin Pan Alley".'

He vowed to keep the Armco Band going, but even with the name Frank Simon fronting it, it was not going to be the same thing without the magic Armco tag. Nor could it work without what was obviously its backbone – the broadcasts. There was nothing to keep the name before the public's eye. There was an even more serious problem. Since many of the instrumentalists were full-time musicians with orchestras like the Cincinnati Symphony, they could not spare the time to go on the road. Once a week in the local studio was fine, but to travel, say, to California? Impossible.

But Frank tried, with all the spirit he had used to go for those early music lessons with Bellstedt. In 1940, he took the band on a tour of Ohio and Pennsylvania. 'A Band Known To Millions – Frank Simon and his famous Radio Band' declared the posters showing Frank leading the band in full evening dress:

> After ten years of brilliant successes as a national broadcasting feature, radio's finest and most popular symphonic band will be heard on its first personal tour. Dr Frank Simon, distinguished American bandmaster, and his famous band will appear before visible audiences . . . audiences that will want to see as well as hear this dynamic conductor and his fifty artist-musicians whose distinctive music is well known to music-loving millions.

The audiences appeared enthusiastic, at Memorial Hall, Columbus, at the Memorial Hall (same name, different location), Dayton, at the Zaneville Municipal Auditorium. When he appeared at home at the Middletown high-school auditorium, Grace Haller wrote in the *Cincinnati Enquirer*: 'If John Philip Sousa ever can be roused from his eternal sleep he must somewhere have stood up and cheered tonight at the rousing performances of his marches by Frank Simon and his band.'

Frank was doubtless raised momentarily from his depression. But he could not keep it up. The bookings fizzled out. With no Armco show and the decision not to play his cornet again, Frank was suddenly like a man who had had his right arm amputated – and his larynx removed. He was, however, astute enough to realize that the band business had changed. If he were going to conduct a band at all, it had to be Frank Simon and His Band. He knew it could never have the same following as the Armco outfit.

The Armco axing was more than just an economic move. It was also a realization that the band business was not what it had been. There were no other big bands working five or six days a week as there had been in Sousa's day. But there was a future: the Cincinnati Conservatory was just a symptom of the enthusiasm there still was for learning about band music. High schools and colleges throughout the country were improving the standards of their bands every term. This was, to use a phrase of half a century later, where it was at.

Now he was going to spend most of his time guest conducting other bands – and the offers for this work continued at virtually the same pace as before – and doing his good works. In 1964, Earl D. Irons wrote to Simon reminding him that 1939 was the year he had personally arranged to have his cornet solo published for him after being shown it at a music festival.

Those festivals were part of his bread and butter existence now and he never failed to take them totally seriously, even though he had earned enough money in the Armco years and had invested sufficiently wisely never to have to worry about his and his family's financial position, thanks to early advice from cousin Julius. As George Crout remembered for me: 'I'd see him walking around Middletown. He always had some project in mind.'

In June 1940 he was in Racine, Wisconsin. He enjoyed it so much that he wrote a letter to the local newspaper, published under the heading 'From a Noted Musical Leader':

> As you probably know, I have conducted bands and taken part in musical entertainments in many cities of the country. But let me say I never saw, heard or participated in a finer program than the one given at your Horlick Field Tuesday night. If you'll pardon the slang, there was a lot of truly 'big time stuff' . . . As one whose life is wrapped up in music, I wish that the US had a thousand 'Racines'.

He was continuing to run his band clinics. William Revelli remembered one he organized for him. 'He gave them instruction on how to warm up. He sure did warm them up!' But Frank was always encouraging 'and helpful', said Revelli.

He continued to spend time with individuals – like the boy he had helped all those years before. Revelli continued to remember that event at Marion, Indiana.

> That boy had appeared before him at 9.30 in the morning and it was now 10 pm. I have never seen anyone more tired. And this little boy was there at the end and went up to him. The boy asked, 'Dr Simon, could you tell me what was wrong with my playing?' He had heard perhaps 60 or 70 players, and really couldn't remember him. He had already written his notes. But he asked the boy to play and there and then gave him a 45-minute lesson. He only packed up when the janitor said he had to lock up the school. So he told him to come down to the hotel and there and then finished his lesson – downstairs in the furnace room, so that he wouldn't disturb the other guests. I said to myself, 'this is a great man'. I wouldn't have done it. I'm dedicated, but I don't think I would have done that. But then it was listening to people like Simon in the Sousa band that had persuaded me to want to join a band and make my life with them. There was Frank Simon on the cornet and Arthur Pryor on the trombone. Frank was a motivator. I don't think he ever discouraged anyone in his life. He would tell people he didn't think they would make it from the beginning, but once they had started with him on a proper basis, he wouldn't say, 'Don't play' or 'Go and sell shoes'.

Revelli listened to the lesson himself 'and believe me, I learned a lot, too. He was a terrific influence. He was a noted person. You said the name Simon, just as you mentioned the name Clarke and people knew who you were talking about.' Some people think it was the fraternity of the band movement that kept him going. 'I never heard Frank Simon say a bad word about any other bandmaster,' recalled Revelli.

Bill Richardson, a retired high-school head now living in Tucson, Arizona, recalled seeing Frank conducting a high-school band at a Mid-West clinic. 'There was this little barrel-chested soloist who played "Willow Echoes",' he remembered for me. 'Frank Simon had tears running down his cheeks. He told the boy: "I've never played it as well as that myself".' The high-school players remembered him for that. They also liked his verbal shorthand. He knew his music terminology, but he did not allow it to overtake him. To a cymbal player, recalled Richardson, he would say: 'Give me a good ching there.' Perhaps that was his greatest success. To give all his audiences a constant series of 'good chings'.

There was also just the germ of a hope that his broadcasting career was not over. In December 1939, extending through the spring of 1940, he conducted a series of radio concerts with his beloved Conservatory band on Station WCKY. The station boasted it was 'powerful as any radio station in the entire United States,' and it was networked by CBS. But four o'clock on a Monday afternoon was not like prime time on a Sunday with Armco and it did not last. While it did, he enjoyed the work originating from the 50,000-watt station, playing pieces like the overture to Corneilus's opera, *The Barber of Baghdad*, works by Moussorgsky, Verdi (the clarinet fantasia from *Rigoletto*) or perhaps Haydn Wood's *A Manx Overture*. To Frank, it justified his work at the Conservatory and his plans for the future. Above all, he was going to spend more time teaching.

He extended his work with yet another attempt at a new broadcasting career – holding a series of band clinics on the air. There was not the instrumentation there had been in the Armco days any more than there was the same quality of instrumentalist, but he still tried to be sure that in addition to the cornets, trumpets and trombones, there would be a flugel horn.

He raised the money for four broadcasts of high-school clinics with the help of Ernest Glover, who was about to become his business partner. But it did not work out. There was no available 'angel'. He hoped he could manage without the backing. Friends told him that art never supported itself – to which he replied that Sousa had never had a sponsor in his life. But Sousa's days were over.

So teaching was now the most important part of his professional life. And every once in a while, a student came along who fired his enthusiasm to an almost unimaginable extent. There was the 17-year-old in particular who got his juices going, the son of the New Orleans policeman. His name was Al Hirt.

16 · *Teacher and Inspiration*

Bourbon Street in New Orleans is an unlikely place to find a Frank Simon memorial. It is a street positively vibrating with the sound of trumpets, cornets and the other instruments with which the director of the Armco Band and the professor at the Cincinnati Conservatory of Music were very familiar. But the music is not his. Jazz, he believed, was a noise people who did not know any better said they danced to – although Frank probably had a different word for it.

Nevertheless, the face of jazz – certainly white jazz – would have been extremely different if Frank Simon had not been around. For one thing, there would have been no establishment on Bourbon Street boasting the regular appearances of Al Hirt, who rejoices in being called the greatest living jazz trumpeter. Because it was Frank Simon who found him.

More than ever in 1940, with no more Armco to take his time, Frank was on the teaching circuit. That year, it stretched to New Orleans, where he had been invited to conduct the Fotier High School Band – which in itself said a great deal both for Simon and for what school bands represented. No classical orchestra conductor of his status would have demeaned himself by waving his baton in front of a collection of schoolchildren. Frank took it as a matter of course – of course, if invited he would go; of course, it was an opportunity to get face to face with the future of band music. And of course, the schools and colleges were already fast becoming the homes of the most vibrant bands in the country.

That was when he met Al Hirt. As he told it, he walked into the huge school – it had 2800 students, all boys – met the band and sized up what he had before him as they started to relax and then rehearse.

'It only takes a few minutes to find out who's got it in the band, who was the outstanding performer.'

He knew immediately where he could find a boy who had 'got it'. 'There was a kid,' he recalled, 'who was going to play a solo that night that I had written and so he walked up to the front and picked his horn and started to play.' The piece was 'Willow Echoes'. The kid was Al Hirt. The choice of music was to prove as lucky for Hirt as it always was for Frank himself. Frank was impressed with the tall, broad youngster – but not overcome. 'He walked up to the front and picked his horn and started to play. He had a lot of technique, but he didn't have any soul or taste in his performance – just technique.'

The germ of an idea was already forming in the Simon brain. He was ready to do a Meredith Willson – except there was no Sousa Band to which to direct the young cornet player, and, saddest of all, there was no Armco Band either. All he could hope to do was to teach him. From that first hearing, Frank Simon felt he could provide the soul to go with the technique.

'Son, can you remain after the rehearsal?' he asked Hirt, knowing full well that he would say yes, he could, but it would not have been nice to act the tough teacher and order him to stay; no, that was not the Simon way at all. 'I'd like to show you a little bit,' he said by way of an explanation that was no explanation at all. Frank took the boy into a side room and gave him a lesson on how he thought the solo should go. 'I showed him how to play it to make something out of it.' And he explained: 'It isn't what you play that's important, it's *how* you play it. How do you like it now?!'

'That makes a different solo out of it altogether, doesn't it?' replied the boy. Frank could only agree that it did. That night, he said, the 165-lb youngster 'played like an angel'. Just as he had told Meredith Willson. 'He had brains,' Frank remembered.

That is the Frank Simon story. It diverges in one important detail from Hirt's own recollection. Al says that he and Frank met for the first time two years later at a band clinic at the University of Illinois. 'My band instructor arranged for me to play for him. I heard he was there and his reputation made it worth while for me to go up there.' The instructor, a pianist named Michael Cupero, knew the value of his young student. 'I'm going to fix it,' he said, 'for you to play for him.' And he did. 'I didn't know why, but he obviously had a scholarship in mind for me.'

He said that he and Simon first met in a studio at the university. 'All right, son,' he says Frank told him, 'play.' Al sat down to feel comfortable with his instrument. 'Don't sit down,' he instructed. 'Stand up.'

'Oh,' said the boy, 'I've always sat down to play.'

'Well,' ordered Simon, 'you don't sit down with me. You stand up. Don't you realize it inhibits your breathing? When you stand up you breathe like a pair of bellows. That's the way to play!'

The rest of the stories converge – up to a point. They agree that Hirt did not have any money. It was an essential commodity for what Frank had in mind – a course of instruction at the Cincinnati Conservatory. Hirt's father's salary would not stretch to paying the fare to Cincinnati, let alone a year or more at the Conservatory. He had other priorities in mind – like feeding and clothing his wife and eight children.

That being so, the Simon treatment came into play. He suggested that the school give Hirt a scholarship – an idea that was close to being laughed out of court. The Depression may have happened nine years before but its ramifications were still being felt. There was an international slump and no one could raise the money. If the Conservatory did not have tuition fees, what *did* it have?

The second part of the Simon treatment was to make it clear that he did not like taking no for an answer. 'He will be the greatest advertisement for the Conservatory you will ever have in your lifetime,' he told George Klusmeier, the manager of the Conservatory, who decided such things. But the Simon influence could go just so far – and no further. Impasse was reached at the point that the Conservatory conceded and offered a quarter of a scholarship. There were only two choices – Al Hirt would stay in New Orleans or Frank Simon would have to pay the remainder of the fees, three-quarters of them, himself. He paid the fees – for four years.

Hirt says he does not know the details. All he knows is that he was given a full scholarship; as far as he was concerned, it was that right enough. Hirt told me he will never forget how Frank expressed enthusiasm for his new student's playing. 'You're a diamond,' he told him. 'But you need polish. And I'm the guy who'll do it for you.'

'Yes, sir,' said Al. 'And he did. Not "I think I can do it", but "I *can* do it".' He jumped at the scholarship. 'I knew I had to move forward and that was the only way to do it. He refined my playing. He taught me how to breathe, always standing up. I needed that. They used to say I was a prodigy. But it was not enough. Frank Simon was my idol and so was Herbert Clarke.' The idea of playing jazz had not entered Al's mind. If it had, Frank doubtless would have been a lot less enthusiastic about him. As it was, he now says 'I dreamed of playing in a band like Frank's or a symphony orchestra. I never thought of jazz until I went to college.' The college he went to was the University of Cincinnati, close to the Conservatory. He studied at the university simultaneously with his once-a-week music lessons.

But it was Frank's influence which was by far the strongest. 'He was a lovely man. Spiffy. So well dressed. A real gentleman.' But it was not his appearance – 'that mustache, always well trimmed' – that appealed so much. It was his technical ability – and style.

Frank was coming to think about his decision to stop playing at 50. He still intended to do it. But with Al Hirt and his other students, he continued to make sweet music – if only demonstrating how notes should be performed. It was not like planning the old Armco shows. Now he could not indicate what he had in mind by simply whistling or humming a few bars. He had to show it on the cornet himself. Even if he had not intended doing that at the beginning, the temptation to do so for his students was too great to resist.

Al Hirt was certainly the beneficiary of that decision. 'If he had to go away for two or three weeks, when he came back, he'd pick up where we left off and and pick up his horn and demonstrate – even if he had not played himself for those two or three weeks. He sounded wonderful. That used to amaze me.'

'Dr Simon,' Al would say, 'how the hell do you do that?'

'Son,' he would reply. 'It's a question of breathing. It won't last long because the muscles in your lips won't be subtle enough. So learn to do it now.'

Al remembers Frank telling him that if he himself had continued to practice, even at this late stage in his career, he would still have played better. Frank Simon playing better? 'Oh yes. For the first few minutes, he was as good as he ever was. But he couldn't keep going. After a few minutes, his embouchure would go.'

For those four years, Al Hirt experienced the familiar Simon teaching style, one to one, standing 'at my arm' at the end of a long studio with a grand piano in one corner and picking up his own horn to demonstrate what he considered to be 'some glitch' in the younger man's playing.

'You didn't read it properly', he might tell Al, 'this is how you should play.' As Al now says: 'I was amazed. I thought I knew how to play, but I didn't. I really did lack that polish. I needed phrasing and breathing. Frank taught me to read music, to divide an eighth note or divide a sixteenth note. I never knew about those things.'

Simon's influence was huge. Al's father, Al Hirt senior, who never rose above the rank of patrolman in New Orleans and who knew nothing about music ('what the hell's a prodigy?' he used to say) had, nevertheless, appreciated his son's latent talent and had encouraged him. 'He used to say "Drop that bat. Get your ass down there and practice." He wasn't like those parents who give up if you can't play like Dizzie Gillespie in six weeks. But he saw what Frank Simon did for me and knew when I didn't need to be told to practice any more.'

It was the kind of vicarious Simon influence that others were to note. 'He had the great Charlier method,' Hirt told me. 'That was a great book on styles and how they should be interpreted. He was big on that. Not just playing the notes, but interpreting them in the right way. You could play the right notes but not in the right style. He was a stickler for that. He had great flair.'

Hirt never forgot that contribution to his fortunes, fortunes that possibly would never have existed without Frank's help. Today, the larger than ever and bearded Al Hirt fills in the remainder of that story. In his strong, deep Southern drawl he told me at his New Orleans home: 'This man was an incredible showman. The greatest influence I have ever had in my life on anything was his influence on style. And his influence on a flair for showbusiness, for entertaining people.'

None of that could have come out in group teaching sessions. But there were those, too, when he conducted the Conservatory band. 'Man, that was a wonderful band.' (Later on, but during Hirt's stay at the Conservatory, the band broadcast for an hour every Saturday evening on the Blue Network, but not conducted by Frank.)

When he taught, Al said, 'everybody listened – with ears cocked.' His conducting was like his playing, Al Hirt now thinks. 'He had a marvelous technique. His cut-offs were very impressive. He had a way to cut off a note which I thought was unusually good. He was like Bernstein in that, and he could have conducted with a pencil.'

Frank had the talent to know not just the way the band was playing but the way individuals played. In the midst of a rehearsal he would say: 'Fred. That's B natural. Not sharp.' As Hirt says, 'I've never known any other conductor – except Billy May – who could do that.' If a player was not playing properly, he would stop him. But if things were right, 'you could see in his eyes that he was pleased'. The emotional Frank Simon was to the fore again. Once more, the example of 'The Stars and Stripes Forever' was cited. 'He would slow down the ending and everybody got worked up and he would go back to the old way. And then he'd get the brass to walk out on to the front.'

There were other examples of his showmanship – like teaching his star pupil to know when and how (with a tug of his arm, as though agreeing reluctantly) to bring his conductor back onto the stage at the end of a performance. 'That was pure showmanship. And so he was to be able to please an audience and have them go with him.'

Frank took Al to a summer band camp with him at Detroit Lakes, Michigan, a chance to learn more technique and more soul. More important, and something he did not tell the youth at the time, it gave Al a free vacation, a luxury he had never had before. 'You're damned right,' he said when I put that point to him. But he was also there to work. Frank was the leader. Al was the cornet instructor, with students of his own. 'Never once did he check on me to see if I knew what I was doing.' The closest he got to that was to ask 'Have you got any talent in there?'

He and the Simon boys became instant friends. The lessons were in the afternoon. But he went out fishing with them and Ernie Glover in the mornings, although not with Frank himself. 'But I don't think Frank Simon ever put on a sports shirt. He had an aura about him – even in the camp he was a spiffy dresser. He always wore a suit.'

Al went riding with David and Joe and he and Joe in particular were a great hit with the girls. It is possible that their success was greater with the girls than it was with the horses. Joe's mount broke a leg and had to be shot. 'Dr Simon was very proud of those two boys,' Al remembered for me. He was also very proud of his pupils. 'He was one of a kind. I never met a man like him.'

Being a Simon pupil was like being a member of a group. Students knew when their fellow-members were doing well. For instance, he constantly told Al of the success of a Texas girl named Jennings McLean, whom he was teaching cornet and for whom he had written a piece called 'Miss Bluebonnet'. That, in a way, was the ultimate tribute from teacher to student. But there were others. In 1941 he went back to New Orleans with Al Hirt to conduct his old high-school band. It was a revealing experience. As Al now remembers, his old trumpet teacher at school behaved strangely during this visit. 'He had it in for me because I now played trumpet better than he did himself. But he was also very, very jealous of Dr Simon.'

Al played 'Willow Echoes' at the concert. (Could Frank have confused this concert with his first meeting with Al? It seems highly likely.) The former teacher was the one who did not appreciate his performance. 'What did you have to go to Frank Simon for, when you had me?' he asked him after the concert. 'I felt like saying, "Do you want me to list it? A? B? C?" But he *had* taught me fundamentals.' But then, that teacher had never written 'Willow Echoes'. 'Dr Simon loved me to play that.' The success of Al Hirt was to prove very significant to Frank. He was to say of his protégé, 'He's rewarded me many times over'.

Yet there was, Al Hirt now recalls, a kind of aloofness about him. 'You didn't really get very close to him.' But that was probably just the teacher–pupil relationship. Before long, he was more like a friend. 'He had a wonderful sense of humor and when he wasn't teaching, he'd tell those great stories. He was also a great public speaker. I had a huge respect for him.'

It appears to have been totally mutual. So much so that Hirt told me he never heard his mentor 'say anything derogatory about jazz'. In fact, his jazz playing only began to take root after he and Frank Simon parted company in their roles as teacher and pupil. 'He taught me to play exactly correct. I remember when I first started playing jazz, people would say to me, "Loosen up, man, loosen up – you're not with Dr Simon now. This is jazz".'

Hirt, in fact, might never have turned to jazz. Had there been Sousa or Armco-style bands still in existence, Al would have seen his future in one of them. But now he had to look elsewhere. He played with Benny Goodman and both the Dorseys before going on the road as a single. Yet some of his most successful early playing was with Arthur Fiedler and the Boston Pops. 'Fiedler was a great admirer of Frank. He used to say they had a lot in common – except that Fiedler was a womanizer. If Frank Simon was a womanizer, man, he kept it very quiet. No. He was a very moral man. Kind of like a father.'

Al Hirt's record albums have won him gold discs and 'Emmy' awards. He has played in Las Vegas and at the Palmer House in Chicago. In 1961 he was featured at John F. Kennedy's inaugural ball and soon afterward established the Bourbon Street Club where he still plays, although he no longer owns it.

He is at a time in life, much older than his teacher was when they first met, when his own style is totally set. I asked him if when he picked up his trumpet and began playing he ever thought 'Frank Simon would have played it like this . . .' 'Oh, sure man, I think that all the time.' He also thinks, when a great success comes his way, 'I wish Frank Simon could see this'. As he told me: 'I think every student thinks that about his teacher. I think that about Frank Simon and I think that about Arthur Fiedler, too.' He has, however, just one complaint: 'I think he was quite proud of me. But he never came to hear me play.'

17 · *The War and After*

Times were changing and Frank Simon might not have known quite by how much. They were changing in the world. Europe was engulfed in war and America was reacting in its own way to it. Franklin D. Roosevelt was re-elected to an unprecedented third term, much to Frank Simon's disappointment and his natural Republican sentiments. The disappointment was even greater in the way bands were – or perhaps were not – being received. Frank may not have realized it, but an additional paragraph he had written in that letter to the newspaper at Racine in June 1940 said a great deal:

> Frankly, I was surprised at one thing – the smallness of the crowd. Threatening weather probably had something to do with it. But even so, I rather expected your park to be thronged to capacity, because of the tradition built up through many fine music festivals of the past.

The truth of the matter was that, outside of the high school or college bandroom, the kind of band Frank Simon was conducting was becoming more and more of a specialist entertainment. People who wanted to hear a band would tune in to their radios. The kind of popular music that was drawing the big audiences came from the swing bands to which Al Hirt was graduating, the Dorseys and the Glenn Miller and Benny Goodman bands and their thousands of imitators. They also had one advantage over a Simon band – in addition to being heard on the air you could dance to their music. The ballrooms and dance halls had never been so popular.

Nevertheless, there was still something greatly infectious about what he did. Both his sons still would have liked to follow in his footsteps – or in the path of the echo of his cornet. But neither of them would have made it, he decided. His advice was that if they wanted to play they should treat a horn as an 'avocation' not a vocation or profession.

David happily continued to play in the school band he had joined at ten and his brother contented himself with practicing when his father was out of the room. It did not mean he did not love his father. Both boys adored him. As a father. Joe would tell me that he went through his early life not knowing who his father really was. 'I didn't know he was a celebrity, to me he was just Dad.'

A Dad who still behaved in some ways in what people across the Atlantic in Britain would have called fairly Victorian. But he knew certain things had to be faced – even if he did not want to face them himself. When the time came, he thought, for David to learn the facts of life, he sent him for a lesson – to a surgeon friend named Walter Reece who explained them to him.

There was no doubt that David was an academic. He was going to make a career as a doctor and nothing would stop him. He earned a place at Harvard and was the apple of his father's eye – for that as for everything else he did. For a man from Frank's background to have a son at Harvard was a magnificent thing. He would have liked Joe to do the same, to go to college – almost any college – but the youngster was not interested. Frank was sorely disappointed but he did not allow it to spoil their relationship. He knew that to Joe as well as to David he was still 'Dad', celebrity or not.

The public memory being what it was, Frank was, in truth, less of a celebrity now than he had been during the run of the Armco show. But in his own field, he was still the top star. And in that field, school music was bigger than it had ever been.

It was, in fact, a huge industry. There were, it was estimated, 4-5 million high-school children in the country, with tens of thousands of them in school bands. All of them needed instruments, sheet music and uniforms. They also needed teaching and in his own branch of academia Frank Simon had no peer.

The strange thing is that he did not feel degraded doing that sort of work after being a national personality. The hurt at losing the Armco job was an injury to his pride. He did not see it as damage to his status. Now that he had decided to concentrate on this branch of his work, he was content to know that he was the best – and was recognized as such.

He had no more hesitation about accepting an offer to conduct a college or school band than he had when he agreed to take on the Toronto Symphony. But they had to meet certain standards. He would consider the ability of the ensemble. If they had limited ability but raw talent, he would accept the invitation, and organize his program accordingly. A first-rate college band would receive no concessions. With them he would attempt the sophisticated repertoire of his Armco years.

It is possible he was just braver than he let most people think. It could not have been easy, after conducting Armco with its symphonic players, having now to confine himself to amateur groups. But no one knew. As far as everyone else was concerned, he was like a symphony conductor going from one orchestra to another.

Yet there was the satisfaction of still playing for the public. The concerts he gave were still selling well, if not quite to the extent of the great Armco years. It was a more specialized audience now and, in its way, a more appreciative one. He had come to terms with his situation. When the axing of the show was first announced he could not even go to all his classes; now he put that behind him. The Conservatory had grown more and more important in his life.

The Conservatory concerts were known to be among the best in the area. Certainly, there were no compromises with the program – twelve items ranging at one from Bellstedt's 'Carnival of Venice' through the 'March of the Little Leaden Soldiers!' by Pierne to the 'US Field Artillery March'. In the background at all times was his beloved Mary, or Maryla as he continued to call her. She continued to be his hostess, to give the best dinner parties in Middletown for important figures in the business, even sometimes joining Frank and the boys at band camps.

Those camps were getting more important than ever, with amazing staffs. In one single camp at Gunnison, Colorado, William Revelli told me, there was Frank Simon and himself, Cliff Bainam, and the United States Navy and Marine Band conductors (Commander Charles Brendler and Colonel William F. Santlemann, respectively). Teaching privately were the leaders of the sections of some of the greatest symphony orchestras and choirs in the country. The students were mostly people from colleges and high schools, who paid to come, to rehearse and have lessons in the morning and go fishing and enjoy sports in the afternoon. 'Frank Simon,' said Revelli, 'had some students who paid to come and who didn't have any talent, but he gave them a lesson every time.'

Joe Simon now thinks that his father was the one who deserved most of the credit for the way the home in Middletown was run. 'He was the most patient man in the world,' he told me. 'She was very difficult to live with and I don't know how he did it. I think by then she had become a manic depressive, but he handled it well. He never raised his voice and I suppose he understood her.'

David sees the picture more sympathetically. He told me: 'She was true blue. He stuck with her to the end.' But then he added: 'They were a good team. She was a lovely lady and shared in his success. She was always there.' David remembers his father saying Mary was pure gold. She traveled with him to his band clinics and to the contests which he judged. Plainly, she saw the way he was being lionized by the people with whom he dealt – and showed nothing but delight that he was.

It was more than his musicianship that attracted attention and such public approval. He had a manner that was all his own and, as the years went by, would change not one bit. Dr Mark Hindsley, then a leading figure in the band world, remembered the time Frank judged a contest at Cleveland Heights, Ohio. Hindsley told me he was always grateful for the note Frank handed him: 'Congratulations, my boy, you have a fine teacher.' He had never met Hindsley, or the teacher, before that day. Later, they got to know each other very well. Like dozens of others, he remembers Frank Simon the public speaker, who could leave an audience spellbound. 'He was a superb jokester.'

One story Hindsley recalled was not filed under the same headings as his stories about synagogue boards.

> He told the story of a church minister who had such a poor memory, he kept his notes in his coat pocket. At the end of the story of the miracle of the loaves and fishes, he said, it was part of the wondrous work of . . . our Lord and Savior (at which point he looked absent-mindedly inside his lapel) . . . Hart, Shafner and Marx.

As he also said: 'He was more than just a peerless cornet player and great musician, he was a great person. Everyone would fall in love with him.'

Frank continued to bring people to the Cincinnati Conservatory and then to appreciate their achievements after leaving. Bob McSpadden, a tenor, got his scholarship to the Conservatory because Frank heard him. It did not matter that he was not an instrumentalist. He went on to play percussion with the band and became a leading tympani player. 'I never would have done so without Frank Simon.' At one Conservatory concert, Bob hit the drum so hard, it split in the middle 'and I fell right into it. I thought he was ready to kill me – except that he laughed so much, he couldn't do so. And when he laughed, the big belt buckle he always wore would jump up and down.'

Frank's card-playing friends saw the same thing time and again. The games continued apace at the Elks Club. These sessions seemed to refresh him. A game of poker, a good joke, a long cigar and a heavy meal and he was a happy man, ready to move on to the next band clinic. Or Sousa Band Clinic, as he sometimes called the events he was now organizing to teach bands how to play the Sousa marches the way the maestro would have played them. All profits of these went to the Sousa Society, set up to promote Sousa's music and his ideals.

In these, too, he was treated as a star and like a star was always given a star's entrance – sometimes three days after the clinic opened. The bands had had those days to get into tune; he arrived in time to, as his son David now puts it, 'Simonize it', to get the rough edges knocked off. Frank Simon's motto was 'Small things are important' and in these sessions he was able to demonstrate just how important. Everyone in the band movement knew that motto and knew and respected the man who coined it. They also knew Frank's own marches. All over the country, bands were playing two Simon compositions in particular, 'The March of the Majorettes' and 'Here Come the Bands'. 'They were good marches,' William Revelli remembered. But he was never a rival for John Philip Sousa or Henry Fillmore. He did not have to be. He still had his own reputation as a player. He was still the most respected band conductor in the nation and his teaching reputation went before him.

Before he would appear, leaflets would be distributed by the high-school band hosting the event – not just duplicated sheets but professionally printed handbills that included potted biographies of the man who was going to be the centre of attraction. 'Dr Frank Simon,' declared one in large type printed on a blue sheet, 'will be guest conductor for the Band Clinic Concert. April 13. 8 p.m. City Auditorium.' Dr Simon, said the leaflet, 'is in popular demand as guest conductor, judge, lecturer for band festivals, contests and clinics in all parts of the country. He is a master showman, dynamic conductor and colorful personality.'

When Frank Simon and his Famous Radio Band appeared at Columbus, Ohio, George Hage wrote in the local newspaper, the *Columbus Dispatch*:

> Yep! They played 'Stars and Stripes Forever' and 'Semper Fidelis' and the crowd went a little mad, the way a crowd will when a Sousa march is played surpassing well. That gives you a capsule conception of how Capital University completed its concert series by presenting Dr Frank Simon and his 50-piece symphonic band last night in Memorial Hall.

He was as busy as he ever had been. But not too busy to make his private correspondence a priority. 'He was a very ethical man,' recalled William Revelli. 'I never heard him speak ill of any man. He may have thought that one man wasn't as good as another, but he didn't say bad things about any conductor.'

It was his main link with other bandmasters, men rarely had a chance to meet between ABA conventions. If they did get together, it would be at the end of a concert, perhaps at 11 p.m. at a German restaurant like Grammers. 'The repartee with Frank Simon telling his jokes and he and the others discussing Sousa and the other great bands was wonderful to hear.' Some he saw when he attended his clinics and conducted *their* bands at music festivals. With others, the only way to make contact was via a letter.

He and Herbert Clarke wrote regularly to each other, chit-chat about fellow bandmasters – one who took offence at being made an associate member of the ABA, not an active one – and news about their families. Clarke in 1941 was getting a little crusty. 'Bill . . . was a great disappointment to me as I wired him to come on to replace my solo cornet who disgraced the whole band . . . turned out to be the dirtiest man I ever came into contact with. Will tell you why I fired him . . . '. Clarke was still director of the municipal band at Long Beach, California, and probably in old age felt he deserved more. In the same letter of November 1941, Clarke writes about how glad he is that Ernest Glover was now doing well – 'he is a good boy, so useful in all ways' – but commiserates with Frank's own difficulties with radio. 'So sorry that you cannot influence advertising agencies over the air, that your band is regarded as the best musical organization which broadcasts. However, perhaps they will realize this later on and we will be so glad to "listen in" again.' The letters went on for another four years, with the same recipe. Except that there was soon a new topic for discussion: the war. 'We are now under the Defense projects out here,' wrote Clarke, 'and the band is being used for many occasions for the Army and Navy, to keep up the American spirit on the Pacific coast which is pretty well protected although some Jap subs have been mighty near the coast and one was captured the other day and towed into our port. Have had several "Blackouts" since the Hawaiian affair. But not in the past two weeks.'

Frank was too old to serve in the forces, too old even to conduct an Army band as he almost had in the previous conflict. But now he had a new function to fulfil – as a morale booster to the people he had taught. From north and south, east and west, old students wrote, telephoned and called to see him. They wanted to see action, but preferably in a service band. Could Frank help? He could and he did.

He knew the leaders of most of the service bands and he was constantly in touch with them, moving immovable objects with his irresistible force.

Mary was soon busy with war work, too. She was one of the 'Gray Ladies', a team of Ohio women who worked in local hospitals, doing auxiliary work. She was based at the Middletown Hospital, serving meals, helping to distribute medicines and sometimes giving patients baths.

Frank was brought in to provide his clinician's services for military bands just as he had for peace-time outfits. But his other work continued as before, as did the correspondence with Herbert Clarke. Frank sent him a copy of Bellstedt's symphonic arrangement of 'Funiculi Funicula' which he himself had published. 'It is so good of you to think of me in sending it,' Clarke wrote. 'You have always been so lovely to me and the longer I live, the more I appreciate your wonderful friendship of so many years standing. REAL FRIENDSHIP without selfishness is RARE! I can count such affectionate friends as you have been to me, on ONE HAND!! Even relatives cannot be relied upon.' Frank merely thought it was a means of showing his own gratitude for the help that Clarke had been to him in those early Sousa days.

In August 1942, the veteran cornetist wrote: 'You have made me very happy Frank in writing me such a nice dear letter which reached me safely last nite [*sic*] and it feels so good to hear that at my age, I have a few sincere friends like you.' But he was despondent. 'Music,' he wrote, 'is about done for and as us old fellows are passing on one by one, there won't be any left very soon.' Three months later, he was writing of the problem all the bands were facing. 'Since the war, I have lost 11 of my best men, thru draft and defense work. It is difficult to replace repertoire players and must have men over 55 years old. So my band has been crippled for three months and still playing two daily concerts.'

Perhaps in his happier moments, Frank could be grateful that there was no longer an Armco band. He would never have been able to maintain its standards. However, the younger members of the college bands were still there, although most of the 18-plus had been drafted. The high-school youngsters were still there, however, and so Frank was kept as busy as ever.

He also kept in touch with his old students who were not going to be involved with military service. On his new notepaper: 'Frank Simon and His Band – A Band Known to Millions – Cincinnati, Ohio' in embossed black letters over a silhouette figure of a band conductor, baton in hand – Frank wrote to Jennings Mclean and her mother in July 1942:

> I never was so busy as this summer at the Conservatory. The band department as usual was large and we had a very nice band with about twenty five taking the conducting [*sic*]. I gave thirty private lessons a week, so you can imagine how worn out I was with the driving back and forth each day from home . . .
>
> At the concert given at the University, the Dean called me over and

> told me he would raise the money for a series of concerts with a fine band for next summer. This has been one of my dreams and of course I will work on it this winter. Jennings will be my solo cornetist and soloist. I am very much pepped up over it.

He was pepped up over his own children, too. David was already training to be a doctor. 'He is in school taking the accelerated course,' Frank wrote to the McLeans, discussing a call his elder son had made from Boston the previous evening:

> Joe has been working this summer as a life guard at our swimming pool. He is going to enlist in Sept and take the V 5 Naval Aviation course at Miami University in Oxford. It is near home, we will have him close for a year at least. Mrs Simon is so absorbed in her nurses aid work at our hospital. They have taken nearly all of our registered nurses.

Frank was never happier than when he was working at home in Middletown. When he gave a concert at the town's high school he could be reasonably sure of packing most of the 1259 seats – which did not make life easy during the hot summer months in those years before air conditioning.

In February 1943, Frank was making one of his periodic assessments about his future. There were the occasional broadcasts, but any hope of reactivating the Armco Band went out with the raid on Pearl Harbor.

There was talk of his replacing Herbert Clarke at Long Beach, California, but it was probably more Clarke's talk than Simon's. In another apparently self-pitying letter from Long Beach, Clarke wrote:

> I resigned from a high position after 60 years of constant professional life in all branches before I broke down and became a 'has been.' I did the same thing when I left Mr Sousa at the age of fifty, giving up a high salary for 'nothing'. In good standing, after making a good reputation all over the world for many years. Guess my pride is worth more than money to me and I do want to LIVE and have a good time while I can walk and go places. So I am giving up $100 a week for 'nothing', in good standing.
>
> You would be just the man for my place. But I recommended James Son, my assistant here for several years as he knows the regular routine of the band with two daily concerts and what is wanted by the city and

> public without hindering the daily concerts to break in a new leader. He is an old Sousa man, an excellent accountant with much experience in that line. Besides I heard some time ago that the city are going to get rid of the band at the end of the fiscal year (June 30). I could not fairly mention some good friend of mine to give up his home and possessions for a few months and then let him down.
>
> Keep this confidential, Frank, but if you put in an application for the job, be sure and secure a five-year contract and they will have to keep the band. I will help you all I can then and be so glad to have you here. You would have a good band of which I am still very proud. No band in the country can do the same work. Just think. We have broadcast every afternoon concert in its entirety for 16 years, WITHOUT A REHEARSAL!

Frank was doing much better than earning $100 a week and enjoying the freelance life. But apply for the post he did. In a reply to Clarke's letter in February ('I wrote you immediately when I learned that you had retired suddenly on account of your serious illness. Thank God you are able to be on your feet . . .') he said he had been in touch with the Long Beach municipality, 'saying that I would consider the position only after I knew definitely that your retirement was voluntary on your part and that there was no trouble between you and the city'.

It was not really a job Frank wanted. Neither was it one that was offered, which was surprising considering the Simon track record. Even so, the Cincinnati Conservatory had seen better days and, almost in the same way he had been chased by Armco until he was caught, he was seriously wondering about taking his old senior partner's job for a second time. In the same letter to Clarke, Frank wrote:

> Things at our schools are in a serious shape. I was told yesterday by the management that the summer school was probably out and that the school might not open in the fall. As I told you, we have lost all of our boys, 98% of which I personally brought to the school. This would be a serious situation for me.

That being so, he said:

> If you feel so inclined and wish to place my name and qualifications before your City Manager, I would be willing to come out for an interview. However, I do not want to make application as it would place me

> in a better position to have him interested in getting me. I think you understand my angle. I have all my assets here; a very expensive home and it would be hard to sacrifice all I have worked a life time for but if our school closes there would be nothing at all for me here.

But the Conservatory did recover – just about and just in time. The schools were very much his main venue. Just occasionally, all was not sweetness and light between him and the school authorities. He conducted the Wellsville, New York, High School Band at a concert held in the campus of Houghton College, a church institution. During the intermission an edict was handed down by the church elders. They would not permit the sin of smoking on college property. Dean Harrington, one of the school players at the time, later wrote to Frank about his memories of that occasion: 'I don't know what you said, but it was easy to tell exactly how you felt about the matter. A few minutes later, I observed smoke rolling out of one of the outside toilets and I believe to this day that you were guilty as all hell.'

Most of Frank's work involved commuting long distances from Middletown, although not all as far as New York. They were tortuous roads in those days before the freeways were built – with no fewer than 60 stop lights between Cincinnati and Dayton, for instance.

Frank had more serious problems. He fell in his cabin at a band camp and hurt his arm so badly that blood poisoning set in. He and Herbert Clarke – now becoming much more seriously ill in retirement – exchanged symptoms in their correspondence.

Frank just occasionally broke his own rule and played the odd solo for concerts. There was the good excuse that so many younger men were in the services, there was no alternative. Bob Hornyak attended midshipman's school in the Navy at the same time as playing in the band of one of America's most prestigious universities, Notre Dame at South Bend, Indiana, in 1944. 'When we heard that Dr Simon would be there to conduct us, it was an incentive,' he told me. But Frank did not just conduct. Once more, he also played – the cornet and the post horn, which he had introduced to the Sousa Band all those years before. 'Even then, he was terrific,' Hornyak recalled.

It was an emotional time. For an emotional man like Frank Simon, almost unbearably so. Bob Griep, later to lead the Fairview High School Band at Dayton, remembered the all-day clinic Frank ran at the Kaiser High School. Between the clinic and the evening concert, Frank went back to Griep's home – to find that there was a draft notice awaiting Bob. He was to report to the Army the following Monday. As Griep recalled: 'You and I left that school together following the concert never to return again. Your eyes filled with sorrow during that concert when you made a sentimental speech concerning my departure and mention of your son in the same breath. Who could forget?'

Joe had begun his flying training and David was at Harvard doing a pre-med course. It was Frank's greatest joy that his boys were able to achieve so much. That could be a reason why he tried to do more for his own pupils – young men and women who did not have his own children's advantages – than could reasonably be expected of a teacher. Much more, in fact.

It was, of course, a continuing pattern, but somehow the war, its dangers and its other attendant problems only heightened his desire to help. William Caiazza was another who benefited from the Simon touch and the Simon attention. He had been spotted by Frank playing horn in his high-school band and was immediately taken under his wing. 'He inspired me,' he told me. He also gave the youngster financial help. When Caiazza told Frank he could not afford to go back to school, his teacher was distraught. When he heard that Caiazza had actually left and gone to work in the family's tiny candy factory, he decided he had to do something about it.

'One evening I was working very late and the phone rang. It was a call that had been transferred from my home. It was Dr Simon.'

Frank's message was as crisp as it was clear. 'I want you to go back to the music business. I want you to save enough to come to Cincinnati.' And he found him a job – demonstrating musical instruments, which gave him the chance to play solos in school bands. He traveled doing just that, all over Indiana and North Carolina. And he took classes at the Cincinnati Conservatory – thanks to a full scholarship that Frank obtained for him.

'He was a towering figure and because I had lost my own father at 13, very much a father figure.' But he did not reap all the benefits entirely. 'I got kinda smart,' he recalls now, somewhat regretfully. 'I did my second year there and never went back. But Dr Simon got me moving.' Thanks to Frank Simon, too, he found a place in an army band. After the war, he played in Broadway shows like *Hello Dolly* and went on to teach music himself in New Jersey. 'But if it had not been for Frank Simon, I would have spent my life working in the candy business.'

During the war, countless numbers were working for the Forces. But, despite what Frank had earlier written to Herbert Clarke, the Conservatory continued to function and appeared to continue to recover. In an air letter (sent via V Mail, letters sent free of charge to troops in tiny, just about legible, Xeroxed photocopies intended no doubt to save weight and space once they had been censored and photocopied) Frank wrote to an Army musician named Paul McCoy. The letter was dated December 1944:

> My dear Paul, It was most pleasant to receive your Xmas card yesterday. Often I have wondered where you are and I am so pleased that you are in a band. Several of my boys are in bands in France and possibly you will run across them one of these days. Harold Flieg, oboist, Ted Crowley, trumpet and Ben Miles, trombone are members of the 7th Army Hdq Band. They have been overseas longer than two years and were in Africa, Tunisia, Italy and now France.
>
> Another of my boys is a WO in France. His name is Raymond Zepp, 36th Div Arty. All these boys are from the Conservatory and are artists of the finest. Many of my boys are in the Pacific area. I hear from nearly all of them and you can imagine how busy it keeps me writing to all of them. It really looks like Xmas here. We had a heavy snow the past two days and it is quite cold.
>
> In spite of the loss of so many of my talented players at school the band is functioning and I have quite a few talented students but most of them are girls.

When the war ended, Frank hoped he could pick up where he had left off. But there were no more radio offers. In a letter dated 18 November 1945, after commiserating with Frank's recurrent hay fever ('You were always so healthy and strong when we were together in the good old days and I was suffering the tortures of the damned with a wicked stomach'), Herbert Clarke wrote:

> So sorry you will not broadcast this Fall. We all were looking forward to listening in to the best band over the air. Hope you will be successful in contacting some other sponsor, so we can hear yours.

Frank was, however, making new contacts all the time, some of which would prove useful in the coming years. One of them was Jack Lee, who was directing the band of the 37th Division National Guard at Columbus, Ohio, and doing graduate research work at the University of Ohio. Frank came to Columbus to conduct the local musicians union band for eight concerts.

'He was the most compassionate man I ever knew,' Lee told me. Someone had told Frank about a march Lee had written during the war called 'The Gremlins' Victory March'.

'Young man,' Frank said. 'I understand you are a composer.'

'I try to be,' said Lee.

'Well,' Frank told him, 'young man, why don't you bring it in to the next rehearsal?' Lee did that.

'Young man,' said Frank, plainly enjoying the Sousa-like role, 'why don't you conduct it?' As Lee said: 'There are very few conductors of any stature who would ask someone to bring in their own music. It is very rare indeed for him to ask anyone to play or conduct it.'

But he was doing more of that now. Servicemen were returning from the war and his Conservatory class, empty for so long, was now almost literally bursting at the seams. There were still the new students out of high school, too. One of them was Gene Blee, who had gone to Cincinnati in 1946 especially to be taught by Frank Simon in a six-week summer teaching program, which included private lessons and a class in band conducting under him. 'Although he had a unique technique, his movements, particularly his use of his elbow as he told us Sousa had done, were things we would never forget.' But it was the cornet lessons he took that were the most valuable.

> He taught me that it was breathing that counted – that the breath was the foundation of all wind playing. He would make suggestions for dynamics, style of tonguing and articulation, if it should be punctuated or more legato, detache or just medium length. That sort of thing. First he taught us to play the instrument and then the music. You can't play the music unless you can play your instrument properly.

When Blee wanted to buy a trumpet it was Frank who got one for him. Not only did he get the youngster a full scholarship in 1946, he also arranged for him to have his first trumpet. 'He made sure that the price was right for me. I had no money at all, really.' But then he had an aim in mind. 'My boy, I'm going to make an artist out of you,' was the phrase that went with a private lesson.

Frank's own cornet playing times in public were really rare now. But he made an exception in June 1946. The newly qualified Dr David Simon, fresh out of his own stint as an enlisted man in the Army, was married and his father joined in the band by playing one of the dance tunes. 'The people there couldn't stop applauding,' David remembers today.

Frank himself was mentally applauding his own lifestyle. He continued to conduct high-school and college bands, held his clinics and his band camps. And he continued being the family man incarnate. He also continued to eat – and now to cook, too. He had perfected his own spaghetti sauce that he could take a whole day to prepare. Now no pasta dish was ready for the table until, like his music, it had been Simonized.

But he still hoped for more. And, apart perhaps from Goldman who still had his own band, he had got so much further than any of his contemporaries. This came home to him in 1948 with the death of his mentor, Herbert L. Clarke. From his correspondence with Frank, Clarke had died a disappointed man. But in death, he was honored for what he was, the greatest cornet player of the early twentieth century and an outstanding figure in the world of bands. A Clarke memorial was dedicated at the Congressional Cemetery in Washington, DC, the same resting place as Sousa's. Frank was there to play a leading part in the ceremony, sponsored, along with the memorial itself, by the ABA, the Pennsylvania Bandmasters Association and the Sousa Band Fraternal Society. Peter Buys directed Washington's four main service bands. Fellow-musician Frank McGrann gave the address. But Frank Simon gave more – his own musicianship. Frank broke his solemn oath never to use his cornet again in public – to play taps.

He seemed to have musicianship also in his private life. In 1949 Joe married the daughter of the same Louis Wolf, who along with his brother had introduced the young Frank Simon and the even younger Mary Chapman to each other. Joe and his bride set up home in Mason City.

That year, Frank made a brief return to broadcasting and conducted the National School Band Clinic of the Air, but it did not amount to anything permanent. For four weeks on Sunday afternoons he conducted a band made up largely of members of the Cincinnati Symphony, but was augmented by students at the Conservatory.

The programs originated on the WLW station which had been so familiar to Frank and, as before, networked by NBC. They were broadcast live from Emery Auditorium in Cincinnati. William Caiazza was one of the students. Another was Gene Blee, who was later to be the principal trumpet with the Cincinnati Symphony, and went on to serve for 32 years. He was part of a trumpet trio.

The idea was to show students who were about to take part in national contests how they should play the music they selected. In effect, it was really a broadcast band clinic. 'But,' remembered Blee:

> We rehearsed in his own studio. You had to be ready with no monkeying around. We were being paid as professional musicians for the broadcast – big bucks. Dr Simon had this great experience from the Armco years, which was so obvious by the way he handled himself in rehearsal and during the actual broadcast. But I can't ever recall a time when he was a hard taskmaster. My most profound memory of him is his gentleness and the affection he had for his students. He was the greatest lyric player of his era. He had the most beautiful control of his right hand to effect lyric vibrato. He could vary it to create intensity. He was also a gentle gentleman.

People still wrote, phoned and met him at functions like the ABA conventions, saying how much they missed Armco. No more than Frank did himself, but there was no point in crying over dropped radio contracts, and the Conservatory band was regaining its strength – even though it had an over-abundance of trombones, 16 of them at one count.

His role as the perfect band expert, however, had not diminished. That was why his lessons were so important – lessons in playing the cornet or trumpet but also still in how to conduct. As before, he told this new post-war generation that a band could play music as well as a symphony orchestra. 'His conducting wasn't very different from that of a symphony conductor,' remembered Gene Blee. 'Frank was an excellent conductor. He assigned the pieces the students were supposed to conduct and he stood by, watching for your mistakes.'

An excellent conductor with excellent contacts. Early in 1950 Gene Blee was drafted into the Army, to be an infantry soldier in the Korean War – except that Frank Simon thought that would be a total waste of talent. He arranged for Blee to join the Ninth Division Army Band, playing a trumpet instead of carrying an M-1 rifle. He later joined the United States Field Band in Fort Mead, Maryland, one of the country's five special service bands.

In 1951 Frank Simon's expertise was called in for a new purpose. Twentieth Century Fox decided it was time to pay tribute to the American band scene, in particular to John Philip Sousa. They were going to film the March King's life, with Clifton Webb – one-time Broadway dancer who in recent years had found a new career for himself as the grumpy baby-sitter 'Mr Belvedere' in the film *Sitting Pretty* – in the main role. 'I wonder if your plans are such,' wrote Lamar Trotti, the writer and producer of the project from the studios, 'that you might consider coming to Hollywood later on to give us the benefit of your advice and information regarding Mr Sousa, particularly as regards his conducting mannerisms? It might be that a week or two at the most would suffice.' It was an offer made at the recommendation of Sousa's two daughters Mrs Helen Abert and Miss Priscilla Sousa. Priscilla confirmed her suggestion in a letter to Frank: 'We all feel that you know the Sousa tradition best of any one and know how father liked his music interpreted.'

So the invitation could not be turned down – until Frank saw what they were making of Sousa's life. He concluded that the film, to be called inevitably, *The Stars and Stripes Forever*, was a travesty of what Sousa had achieved and refused to co-operate any further. The Sousa film – called in England *Marching Along* after Sousa's own autobiography – came and went. Leslie Halliwell in his standard work *Halliwell's Film Guide* described it as a 'low-key musical biopic with predictably noisy numbers'.

Frank's refusal to have anything to do with the low-key musical biopic was a rare moment of pique, but he thought he could do better leading the Sousa clinics and the Sousa Band Fraternal Society. Nevertheless, it did not stop his joining five other alumni of the Sousa Band at a reunion preview of the movie in December 1952. 'If you knew Sousa like we knew Sousa – oh, oh, oh what a guy!' was what the Cincinnati *Times-Sun* suggested was the theme song of the occasion. That was a distinctly happier theme than their review of the film, based on the Simon report. 'It was bad biography,' Frank told the paper. 'The chronology of his march composition is way off.' Another of the ex-Sousa musicians said he was sorry there was not more of Sousa's personality in the movie. In particular, no mention of the time one man remembered when a bandsman tried to smuggle a woman onto the train with him. He could not understand how such a poignant moment could possibly be omitted. As he recalled: 'The woman went fast. And so did her friend.'

Frank was less disenchanted with other events of 1952. That was the year he was a guest conductor at a Sousa clinic at Durham, New Hampshire, along with veterans Gus Helmecke and Samuel Harris, who between them had to listen to no fewer than 51 Sousa marches being played. The veteran Sousa drummer, Helmecke, wrote: 'Frank Simon conducted and his interpretation was like Sousa's. Frank did an excellent job. I gave them the usual fanfare and all seemed to enjoy it. The university band was excellent.'

Occasionally – just occasionally – Frank allowed himself a little whimsy apparently at the expense of the March King's sacred requirements. As he did in November 1951, he would conduct a piece called 'Paraphrase Marching On' – which was 'The Stars and Stripes Forever' but distinctly not the way the 'Governor' would have wanted it played. Instead, he featured the march as Elgar, Strauss, Liszt, Wagner, Rossini and Bizet would have played it. There was, however, a final apologia – the end of the piece featured the pure march. Other composers and songwriters, Irving Berlin among them, would have reached for their telephones and called their lawyers' numbers at such parodies. Sousa, of course, was no longer able to do that and Frank Simon must have had a better knowledge of the March King's sense of humor than the writings about him seem to indicate.

There were plenty of awards coming Frank's way now. He was

made an honorary member of the Band Fraternity, Kappa Kappa Bi (later to be changed to life membership of the Grand Chapter) and of the National School Bandmasters Fraternity, Phi Beta Mu Alpha and then in the early 1950s an honorary citizen of Texas.

His influence with younger people was as strong as ever. Gene Young was a regular private student going for his Saturday lessons at the Central Avenue house. 'He was such an imposing figure,' he remembers now, as the conductor of the Goldman Memorial Band in New York. 'He had enormous dignity – perhaps because he always wore a tie.' He also had the dignity of being the supreme teacher, passing on to Gene what he thought he could manage as a cornetist.

Even when he was a child, Gene Young felt that Frank Simon treated him almost as an equal. He would introduce him to his wife: 'Mary, you remember my prize pupil Gene Young. He is going to play from the St Jacome method book.' As Young now remembers: 'I always felt he was letting me into a *sanctum sanctorum* when I went to his house.' The enthusiasm carried through to the lessons themselves. 'His transcriptions of symphonic works were quite remarkable,' Young told me. 'Frank loved the symphonic works, from Smetana to Tchaikovsky. In the '50s, he was working to have band music upgraded. But he also knew it was showbusiness and that was his big success.' He continued to fight for the dignity of the band.

> There was a snobbery, with bands for the most part being looked down upon because it was easier to form a band than an orchestra, just as it was easier to play a saxophone than a violin. The bitter irony was that Frank was such a believer in bringing music to young people, initiating them in the grandeur of the whole spectrum that music offers, that it was in many ways the antithesis of most music education. He used the band medium to introduce people to the operation of music and the symphonic repertoire.

One of the first things he taught Young was the role of the cornet in the band. 'He thought of it as the soprano or mezzo-soprano voice. But he told me, "You can't play the music if you don't know the text, the meaning of the text." I always thought of him as more a teacher of music than just of the cornet.' He had his own style, as much of manner as of teaching.

> He would take me down to the basement. But he wouldn't say, 'Let's go down to the basement.' He would say, 'I think I have something in the library that might interest you.' That way, he commanded respect. He never lost his temper. He was never inhibited. I've seen him get perturbed at rehearsals. He would speak more slowly – and that was almost a coded language. The bandsmen knew they were being chastised. He made it feel that if you didn't play the music properly, you were the ones who were missing out, that you were disappointing him by missing all your opportunities. To hear someone who was actually in Sousa's band, that was remarkable.

He emphasized the importance of the work he gave his students, Young recalled, by giving credits to the original composers or arrangers. 'When he taught me Bellstedt solos, it wasn't the way Simon did it, but he would say, "This is how Bellstedt would play it. This is Bellstedt's way and how he taught *me*".' Gene Young went into Temples with Frank and together they played 'Eli Eli' there. 'When he taught me, he didn't run around the scale like a man possessed, expecting me to do things that were almost impossible. He sang it – like a cantor. His Jewish background seemed to me to be very important to him!'

Gene was one of his students when Frank had an automobile accident in 1953. In the depth of winter Frank's car skidded and left the highway. He was not badly injured but he cut some of the tendons and ligaments in his hand and his great fear was that he would never be able to control a cornet again. Fortunately, his son David was nearby – close enough to be with his father as he was taken into a local hospital and close enough, too, to call on one of Frank's closest friends and poker-playing buddies for help.

Dr Walter Reese, a surgeon and eminent war veteran, was a man in whom both Frank and his son had an infinite trust, particularly since those early lessons in the facts of life. He performed the operation while David stood over his shoulder at his request with a copy of *Gray's Anatomy* to help him identify the tendons, nerves, arteries and muscles. The brushing up was enough for the damage to be repaired so that Frank could continue, as he put it, to 'noodle' with his cornet when helping his students. Joe was in the operating room at the same time, like David's, a supreme gesture of love by a son for a father.

Gene remembered: 'He had been told he might never be able to play his cornet again, but he worked squeezing rubber balls in his hand and after a year was able to do so. To me, he still sounded great.' And so was that influence. Frank drove his young student to lessons at the Cincinnati Conservatory in his green Lincoln sedan, listening to the radio and playing one of his favorite games – guessing the title of pieces of music from the opening bars. Gene Young saw the problems that Frank faced.

> He knew he was becoming an anachronism. Band music was on the way out. And it wasn't just the rise of pop music. Symphony orchestras were increasing their following. The LP had come in and more people were schooled in the classics. His only hope was to keep band music going in the schools and largely through him it was.

In 1954 there was a little more band music to be heard than before. It was the Sousa Centennial Year and all over America concerts were held – many of them conducted by Frank Simon. 'Music just seems to flow from Frank Simon,' wrote Priscilla Sousa. The band director of the University of Wyoming, Edgar J. Lewis Jr, wrote to Frank: 'Your excellent conducting, coupled with your ability to convey the authentic interpretation of the Sousa music, was appreciated and respected by all of us.'

Frank set himself a target – to get Congress to adopt 'The Stars and Stripes Forever' as the national march. It took time, but the scheme eventually bore fruit. His principal task had to be with the younger generation. His work at the Gunnison band camp in the mountains of Western Colorado was another means of getting over his messages to young people with talent. The only problem Frank experienced at these was of food – or rather of a lack of it. Al Wright's wife, Gladys, who was one of the students at the time, remembers when the camp's organizers found a new place for the customary camp banquet – except that it ran out of food. No crime was greater in the Simon book. 'So we had an extra hour on the program and we were all let loose on the town. There were only two restaurants there – and both were closed.' But he did like the achievements of the students. 'He accepted their limitations,' said Al Wright. 'He no more expected them to play like professionals than anyone would expect a college football team to play like professionals.'

So he went on teaching, improving the standards of his students. In 1953 he was in Moose Jaw, Canada, holding a clinic. His subject: written notes. 'Notes are only a means to an end,' he declared in a lecture. 'Staffs, key values and so on are just marks on paper. Until those marks cause a mental reaction in the young student's mind, they do not become music.' That was what he always managed to achieve: a mental reaction. But there were his own reactions to consider. He had come into conflict with the Conservatory officials, who wanted what they thought were new teaching methods in the curriculum. So Frank resigned. It was an unhappy moment for him, only partly compensated for by taking on a few brief teaching sessions at the rival College of Music.

But there were other considerations he had to make. At the age of 65, the most important one of these was his health. In 1955 his doctors diagnosed a condition that meant he was virtually going to retire – and to move to Arizona.

18 · *Twilight in Tucson*

The idea of Frank Simon leaving his native Ohio turf seemed in itself revolutionary. He had been born in Cincinnati, lived most of his life in Middletown and established his greatest career milestones in that city. But now those milestones seemed to be lying on his chest – every time he breathed. He was suffering from breathing difficulties that did not affect merely his cornet playing. Any kind of breathing at all was bringing difficulties. He saw doctors who, he was told, were the finest specialists in the land and the diagnosis was clear: he had emphysema. The only cure: to find a dry climate. He chose Tucson, Arizona.

The move was a good indication of how serious was Frank's concern over his health – to say nothing of his family's. Perhaps even more than he was a musician, Frank Simon was a family man. Mary, of course, was going with him. But he was having to leave behind not just his sons and daughters-in-law, to whom he remained remarkably close, but also a new generation of Simons, his first grandchildren.

The compensation of seeing them at Christmas (the best time of year to be in the hot, sunny Arizona climate), of occasional fishing trips and more opportunities to watch his beloved baseball at first seemed of little consequence. Even the chance to live in a luxurious ranch-style house in the middle of an orange orchard (it had grape-fruit, too) was hardly enough. But the doctors' warnings were. He and Mary sold their house in Middletown and flew west.

Their home at 6914 Orange Grove Circle was, Mary wrote, an 'opportunity [for] taking life easy and raising oranges and grape-fruit'. A swathe had been cut in a citrus orchard to make way for the house. Of all the residences Frank had had, the Middletown homes with Mary, the apartments in which he had lived with his parents, the hotel rooms on the road with Sousa – even if they did change the sheets every day – this was the closest to paradise. But it was not quite home. Mary was even more apprehensive about it than was Frank himself and, although he got to taking the vast change in their lifestyle in his stride, she never would.

What Frank had, of course, was the camaraderie of the bands. He had friends in Tucson as he had in every city in every part of the United States. Wherever he went, had he chosen to do so, he could have put a pin in a map, driven to the spot, looked in a local telephone book and rung up an old student, a fellow-member of the ABA or an old associate from the Armco days who happened to be living there. What was more, he could be pretty sure they would be pleased to see him.

In Tucson, he found Jack Lee, the young National Guard conductor whose work Frank had played ten years earlier. Now Lee was able to return the compliment to the 'most compassionate man' he had ever known. The much younger man was by now director of bands at the University of Arizona, just a stone's throw (as stones were thrown, that is, in the wide-open spaces of Tucson) from the Simons' home. Lee was so delighted to have his mentor on hand that he offered Frank a part-time job: Visiting Professor of Bands. He could give lessons whenever – but only whenever – he wanted to, usually on just a couple of mornings a week.

It was a position he accepted with the same kind of enthusiasm with which he had agreed to join the Cincinnati Conservatory all those years before. Now he was not looking for kudos. He had had that. He was not even looking for money. At 65, he not only did not need it but he also had to accept that he was well and truly retired, that there would never be another Armco Band – and, truth to tell, he probably did not want one. The teaching he did at Arizona was enough to keep him out of the house and, most important of all, for a very good reason. He was not at all like those thousands of other retired men who had to look for excuses to save face. But as Jack Lee told me, he had no reason to feel there was anything selfish about his new life. 'This gave Frank Simon a chance to develop wonderful players at the university.'

Once more there were opportunities to use all the old techniques – not just of cornet playing but of the Simon kindness and generosity. Occasionally, there would again be a talented student who could not quite afford to continue college – an old story in Frank's teaching career but usually a genuine one. Early on in the Arizona period he discovered a girl from Colorado who measured up to the best of his Cincinnati students. 'She found he was here and did everything to attend his classes,' Jack Lee recalled for me. 'But she could barely afford to eat.' Frank's answer was to pay for her tuition himself. When Lee's own son wanted cornet lessons, Frank took him on – without taking a cent in fees. He was also generous to Lee himself. When Jack wrote a book on conducting bands, Frank wrote a foreword describing his style as 'original, clever and exciting'. In the same piece, he quoted Tolstoy: 'Art is a human activity . . . that one person consciously by certain external signs conveys to others feelings he has experienced.'

Frank Simon was conveying that all the time. From the first tap on the music stand at concerts (Lee says he was the only conductor whom he ever knew who actually performed that action so often caricatured in the movies) to the reverberation of the last note, he was teaching his own experiences. Just occasionally, as before, he allowed himself to get crusty – as the time he auditioned a boy who had been taught to play cornet by rote. He made a very good sound, but could not read a note. 'My God,' he said to Jack Lee, 'what sort of students have we got here?' Lee replied: 'That's why we've got you here, Frank.'

The word that Simon was around spread. Suddenly, there were applications from all over America to join the university – each of them specifying that the main reason was that they wanted to study in Frank Simon's classes. The first was Patsy Leonard from Charleston, South Carolina. Her father, a band director, continued to send his best students to the University of Arizona long after Patsy graduated. 'We started then to realize how vitally important Frank was for us,' said Lee. 'I had students but I didn't have time to Simonize their work with polish the way he did.' When Frank was really happy with a student's progress, he would ask the name of the youngster's teacher. 'Ah,' he said if he recognized the teacher's name, which he usually did. 'The apple never falls far from the tree.'

Frank had developed his teaching style now, with his students learning almost as much from the stories and anecdotes as from the techniques of developing an embouchure. 'Band was more than a four-letter word,' said Jack Lee. 'He fired his students with enthusiasm. His love for Sousa gave the students a new respect for their own band and for themselves.' And he did continue to play himself – even if in his own mind the sound that came from his lips was nothing like the sort he had made in his Sousa or Armco days. But the enthusiasm he saw for his work was reward enough. 'Usually,' Lee added, 'at every concert I'd have him do a piece and he'd go into the library to get one out specially for the event.'

Frank found the whole experience totally rewarding. So much so, that the library there became a whole new dimension in both his and the university's life. He installed his own massive 20,000-document collection at the university and when he felt totally at home there, he took one of the most significant and irrevocable decisions of his life. He let it be known that he never wanted it to leave the institution and that, when he died, there it would stay, fully cataloged and filed in perpetuity. Nearly four decades later, band students could still go into that same library room – although it was about to be moved – and under a picture of the full-faced, mustachioed black-uniformed Dr Frank Simon pull out a card that read: '9498. Our Bugler' or '9016. Ta-ra-ra-Boom-de-e'. Number one was 'Bride Elect – Sousa'. The card for 'Willow Echoes' reads 'Dedicated to my friend, August H. Schaefer'. All Ferde Grofe's arrangements for Armco were included. So the historical dimension of the gift was an additional bonus. It was a vitally important development in the history of the university. As Jack Lee told me: 'He had more band music than we had ever had before. In one go, we tripled the size of our library.' In a letter to Frank, expressing his appreciation of the gift, the university President, Richard A. Harvill, noted:

> In accord with his plan, all coming generations of students and all faculty members of the school of music will benefit greatly from the availability of this library and through the career of each student and each faculty member the influence of the library will be carried to every community in Arizona, every state in the Union and to many other countries of the world. The university appreciates deeply not only this

> wonderful plan itself, but also the interest and faith in the program of the school of music and that of the university as a whole which led you to make these arrangements.

Frank now wore an air of both contentment and resignation. He was content with his life and resigned to the fact that he was in retirement and should enjoy it while the opportunities presented themselves. That being so, installing his library at the university made a great deal of sense. It was not, however, the only bequest he made. One of the hardest things for him to part with was the gift that John Philip Sousa had made to him just before he died – the original score of 'The Stars and Stripes Forever', which he now handed to the Smithsonian Institution in Washington, DC.

But he was closer to his main library, both physically and spiritually. For ten years, the campus at the University of Arizona echoed to the sound of music that Frank Simon made his own. The cadences were rich. The brass was sweet. The percussions were boisterous. The winds smooth. *Almost* the way Armco had been in its great days – although asking for the perfection of those days was demanding too much. But it brought enjoyment to the players and delight to the audiences.

There was a further dimension to his life in Arizona. Having Frank Simon's friendship meant more than just enjoying his music. Jack Lee and friends also enjoyed his oranges which he brought into the university by the caseload virtually every week in season. There was also a whole new audience for his jokes. 'Watching him enjoying his own jokes was like seeing fruit jelly wobbling on a plate,' said Lee. 'Whether they were funny or not, he laughed so much, you laughed with him. In the end, it was hilarious – even though you might be saying to yourself, "Why am I laughing at that terrible joke?"' Like the one of the Jewish conductor who performed in five–four time. It was not a story ideally intended for retelling, but it looked good enough for Frank to virtually convulse himself and for his stomach to rise and fall like a pump. The conductor called, 'One, two, three four . . .' and then shrugged his shoulders. Frank loved the tale and his students could not help loving it with him. Equally, if he himself heard something he did not like, all the old Simon emotions came to the fore. 'He'd cry at births, deaths, weddings. He'd cry at darn near everything,' Jack Lee told me.

Frank used the old Sousa methods in his teaching. He taught the young bandsmen and bandswomen how in the second strain of a march the clarinets would play. Then the second time around, the trumpets would take over from the clarinets to give it a different sound. He may have told the students it was the Sousa way. As far as they were concerned, it was the Simon treatment – and that was all they wanted to know. 'It *was* like Sousa,' said Lee. 'He not only wanted a contrast of melodies but a contrast of color, too. He asked clarinets to play an octave lower in indoor concerts than they would play marching outdoors, because that was how Sousa did it.' He still conducted bands in other parts of the country, although not as many as before, still took the occasional clinic, still even appeared in the rare broadcast. But his contacts with students was the most important part of his professional life.

Just occasionally, Lee remembers, he found the job of conducting a bit too strenuous. Sometimes, his arms were a little unsteady – so he dictated the directions to the younger man who conducted in his stead, following precisely what Simon wanted. But most of the time his beat was firm and precise as he wanted it to be. And that was one reason why he still so much enjoyed the occasional summer music camp, like the one still held at the Gunnison Western State College of Colorado. Gladys Wright (the first woman elected to the American Bandmasters' Association membership) was at the one he attended in 1956, sitting in on a Frank Simon class:

> He took a girl who played trumpet and we all listened. He was a fantastic teacher. He worked on note separation and style. After about half an hour, she sounded as if she played five, ten or 15 times better. It was one of the best examples of good teaching I ever saw. When she came in, her notes were too long and without the right accents. There was no separation – what she had been doing was playing notes instead of music. He taught her the basics of that kind of music, which note to put the accents on. She was plainly a bright girl but after Frank Simon had taught her in that one lesson, she didn't even sound like the same girl.

Sitting in on one of those lessons was an eye-opener on its own. He had his own style, perfected as it had been over the years. He still never shouted at pupils, but now he seemed a little more matter of fact. 'Cut your notes short,' he instructed without coloring the command. 'Don't put your tongue in the mouthpiece. Do a *tut* and a *toot*.' Gladys's husband, Al Wright, saw it, too. 'There are natural teachers,' he said. 'Frank Simon was one.'

It was not just a listening session but also a chance for him to demonstrate his own abilities. 'Simon's Concert Band' played at a 'Twilight Band Concert' and featured the 'Athenian Overture', a march Frank had written himself ('The Statesman'), as well as 'The Stars and Stripes Forever' and scenes from *La Bohème*. It was also an opportunity to put forward his most deeply felt musical theories and philosophies. As he prepared to conduct his first concert of the University of Arizona Band ('The Pride of Arizona' with Jack Lee leading the first half, Frank the second) he told the young musicians: 'What we want to do is to show the public a band is in no way inferior to a symphonic orchestra. Reeds and brasses can produce music of the first quality without the supplement of a string section.' He had said it before and other people had heard it before. But it was a rather good pep theme for the band – which he now said was 'the best in the country'. It was precisely what he was expected to say, but it was also a tribute he felt like paying to Jack Lee. Lee, he told the youngsters, 'brought the University of Michigan's band to its highest state of perfection for its working the field. But here he is bringing the band to a higher level of attainment.'

It was a fulfilling new life for him despite the problems of settling down so far from his roots and from those of his family. He found a new group of friends who loved his jokes, new neighbors to enjoy his spaghetti sauce and then, when the weather got too hot in summer, went back north. He and Mary either stayed with David and his wife or with Joe and his. Sometimes they all met up in Canada on a fishing expedition, usually good excuses for fishing stories and jokes. And at Christmas he and Mary entertained the children at home.

If ever a man settled into the Arizona way of life it was clearly Frank Simon. He met his children at the airport, wearing a ten-gallon Stetson hat, cowboy boots and a 'bolo' string tie. When in Tucson, act like a Tucsonian. But he also acted like a bandmaster. The fact that he had officially retired was not allowed to interfere with the acceptance of engagements he considered important.

Very soon after the retirement officially began, he was off on his travels again, this time to Iowa to conduct the state university's symphony band. The concert was held very soon after another of those sad milestones that were more and more dotting his years – the death of a colleague. This time, it was Edwin Franko Goldman who had gone, an event that moved him both because it was the passing of a man he sincerely respected and because it only served to remind him of the frailty of the life of a man in his mid-60s. Goldman was to have conducted the band himself, leading them in a composition written specially for the occasion – his new march, 'Iowa'. When Frank gave the downbeat for the march to begin, it was its first public performance. The audience liked it so much, the band played 'Iowa' a second time as an encore. Soon afterward the Simons entertained Goldman's widow at their new home. It was a pleasant enough experience for all to want to do it again. Mrs Goldman's visit was followed by one from Sousa's daughter Priscilla, who had so wanted Frank to advise on her father's filmed biography. He took them on trips through the Department of Fine Arts at the university where his band department was situated.

Somehow, the further he was from home, the stronger his roots became. To his friend Seymour Okun, then bandmaster of Frazer High School at Frazer, Michigan, he wrote about his new activities but could not resist an old joke, the one about the synagogue and the chandelier. He had embellished it over the years. It was the Jewish New Year that he wrote Seymour, 'It is not too late to wish for you and your dear ones a year filled with the best of health, nachus [joy and pride], prosperity with abundance, in abundance.' He wrote on the eve of the sacred fast of Yom Kippur, the Day of Atonement, which begins with the recital of the Kol Nidre prayer:

> Tomorrow night is Kol Nidre and it brings me to ask if you have by now had my arrangement copied as well as the vocal arrangements. Next week I am to make some tapes of the Kol Nidre to present to several publishers for publication. Will also have a full score made as well as a condensed one.

Clearly, even in retirement he was planning ahead. But that did not mean he ever would forget the Sousa days or the Sousa influence. He talked about them constantly, to his family, to his fellow-alumni when any found themselves in Tucson or when he bumped into them on his visits. You did not have to be too observant to notice that Frank had a new habit now which a psychiatrist would have delighted in analysing. When Frank talked, particularly when he got excited about the Sousa or Armco days, although not exclusively then, he appeared to be running his fingers over the keys of an imaginary cornet.

Even if he had wanted to forget his days as the great virtuoso (and he would not), the passing of events and of even more friends prevented his ever doing so. Goldman's death was followed just a few months later by that of Henry Fillmore. Frank pasted the death notices in his scrapbook and told more stories about their subjects, like the time Fillmore composed a tune for his pet dog Mike and the dog barked in unison with his master's directions.

In 1957 he and Mary were principal guests at a Sousa reunion dinner, a wonderful opportunity for more stories which Frank, of course, failed to ignore. Four years later, the 1961 Sousa reunion departed from usual practice and did not merely feature Sousa's music but Frank's too, along with works by Bellstedt, Clarke, Pryor and Meredith Willson, among others.

In the meantime, Arizona was doing him honor. He was presented with the university's 75th anniversary Medallion of Merit. They chose for the occasion the half-time ceremonies during the Arizona–West Texas State football game on what was decreed to be High School Senior Band Day. He was so moved that he wrote a march especially for the university, called 'Here Comes The Band', which was subsequently adopted as one of its official marches, played at nearly all its football matches. The citation reads:

> In commemoration of its founding on March 12, 1885, the University of Arizona awards to men and women of outstanding achievement, or distinguished service to their communities, the state or the university, its anniversary Medallion of Merit.
>
> Presented to: Frank Simon
>
> Distinguished American band conductor, cornet soloist and music educator, he is the composer of many fine compositions for band and solo instruments. From 1914 to 1921 he was the featured cornet soloist

and assistant director of John Philip Sousa's band. For twenty years he was artist trumpet teacher at the Cincinnati Conservatory of Music and for ten seasons conducted the Armco Radio Band featured on NBC. A charter member of the American Bandmasters Association, he is Past President of that organization. A member of the University Faculty since 1955, his generosity in presenting to the University School of Music his exceptional library of band music of more than 3,000 compositions has brought distinction to the University. The advantages this gift affords through its influence on students and members of the Faculty will be reflected on communities throughout the State and Nation. Eminent musician, composer and teacher.

Given at the University of Arizona this 29th day of October 1960.

But no matter how strong was his attachment to his new home, he still wanted to get back to Ohio. In June 1961 he was given the first life membership in the history of the Cincinnati Musicians Association. Twenty-nine other musicians with local associations were similarly honored.

Once back on home territory, it was difficult to keep him away. A year later he was on the rostrum at an event that got all the juices going. 'This scene in Sunset Park warms my heart,' he said. He was not only back on familiar territory, but also in a more than merely familiar environment – conducting the Middletown Band, which he had first led at 14. It called itself the Summer Band now, but he knew its origins even if the audience at the park did not. His voice, of course, choked with emotion.

There was yet one more cause for those emotions and memories that month. Now Bennett Chapple had died, too. The passing of the Ironmaster was a moving event that hit Frank more deeply than many similar notifications he was receiving now. Chapple, he said, had 'stood by me 100 per cent' and had found the money for some of the Armco Band's earliest concerts – at one time to the extent of $6000, a huge amount at that time. More important than Chapple's business help, Frank recognized he had lost another friend. And even more than that, it seemed to put the final lid on any remote chance there might have been of reviving the old Armco days. He had known for years that that would have been an impossible slice of pie in the sky, but he could still have nurtured the distant hope. Now the distance was just too far to contemplate.

In November 1963 he conducted a massed band of 31 high-school bands in Cincinnati, hailing not just from Ohio but also from the neighboring states of Kentucky and Indiana. There were 2000 young instrumentalists playing simultaneously during the half-time break in the Cincinnati–Dayton football game. To be seen by the musicians, he had to mount a makeshift platform by ladder, formed from a series of planks resting partly on a three-wheel Isetta car owned by his old student, Bob Hornyak. 'My God, Bob,' he appealed as he climbed the steps, 'hold on to me. Don't let me fall.' As Frank conducted, Hornyak held him by one leg while one of his assistants clutched the other. Even without the hefty dose of sheer fright from which he was suffering throughout the whole performance, it was virtually impossible to control such a huge ensemble – and it sometimes sounded it – but it was perhaps the most spectacular band concert of all time.

Hornyak remembered the bands gathered for the occasion, all of them puffing out their cheeks with every bit of might that the (to use one of Frank's favorite phrases) good Lord gave them. They ranged, he told me, 'from the sublime to the ridiculous. You had a little 25-strong country band of questionable ability, standing next to a very successful high-school band of 150 with many fine players.' Nevertheless, it was perhaps the finest of all the honors he had ever received. It was like a benefit concert for a great singer, a dinner for a master chef, a celebration game in tribute to Babe Ruth.

Afterward he made the inevitable speech. He said he had not been daunted by the experience. 'It's often a chaotic state because no bandmaster ever plays in the same tempo as another. So I get up there and wave the biggest stick I can carry. Rhythm is something you have to feel. It's like a clock, you know.' He told his young musicians, fighting back the emotion in pauses in his talk: 'Make the best of your life. Time flies by quickly. You have a wonderful opportunity to develop yourselves in the fine arts. There is always room for fine artists.'

About now he wrote what was to be his last march called 'The Little Giant'. Written in five flats, it was dedicated to his now old friend Jack Lee, but to date it has never been published. Publishers say they find the key too difficult. But then that *was* Frank Simon. He did not believe anything should come easily.

As always, Frank seemed as proud of his 'boys' as he was of his own achievements and responses. This was Meredith Willson's year. His Broadway triumph with *The Music Man* was followed with a world premiere – in Mason City, of course. Frank could not have been happier had he himself been leading the 101 cornets which followed the march of the 76 trombones. As it was, he more than contented himself by being the judge for a four-hour 132-band parade which marched through the streets of Mason City.

But it was back in what he would still consider home that the real honors now came. The Cincinnati Conservatory made him their conductor emeritus, and he was interviewed on local radio programs, in all of which he used the opportunity to 'plug' his philosophy. 'Over four million kids play in school bands,' he told the WLW 50/50 Club show, pleading for respect for the work the school outfits did. 'Without them, the publishers and the music instrument makers wouldn't be able to stay in business.'

Frank returned for one night to the Conservatory itself, now a division of Cincinnati University. Ernest Glover, who had succeeded Frank as conductor of the Conservatory's 'symphonic band', invited his old friend Frank (they had just made up after a long-running personal row) to conduct the second half of a concert at Cincinnati. At the same time, his former student Jack Watson (now Dean) presented a certificate declaring: 'The President, Directors and Faculty of the University of Cincinnati have the honor to confer upon Frank Simon, founder of the Band Department of the Cincinnati Conservatory of Music in 1932, the title of Conductor Emeritus of the College Conservatory Symphonic band of the University of Cincinnati.' Frank shed more than a few tears as the framed citation was handed to him. Frank himself was allowed a moment of reflection. 'I'm very happy to have so many wonderful years in music,' he declared. 'It's been very wonderful to me, very kind to me. The most rewarding thing to me has been the fact that I've brought many, many hundreds of students to Cincinnati's Conservatory and to see what has happened to them. They are holding the finest positions not only in musical education but in the professional life of this nation.' It seemed that events in his life just got more and more important. When he conducted the band, it may not have been the greatest demonstration of his skills but he had never been prouder. If there had been a meter to measure such things, every discordant note, every bang on a drum that was slightly out of time would have registered off the appreciation scale.

At the end of the ceremony, Frank thanked Jack Watson for organizing it. 'Thank you, Dr Watson, from the bottom of my heart,' he told him. Watson was among many students who had made 'distinguished' contributions to music, he repeated once more. In fact, the list was so long he decided not to attempt it, at the ceremony at least:

> I've lived quite a long life and the good Lord has been good to me. I prize more than anything else in my life whatever contribution I may have made to young people, not just musically but in character and dependability and loyalty and to work for the highest ideals of the greatest art in the world. That has been the most rewarding thing in my life.

There was more to the renewal of friendship with Ernest Glover than the mere fact that the two men attended the same ceremony and conducted the same band. Even more than that, they were actually talking to each other. It seemed to take years off both of them. No one doubted that all was well again when they sat together at a 1963 dinner at Mecklenburg's Garden, the kind of German beer garden restaurant that only had to put bratwurst on the grill for Frank Simon to smell and to run – even from Arizona.

David thought that the feud between his father and the old deputy director of the industrial band had gone on long enough and organized the reunion at the restaurant for as many former members of the Armco Band as he could find. But above all, it was intended to be a reunion between Frank and Ernest. It worked – after having to use a considerable amount of persuasion to get Glover to attend. The two old musicians put their arms around each other and old times became new ones. As David Simon now recalls: 'People got up and started roaming around the tables, talking about their happiest days with Dad's band.'

The ABA did as much as they could to honor him. They presented him with the Edwin Franko Goldman Award, which went very well with another high ABA honor: he became its fourth Honorary Life President, following in the footsteps of the first,

Sousa, the second, Goldman, and the third, Albert Austin Harding. The *Cincinnati Enquirer* noted:

> . . . who can forget Dr Simon himself with his gold cornet and the solos he played with the difficult triple-tonguing that separated the men from the boys on that instrument. There isn't a Cincinnatian of middle years who doesn't look back fondly to those Armco Band Sunday afternoon concerts in the parks and the clear tones of Dr Simon's cornet ringing through the soft summer air. They don't have bands like that any more and they just don't play the cornet like that any more.

It was a fact that Frank hated to admit, although to himself he did. He felt himself an old dog and had no interest in learning any new tricks. Although now, when he had a conducting engagement, he did begin to change his programs somewhat. He played medleys from the works of composers like Richard Rodgers, whom he admired greatly and would feature selections from other Broadway shows.

He liked New York because it was an opportunity to see those shows which he continued to enjoy. He also liked certain Italian restaurants, where he would almost concede that he could get a spaghetti sauce almost as good as the one he made himself.

These were all awards for past services, but Frank's services and generosity were of the present, too. In the summer of 1964 he conducted a Sousa concert at Dayton, organized by an old friend, Don Bassett, who had been first clarinetist in the Armco Band. Thousands of similar events there had drawn no more than about 300. 'It needed a shot in the arm,' he later wrote. 'To make a long story short, this event drew approximately 8000 people according to park officials, police and city officials. They turned hundreds away, no more parking space available. It proved to be that with publicity, proper rehearsals and diversification in the program, a band still can draw music lovers.'

It certainly did that – and in a way no one could have predicted. If Armco had ever contemplated reviving their old shows, this would have convinced them. But that was another slice of his favorite pie in the sky – and, as it turned out, so was the notion that a Frank Simon well into his 70s could do what he had done even in his 60s.

Soon after the Dayton concert Frank was taken ill, rushed to hospital for immediate surgery for polyps of the colon. He was ill and feeling sorry for himself. As a tribute to an old friend, he was immediately taken under the wing of Dr Benjamin Felsen, Professor of Radiology at the University of Cincinnati. Very unusually, but because of his affection for Frank, the professor took full charge – even to the extent of personally administering the barium enema necessary for the preliminary X-rays. He told his patient to hold his breath. He did so. And he kept it held so long that one of the residents standing by even thought he might have died in the attempt. But after playing the post horn in Sousa's band it was all in a day's work – or a day's treatment. Old habits die hard.

He stayed on in Middletown, living for a month's convalescence in what had been the center of his best card-playing but which had become the Manchester Motor Inn, with a huge photograph in the lobby of the marching Middletown band, led by a certain 14-year-old named Frank Simon.

He might have yearned for the opportunity to feel well enough to lead a marching band now, but he was not much in the mood even for card playing. He was not allowed to move further than the bathroom. Later in Tucson, he was ill again. There, a second operation was performed, this time for gallstones.

Frank was even less in the mood now for staying in Tucson, yet he agreed to serve on the university faculty for another year. But one thing he kept on doing: writing his letters and receiving them from dear old friends. On 28 August 1963 William McFee wrote to him:

> No man is lonely so long as he has the solace of good music. He may be old and bereft of friends, but the wonderful sounds that come through the night are comfort to his soul and a reminder that the Supreme Creator of all the Universe gave to him the greatest earthly gift of all, music. With it, and in it, he not only sees the stars, but he hears them, the eternal music of the spheres, and perhaps, who knows, even the voices of angels. There are words to be written, words to be heard, and words to be read, but great music surpasses all of these in its universal understanding and appeal to the best in mankind. Music is the joy of joys that brings surcease from sorrow, erases the cares and troubles of the day, that comforts, consoles, and gives a deep inner spiritual feeling of earthly triumph when all else seems lost. This is music, God's greatest gift to mankind.

Frank himself was always something of a gift to his friends, too. The University of Arizona always thought so. In a letter to Frank, the Director, Andrew W. Buchhauser, said of him 'We are proud to know you as a manly musician and as a musicianly man.' It said a great deal.

There was now a regular correspondence between himself and Lynn Sams, a retired music instrument salesman now living in Napa, California, who it later turned out had been the real model for Harold Hill, the salesman in Meredith Willson's *The Music Man*. He may have been a bit of a rogue, this real-life Music Man, but he was a wonderfully warm friend, a faithful correspondent and, most important of all, shared Frank Simon's sense of humor down to the last cackle. Rarely did a letter pass between them that did not end with at least one joke. But it was also equally rare for there not to be a commentary on the state of health of both Frank Simon and the music business. In one letter to Sams Frank wrote in 1964:

> I have signed up for one more year in the University here after which time we expect to move back to Middletown where we still have many old friends. I love to do guest conducting engagements which give me more satisfaction than teaching, but I confess to you that the many hundreds of fine students and performers I have taught and started out on a musical career is the most rewarding part of my life.

If these letters were details of a man's reflection on his current life and what had gone before him, there was always room for a joke.

Truth told, Frank would have loved to work more but he knew he simply could not do so any more. Another note to Sams was less encouraging: 'You know, Lynn, the good Lord willing, I will be seventy-five come November 26th. It's time to dig a hole six feet deep and tenderly lay my instruments away for good. They have done OK by me for nearly sixty-five years.' There was more to it than mere sentiment. 'It makes me sick,' Frank wrote in another letter, 'when I pick up my instrument while teaching and hear how perfectly lousy it sounds today. There was a time when I really had it, but I never practice a note any more. That's why I feel like giving my instruments a decent burial.' The instruments might have been ready for an immediate coffin, but not Frank Simon.

Immediately after the enforced month's rest – allowing Mary to answer most of the letters and get-well cards that he received – he drove to Missoula, Montana, where he had a Sousa concert to conduct. There was another Sousa concert at Dayton that attracted 8000 people. He said he did it because he had been told by the Dayton organizers that the municipal band needed a 'shot in the arm'. 'It proved to me,' he wrote in another letter to Lynn Sams, that 'with publicity, proper rehearsals and diversification in the program a band can still draw music lovers.'

He and Mary went back to Mason City to spend some more time with Joe and his family and after that took off for Canada to fish with his two sons and two grandsons. One of those grandsons, Frank Simon II, now a successful businessman (appropriately, in the fish business) recalls a grandfather who made a lasting impression on those fishing expeditions. 'He was kind, patient, very funny and taught me more about fishing than anybody I know,' he told me. He also gave the young Frank his own King cornet, but the boy had no more talent in that line than did his father, David. Frank might have hoped that somewhere along the Simon chain there would be another professional musician, but he did not say so and certainly did not encourage a vocation where his idea of an *a*vocation was more appropriate. As it happens, all Joe's children played musical instruments, but none of them professionally, except one daughter, Karen.

Simon was rather more concerned about the health of the nation. It was election year and Lyndon Baines Johnson, who had taken on the presidency after the assassination of John F. Kennedy, was fighting his first election for the White House. His opponent was the right-wing Republican, Barry Goldwater. Frank watched the campaign with all the enthusiasm he usually reserved for the ABA. 'LBJ', he wrote in another telling letter to Lynn Sams, 'in my opinion is the greatest double talker in the country.' He added:

> While Goldwater has not been as discreet or politically wise as he should have been, I admire his courage in stating his convictions and I think he is thoroughly honest. Rather than lose my vote both Mary and I will vote for him. I have read the story of how LBJ and his wife got to be worth approximately fifteen million and the facts of the story [are] not pretty.

He had firmer plans now for his own future which he hoped would be a lot more 'pretty'. 'I want to retire and move back to my old hometown [Middletown] to be nearer my dear ones and a lot of old friends in my remaining years.' After all, he was about to become 75 and thought he was entitled to think along those lines. His 75th birthday was not quite the secret Frank imagined it would be. David had been planning things for his father to commemorate the event.

19 · *Final Honors*

It was not just the Frank Simon career that was drawing to a close. As far as he was concerned, the whole world of popular music was, too – or it had gone that way already and was merely awaiting what he might have considered a decent burial. Rock'n'roll had headed what were now known as 'the charts' for more than a decade, but he hesitated in using the expression. 'I was trained to be a serious musician by the best teachers money could buy,' he said in the 1960s. 'But do I like the current popular music? Well, they say you can't teach an old dog new tricks. I'd rather drive a garbage wagon than be a jazz musician. I hate it. It's only for the feet. There's nothing for the mind and heart.' It was a sentiment straight from his heart, but he did not offend his old pupil Al Hirt by letting him know how he felt – not, at least, in those terms.

When the poet Richard Armour put his views on paper in the unlikely pages of the *Wall Street Journal*, Frank commented: 'I subscribe to this 100%.' This was:

> Guitar sales are up
> We have been advised.
> And I'll have to admit
> I am not surprised.
>
> Oh, if I were rich
> The supply would be dwindling
> I'd buy up a million
> And use them for kindling.

Another time, he heard a program of modern music which he described as 'filled with nothing but dissonances, constipated fifths,

Hebrew sevenths, ninths and thirteenths, with brass clashing and the percussion booming their damn heads off.' When he attended another concert and saw several of his contemporaries walk out in evident disgust, he told a friend 'I said to myself "Amen".'

There were plenty who said 'Amen' to him and to what he stood for. He kept in touch with the few people who were perpetuating his kind of music. He kept writing letters to them, like a note to his old student Gene Young, in which he heard about the death in an auto accident of another pupil, Harry Lansdale. Frank wrote:

> Needless to say, this sad news has completely unnerved me and brought me such pain at heart that I am unable to express myself. It has left me breathless. Like yourself, he was a super talented boy – with a great future. He was brilliant and a good boy, too. My heart goes out to his dear, devoted parents, to whom I have just written. Just how they will bear this irreparable loss is in God's hands.

By now he knew he was in God's hands himself, which was perhaps why he said 'Amen' to things with which he agreed. Now, however, there was an opportunity for old bandsmen to say 'Amen' to the wisdom, kindness and musical brilliance of . . . Frank Simon. His son David wrote to 2000 people who had known his father over his long career and invited them to contribute letters or other messages to a volume he was going to present to Frank.

Almost everyone of them responded – colleagues from the Sousa days, men and women who had known the child Frank Simon and recent students who had sat at the feet of the septuagenarian professor, old members of the Armco Band, middle-aged men who now ran their own bands but admitted they would have been nothing had they not attended his classes at the Cincinnati Conservatory or his clinics.

On top of it all, the City of Cincinnati declared 26 November 1964 to be Frank Simon Day. They awarded him their gold seal, an honor passed to very few. The Mayor, Walter H. Bachrach, said: 'Your outstanding contribution to the world of music will long be remembered, here in Cinncincinnati and throughout the nation.' Frank replied saying how much he, 'in all humility', appreciated the honor, but he was probably happiest of all with the letters from old friends and colleagues.

They recalled concerts, classes and clinics. They wrote on their own embossed, headed notepaper and on lined sheets torn from exercise books or from legal pads. They wrote under the crests of military bands, or with pictures of musical instrument factories at the top of the sheets or below the ever-recognizable badges of municipal institutions. They all had the same message: 'Frank Simon, you were terrific.'

The city of Middletown, in the form of its commissioners – Chairman, Vice Chairman and three others – did not declare it Frank Simon Day, but they sent a note of congratulation 'on behalf of the citizens of the City of Middletown and the City Government. We wish you a happy and blessed birthday and also extend our wishes for many more happy ones in the future.'

Armco remembered him. C. William Verity, Jr, Vice President and General Manager and grandson of George M., wrote to Frank:

> What a pleasure it is for me to express to you my best wishes for a happy birthday . . . What wonderful memories of the past came to me as I write to you today. The name of Dr Frank Simon not only brings back memories of your contribution to the cultural history of this area, but also of a love affair between a musician and a company. You brought happiness, good music and fame to Armco and to Middletown. We are all indebted to you for this.

Logan Johnson, by then the company president, wrote 'We treasure the twenty years you devoted to the Armco Band and what it did for us.' He also sent a watch inscribed 'To our good friend Frank Simon – Armco Steel Corporation'. In reply, Frank recalled his time with the Armco Band: 'Those years with Armco stand out as the greatest achievement of my musical career and I shall always be grateful for the opportunity to have been a part of this great human organization.' The manager of the Middletown plant, Don Holstein, wrote: 'It is hard for me to realize that the Armco Band has been off the air these many years.' The assistant manager, Ralph J. Wright, said: 'I believe that I was closer to you and your band than most people because, as you will recall, you and Ernie Glover were constantly trying to get me to place your musicians in the mill. Also, you will recall, this was somewhat of a problem because no musician wanted to work on a job which might cause him to injure his fingers.' The name Ernest Glover came up again and again in the letters. Glover himself wrote, thanking Frank 'who was to become my greatest friend and font of inspiration'. A great many people knew that. Keith Harman wrote to his old colleague:

> The greatest thrill of all was to see you and Ernie Glover sitting together at Mecklenburg's, at the Armco reunion in July 1963 – friends again for ever – and *my* friends too. I'll never need a camera or even a photograph. I'll always see that again in my mind's eye.

It was a great moment for old memories, particularly those shared with old friends. Richard Dowling struck a very personal chord:

> True happiness consists not in the multitude of friends but in the worth and choice. The pleasant thing about having a birthday as you grow older is that you realize that you have given to mankind the best gift you can. You gave to the citizens of the Miami Valley a great cultural development . . . My wish for you is an old age serene and bright and lovely as a Lapland night.'

This was the time that Meredith Willson wrote, saying that 'in the big parade', there was really only one cornet behind the 75 trombones – Frank's. Al Hirt wrote thanking him 'for all you've done to help me. I'll never forget you! May you live another 75.'

Frank knew all that. Results had spoken for themselves. This being so, perhaps the most gratifying letters were those from some of his new students, all of which seemed to prove one thing: at 75, his touch was still firm, strong and melodic. There was one from Jim Lee, who wrote in pencil: 'Now that I am in high school I realize the importance of all the experiences and scales you have taught me.' An older ex-student was Barbara Mason. 'Do you remember the day I entered your office for the first time?' she wrote. 'I was extremely nervous. I felt that such a great musician as I had heard you to be would certainly have no patience with a student who couldn't blow her way out of a paper bag.' She worried about the looks Frank gave her and was even more disturbed when he looked at her cornet and said 'Where on earth did you get that old tin can?' He lent her the money to buy a new one – and stay at school.

The letters transcended the generations. 'What a joy it is to join your thousands of friends in every part of the United States in wishing you a happy birthday,' wrote Richard Franko Goldman, Edwin's son: 'So far as all the Goldmans are concerned, I don't have to tell you how much we all love you. You were one of the few people in the world of whom my father thought as a good, close, valued and trusted friend. And I hope you know that this is the way I feel about you too.' John Philip Sousa's daughter, Helen Sousa Abert, wrote to tell him: 'What a full life you have had! A brilliant performer as a soloist; your years with the Cincinnati Conservatory, the conductor of the Armco Band, the University of Arizona and for me an important one, the clinics you have organized to show the correct interpretation of Sousa music.' Then she quoted from her father's autobiography *Marching Along*: 'From the ranks of the band have arisen several men who are now conductors of their own bands; among them Frank Simon. I am proud to call him a graduate of Sousa's Band.' She added: 'I know that my father had a very high regard for you, not only as a musician but in many other ways. So on this felicitous occasion, I salute you in his name and in my own.' From the law offices of Wexler, Mulder and Weisman, Bob Morris recalled his own father's days in Sousa's Band:

> As you might suspect, my earliest recollections are filled with the mementos of my father's Sousa years and my first-hand knowledge of you comes through the many photographs collected by my father. In truth, there was a time that the only band members I could identify were Mr Sousa, Dad and you. Later, you came to represent a letter I received from my father, the fellow who had a vast store of wonderful and funny tales and the heartiest laugh.

Jack Lee wrote in his letter:

> I like you because you inspire others. So, regardless of the fact that you are the Dean of American Band Masters and a very generous individual, I will always feel I have had a rare privilege in knowing you and having you as one of my best friends.

Writing on the notepaper of the City of Piqua, Ohio, Robert M. Hance Jr told him:

> My sole ambition as a boy was to become another 'Frank Simon'. Unfortunately, as the years passed, I found that I could never do this

> and, further, I am sure that no one else could duplicate the accomplishments which you have made in the pursuit of your particular career. As your student, however, I want you to know that you created impressions with me and afforded me an inspiration which has stood me in good stead throughout my complete life.

The bandmasters were delighted with the opportunity of doing nothing less than jumping on the bandwagon. 'How glorious were those days when every young cornetist in the Malden High School Band would rush into rehearsal with, "Did you hear Frank Simon yesterday? Wasn't he great?".' That was the memory of Chester E. Whiting, in 1964, sitting in Frank's old place as President of the ABA. Robert M. Barr, Director of Music at Glynn Academy at Brunswick, Georgia, a man frequently looked upon as a second Frank Simon because of the influence he had on his old students (and selected by *Reader's Digest* as one of their 'unforgettable characters') wrote in his letter to Frank: 'It is only fitting on this day set aside to give our thanks for our many blessings that we also thank our own God for blessing us with the privilege of having associated with such a great Man and Musician.' Jennings McLean rushed to convey her wishes to her teacher and mentor. 'What a joy and privilege to address my affection and congratulations,' she wrote from San Antonio, Texas:

> Heritage and talent are gifts from our creator and for which one never ceases to be humble, but is it not the hand of our earthly teacher and guide that allows us to develop and use these possessions? No greater gift has been afforded me in my musical life than the honor of knowing, studying and playing beautiful music with you.

That influence was what so many people referred to.

Jack Mills of the famous Mills Music Publishers in New York, the organization which had pioneered the distribution of band music, said:

> Between us there is more than a century of professional music. Your encouragement in our early years of educational music publishing has always been remembered. Our twenty-five years in this area has been most productive and its growth is due to the strong belief and pioneering of music's role in the schools by such as Dr Frank Simon.

There were always more letters from his old pupils. One, George E. Reynolds, by then Professor of Music at Dickinson State College, North Dakota, signed his note 'Your devoted pupil'. He wrote:

> A little curly-headed cornet player from Dodge City, Kansas, joins your host of grateful friends in saluting your 75th birthday, wishing you many healthy, happy years ahead. Thanking you for the privilege of your friendship and very proud to have a share in your dynamic and influential role in music in our time.

J. T. 'Scotty' Lenoir from his home in Temple Terrace, Florida, wrote:

> For twenty-eight years I've been planning this letter. And several times a year for the past fifteen years I've tried to write it. How do you tell a man that you've had a full, useful and exciting life because of his influence? Would he believe you if you told him he was largely responsible for your great joy of living?

Then there was Jimmy Henderson, who wrote on the notepaper of the Jimmy Henderson Orchestra from Sepulveda, California:

> Some twenty years ago you gave me a start by bringing me to the Cincinnati Conservatory of Music. It was at that point in my life that all of my boyhood dreams of becoming a professional musician became a reality. Those wonderful years of association with you have had a profound influence not only on my career, but my personal life as well. For this I will always be sincerely grateful.

Hundreds of others wrote similar things. They asked him to put his memories onto tape. They wanted to pick his brains about his and their pasts. Robert L. Bierly, commanding officer of the United States Army Field Band, told him: 'Each time you have appeared with the Army Field Band, the men were exhilarated and felt that you had given them something by way of instruction and inspiration. I felt the same way just by standing back and watching you perform.' There was another letter from the United States Air Force band. Captain Harry H. Meuser wrote: 'The experience I gained from you was invaluable.' All in all there were over 800 letters.

All over the Cincinnati–Middletown area there were celebrations to mark the Frank Simon anniversary, which, quite rightly, fell that year on Thanksgiving Day. The Cincinnati Conservatory had now merged with the city's College of Music, two institutions which both had a Simon connection. To mark the birthday there was an occasion that went into the local music history books, what came to be called the Frank Simon–Ernest Glover gala concert, with the two veterans sharing the podium at Cincinnati's Eden Park, a venue they both knew as well as they remembered the score of 'The Stars and Stripes Forever'. After the concert, the two friends joined Dean Dr Jack Watson and other people from the Conservatory at Grammers, one of Frank's favorite German restaurants. 'I remember Ernest mixing some light and dark beer for Frank and he loved it,' Watson recalled for me. 'Ernest was so pleased that *he* had pleased Frank.'

There were other experiences for Frank's life-memory book. Arizona University decided to mark the 75th birthday by awarding him a copper plaque. Frank told the university authorities:

> I must have heard from six or seven hundred of my former students. The most rewarding part of my life is not what I did as a performer or an artist or bandmaster, but what I did to help boys and girls get somewhere in music. Now those students are going ahead developing other youngsters. That to me is the most worthwhile thing I have done.

What was not so worthwhile, or so it appeared at the time, was the typical Simon reaction to all the excitement. Back home on the orange grove he was taken ill. If at first it looked like just the usual symptom of happiness or despair – the collapse at the Sousa audition, the total feeling of disaster after the end of Armco – both he and his family were given the truth; he *was* ill. Frank was rushed to St Joseph's Hospital in Tucson, suffering from severe headaches, dizzy spells and shortness of breath.

The diagnosis of the internist he consulted was high blood pressure combined with heart trouble. It was the first time he had been told there was anything wrong with his heart, although he was assured it was not serious. What *was* serious, however, was the fact that he was overweight. After ten days, his weight went down from 205 pounds to 179 and the doctors sent him home. In a letter to Lynn Sams he wrote: 'I still have to lose some beef – most of my weight loss was the water they rid me of.' If this news worried Sam, the last paragraph was probably the saddest of all: 'I have nothing in the line of humor to send you today – knowing how we both enjoy a good laugh. Next time I come across a gem, will send you the first copy.'

He was well enough to go to Washington, DC, the following April to conduct a concert which was going to be the first step in setting up a fund for a Sousa memorial at the Kennedy Center. Questionnaires were sent out to all the known surviving Sousa Band members. They filled in the necessary details – 'Jerry Cimera, trombone, joined 1914'; 'Roy M. Miller, 1920–1926, clarinet'; 'David Piates, 1919–1920, clarinet'; 'Gerald "Jerry" Huffmon, cornet'. The questionnaires alone represented a fascinating history of band music. Just occasionally there was a sad note scribbled at the bottom of the form: 'I regretfully report that my father, Charles C. Thetford, passed away last June 14.'

Frank himself liked to think he was still the man he had been 20 years before, but he was not. In October he was back in hospital, the Christian R. Holmes Hospital of the University of Cincinnati. He arrived at his old home town to see family and friends and was immediately taken to the hospital, where he was admitted. Once more it was high blood pressure, but as he acknowledged to a friend in a letter from his hospital room, it had reached 'alarming proportions'.

He was on a very strict diet of 800 calories a day and his weight was down to 183 pounds. 'Must take off at least ten or twelve more pounds.' Four days later, his weight was down another four pounds 'and other symptoms which I had have disappeared and once again am feeling well enough to leave here the first of the week'.

There were, however, other worthwhile things and they did not all revolve around his orange orchard in the sunshine of Arizona. Mary, in particular, was homesick. Frank, in those reflective moments that encompassed his life more and more and which continued to make his eyes glisten, contemplated some of the things he had missed – the opportunity to see his grandchildren grow up on a weekly, let alone daily, basis; the chance to spend time with his sons just when he fancied doing so, not merely because there was a note to do so in his calendar. There were friends who worried about the work he was still putting in. Bill

McFee, his old Armco colleague, pulled no punches – although he may have expected to get one in the eye for his trouble. 'Frank,' he wrote, after explaining that he probably knew him better than anyone except Mary, 'it is time for you to quit and hang up your wonderful, wonderful laurels! No man in concert band music has ever had the great success that you have had, not even Mr Sousa. Who knows better than I? More than anybody else, you helped found the American Bandmasters Association and I am sure all your contemporaries love you and respect you for it.' Frank partly – only partly – took it to heart. Somewhere, he knew, there were more laurels to earn before he rested upon them.

Confirmation came in what was for him an unusual way. Two albums were released in 1965 by the American School Band Directors' Association, directed by Frank Simon and called *Sounds of John Philip Sousa*. Clearly no one else knew as much about Sousa's music as did Frank. But that was not the end of it. A booklet was included in which Frank wrote what the profession called the sleeve notes. But these were not just bare details of each piece of music. He wrote his own memories of Sousa, the March King, and then, under each title, precise instructions on how John Philip himself would have played the piece – not as the notes dictated on the sheet music but as Sousa would have conducted the work, 'clarinets first, then trombones . . .' There was this, for instance, for 'The Free Lance March':

> The introduction is played as written with emphasis on the marcato markings. Now in the first strain, first and second measures, the marcato notes must be firmly attacked. Great persistence must be taken to see that the rests get their full value of time . . .

The rehearsal techniques, as they were called, were dictated by Frank to Mac E. Carr, President of the School Band Directors' Association and to Frank's old friend Seymour Okun.

But all this was very much what he thought was going to be a final fling. Finally, in November, he resigned his position as visiting professor at Arizona University. The President, Richard A. Harvill, wrote to him: 'I cannot overemphasize the extent and quality of your services to this institution during the ten years that you have served so well. Your eminence in the field of music and your outstanding contributions over many years brought distinction to the University of Arizona.'

The move came in May 1965, when Frank and Mary packed up their belongings and went back to Ohio – not this time to Middletown but to a new apartment at the Hammond North, on Hamilton Avenue, Cincinnati. It was a brand-new 19-story-high building 'with every modern convenience'. He wrote to Lynn Sams: 'They finally awoke in Ariz. They have over twenty applications for my position but have not filled it as yet. What they want is a big name with damn little pay. I hope they find it – but it won't be easy.' Frank was not usually like that. But the taste left from the orange grove was of sour grapes. He thought they were totally justifiable.

And what about his emphysema? His Tucson doctor said he did not have it – after spending some $10,000 on various tests and treatments over the years. His son David was not surprised. 'I think he just had congestion,' he now recalls. Frank was pleased to hear the news, but as he wrote to a friend at the time: 'After I spent a small fortune on medication, inhalations etc. to find out that I did not have emphysema, but what I have is a post-nasal drip, which I control quite well. I find that rest is so essential since I do have a slight angina, otherwise I am OK.'

Not everybody realized Frank had moved and sometimes when that fact was combined without his fame extending beyond the world of music, things did not always work out to his advantage. In July 1966 he sent an angry letter to a restaurant in Tucson which had sent him a bill for $18.30 for a meal he had not eaten. Someone had charged the meal in his name – two months after leaving the city. 'I could never in my life believe that such a trick would be done to me,' he wrote. 'I hope you can find out who did this very low thing . . . In addition I have never charged meals anywhere in Tucson and have been in your Speedway Restaurant many times. Always cash.'

He was much happier *earning* that cash. Even at the age of 76, long after he had allowed the thought to cross his mind that it might have been a wise thing to bury his horn six feet under, he still thought of retirement as a dirty word. He was pursuing still what was now known as the Frank Simon Sousa Clinic and Concert. He even had a manager, David L. Chapman. Chapman sent out a series of letters informing interested parties: 'You will be interested to know that Dr Frank Simon – acknowledged as the most authoritative interpreter of the music of John Philip Sousa – is available for a limited number of engagements this winter and spring.'

He did have other things to do, however. In the fall of 1965 he was brought back to the faculty of the Conservatory, by then part of Cincinnati University. Dean Watson wrote to him:

> I am writing this in the hope that you will be interested in returning to your home-town and joining the faculty of the institution for which you have done so much, including funding its band department. . . . The determination of your teaching program and schedule would be completely up to you and you would be free to take time off whenever you wished.

There was a slight catch:

> We cannot offer you the kind of stipend that your wealth of experience, your great talent and your international professional standing warrant, but perhaps, in a way our eagerness to have you with us once again will make up to some extent. We can, however, offer you $5000 for the academic year. I sincerely hope you find it possible to join us.

He not only found it possible, he found it exciting. Fifty years earlier he would have jumped over a music stand to show just how exciting he found it. He wrote to a friend: 'They were anxious to have me back and have made it very easy for me. I have six students, all music majors and I am so pleased that all of them, with one exception, have real talent and dedication. This makes it a joy for me to teach.' But he did not want any more students added to the list. As he approached his 77th birthday, he wrote to Lynn Sams: 'I never wanted to completely retire, so long as my health would permit and I can make a contribution to those whom I teach.'

What Frank did not know was that his $5000-a-year salary was paid by his son David. The young doctor knew how important it was for his father to have a fairly full-time interest. Had Frank known of the filial assistance he would doubtless have been a less happy man, so the background to his 'stipend' was never revealed to him.

Getting him to join the Conservatory was the sprat that was used to catch the mackerel. As David Simon now recalls: 'I missed him and I also knew that my mother hated Arizona. I thought that would bring him home.' The younger Simon and Jack Watson talked about it and cooked up the scheme for a less-than-heavy schedule at the salary that David would pay. 'But as far as we were concerned, it was a thoroughly professional arrangement,' Jack Watson told me at his home in Florida. 'We didn't have any money at all in those days. I inherited a budget when the institution was privately owned – by the Cincinnati Institute of Fine Arts which wouldn't let it go under, but wouldn't pour any money into it.' Since 1962 it had been part of the university, but the budget was unchanged. He had a faculty of elderly, not terribly talented men. 'Frank was elderly himself, but he had so much talent, it was wonderful to have him back.'

He *was* back among his own – the same dapper man of old, although there were no spats over his shoes now and occasionally he still wore a bolo tie. 'There were lots of students who wanted to study with him,' Watson recalled for me. 'He was dynamic. He was very alert and very interested in young people.' But there was that other side that kept coming up. 'He was so emotional about being back,' Watson recalled for me. 'He was with old friends. It was the same plant where he had worked before, but it had deteriorated since he was there before.'

So had Frank's health. Soon after moving to his new home, Frank had a serious fall and hit his head, but it did not appear to have any lasting effect. Being back in his home environment and teaching once more seemed to have performed miracles for him. Ernest Glover, who had taken over from Frank as head of the band program – and who also still ran the brass department of the Cincinnati Symphony – had something to do with it, too. He had been trying for some time to get his old friend back on to the faculty, but it was David Simon who clinched the deal. 'Ernest would shed years when he was around Frank,' said Watson. 'The students tended to follow him around, stop him and talk to him in the hall,' he added. 'That is one way you can tell a good teacher from a bad or indifferent one – those the students can't wait to get away from.' The other members of the faculty were as delighted to have Frank back as were his students. Watson would consult him on ideas and techniques (and ask his advice about trumpet mouthpieces).

In November 1966 Frank was surrounded by the few who remained of his old friends. Ernie Glover and the by-then 95-year-old Richard Dowling ('I think he has perhaps done more good for the city of Middletown than any other man who has lived here') were sitting next to him at a lunch organized by the Optimist Club at the Manchester Motor Inn, the Middletown scene of so many laughs, so many card games. This time, there were lumps in the throat, catches in the voice and tears in the eyes as he remembered the people who had influenced his life, as he went through the various stages of his career and summed up the music business – then, after steel and oil, the third biggest in the nation, taking into account the players, the writers, the publishers, the uniform and instrument makers, the recording companies. But he issued an appeal for the music of Middletown: 'I know you have some form of an orchestra here in Middletown now. Everything cultural needs support; it needs your help, no matter how little, your presence there shows that you're interested in things that the Lord created. You know music is divine and helps these little things that are culture in your community.' He went on: 'As I said before, man doesn't live by bread alone, you have got to have these things for the benefit of our young people.' He finished his talk: 'I want to thank you for listening to my rambling story and I hope to see you again some time.' Judging by the response he got, the thanks were all on the listeners' side.

It was more than just an Optimist Club occasion. It was another one of those Middletown days – a family event. It was true that Frank still loved his own family above all else. David's marriage had come to an end now and he was anxious that his father approve the choice of a new bride. One woman he met the older Simon did not like at all, and David took his advice to drop her. When he eventually met Jane, who became the second Mrs Simon, Frank was delighted. 'My impression of him,' she says today, 'was that he was a very gentle, sweet man. He loved people very much.'

The two generations of Simons were present the day that David had decided to announce his engagement to Jane. It was the day of another Sousa memorial concert at Dayton. When Frank had finished conducting, David noticed his father was not feeling at all well. He appeared to be giddy and he was swaying on his feet.

Fortunately, the younger Simon had his medical bag handy and administered some nitroglycerine while his mother was conveniently got out of the way. Back home, he seemed to recover and he heard with considerable joy of his son's forthcoming wedding plans.

Once, David and Jane spent an afternoon at the racetrack before going back to the senior Simons' home for dinner. 'He had spent all day making his spaghetti sauce, which we loved. He was so pleased he could please *us*.'

He made another radio broadcast on WLW's *Fifty-fifty Show* in which, this time, he attacked modern music. 'The teenagers have taken over,' he said. 'Advertising agencies have decided what we hear. It's music for the feet.'

So he was busy teaching music for the mouth and the hands. There was every reason not to confine his talents to the people who paid for lessons. So he made a recording of 14 high-school musicians, which actually went on sale. If that was not enough, he took a trip to Canada – not just to fish but to teach for the 'Separate School Board' in London, Ontario.

'Simon Still Precise, Pals Say,' declared the *Middletown Journal* when he helped to conduct a concert by the Greater Cincinnati High School Band and the College-Conservatory Exposition Band in May 1966. It was an important occasion. Ernie Glover and Ferde Grofe were there. Grofe – whose expenses for the trip had been paid by David Simon – conducted his *Mississippi Suite* from his wheelchair (he had had a stroke the year before). As far as Frank was concerned, it was important, not simply because he was conducting the bands, but because during the intermission the university presented him with their honorary degree of doctor of music. The old adage that honor comes late at home was never truer. The University President, Walter C. Langsam, wrote to Frank offering the degree – 'in the hope that this news may please you as much as it does me'. When Frank read the letter, he sat down and cried. At the ceremony itself, he cried again. The citation read:

> FRANK SIMON, native of Cincinnati; inspiring and inspired musician; talented teacher and composer; venerated mentor of youth.
>
> Virtually without parallel, his career fairly rings with the sound of music. His prowess as pupil under one of Cincinnati's – and America's – greatest cornet teachers, Hermann Bellstedt, won him a place, without

audition, in John Philip Sousa's Band, of which he soon became Premier Soloist and Assistant Conductor. His Armco Band, heard weekly for many years on a nationwide radio network, was a favorite throughout our country. Responding to his ability to discover and encourage young musicians have been such notables as Meredith Willson and Al Hirt. He served also for more than two decades as a popular member of the Cincinnati Conservatory Faculty, and organized the outstanding Symphonic Band. Following retirement, he moved to Arizona. His many and varied honors include the Honorary Life Presidency of the American Band Association and the Edwin Franko Goldman Award of the American School Band Directors Association. By virtue of the authority invested in me by the Board of Directors of the University of Cincinnati, I hereby gladly confer upon you, Frank Simon, the Degree of Doctor of Music, *honoris causa*.

Walter C. Langsam, President

But if these were tears of joy, he was not totally happy. He had bursitis in both shoulders 'and I mean bad', he wrote to another friend. He was watching the Pittsburgh Pirates playing the Cincinnati Reds on television, which he enjoyed. But there was something that excited him more. He finished his letter: 'Now Mary is calling me for lunch, which is sweet music to my ears.'

News of the degree traveled fast. Dr Richard A. Harvill, the University of Arizona president, wrote congratulating him: 'You have made tremendous contributions to music in this country . . . you have enriched the lives of many. Musicians everywhere join with your students and colleagues in gratification at the distinction conferred upon you by the University of Cincinnati.' In reply Frank said he was completely taken by surprise. 'Teaching,' he said, 'I regard as the most rewarding part of my musical life.' Frank wanted to stay at the Conservatory for as long as he could. He was the only Cincinnati University professor who had been allowed to remain there after 75.

Now he was impressing people by showing that he was virtually the same man he had been a decade earlier. True, he did not pick up a cornet and demonstrate 'Willow Echoes' the way he used to do, but his conducting was to the old standard. As Jack Watson recalled:

He was very precise with the stick work. Very legitimate. Not big and flamboyant but he conducted in a small area, very intensely. His tempos were wonderful. He could make subtle changes with his marches. You

> wouldn't have heard them from anyone else. Just as it took a Von Karajan to bring out Viennese waltzes properly. There would be a repeat, just a slight difference in tempo, a little slower, a little more rhythmic.

Frank did vary his approach. 'He had an overall pattern, but he didn't keep to the same idea all the time. He was wonderful. No sign of age either. It probably cost him a lot more energy but it didn't show.'

He was back to writing jokes to Lynn Sams – like the one about the Irishman who wrote a letter to God, saying he needed $50 urgently. But because he could not afford the price of a stamp to the heavenly address the letter was intercepted by the postman who read the envelope and then took it with him to his masonic lodge that evening. The masons were so impressed they had a collection and sent the man $25. 'Pat received it and sat down with another letter to the Lord, in which he thanked Him for the money but pointed out that he had asked for $50, but only received $25. He continued "Next time, dear Lord, send it through the Knights of Columbus as those damn Masons stole half of it." If that makes your belly go up and down, I know you enjoyed it,' he wrote – and his own belly went up and down as he signed the letter.

In another letter he told the story of the tailor who was taken by a wealthy customer to the circus. The man was a circus nut, but he could not get his tailor to share his enthusiasm. He was not moved at all by the clowns, hated the animal acts and was pretty bored by an acrobat. Finally, there was a high-wire act, a man who did somersaults on the wire at the same time as playing 'The Flight of the Bumble Bee' on his clarinet. The man asked his tailor, 'Now, what did you think of that?' 'Since you asked me,' said the little man, 'a Benny Goodman he is not.'

All Frank wanted to do was to remain a Frank Simon. But he no longer even owned a cornet. Both of his instruments had been given away to his two grandsons. If that was a demonstration of the way he felt, he put his thoughts in writing at this time:

> I was trained to be a serious musician by the best teachers money could buy. If I had to do it over again, I'd be a musician for my own pleasure, but I'd never make it a life work because it's the most insecure profession in the world. But I have no complaints. Listen, the Good Lord has been good to me and I have done well in music.

That was a classic understatement from a man who always had tended to understate his successes.

As he and Mary approached their 45th wedding anniversary most people would have said they had the perfect marriage, but Mary was becoming quite a problem both for him and for the rest of the family. 'She became quite difficult,' David Simon now remembers. 'But she had a lot of tragedy in her life.' Her father had died when he was 27, her sister Ruth – common-law wife of the actor Noah Beery – had died in Mary's car, and her best friend had died after a tragic fall in the Simon home.

But there was even greater unhappiness to come. Frank himself plainly was not the man he had been. He was once more overweight, even though his son David had put him on a rigorous diet and had committed the sin of sins – taken his cigars away from him. His son Joe recalled: 'One day they put this plate before him. His jowls dropped. Finally, he said, "If I have to die two years earlier, I'm going to carry on eating and smoking."' 'He loved food', as Joe said: 'Whatever he'd see, he'd eat.' His spaghetti and sauce and even corned beef and salami remained part of his life. Weighing about 230 pounds, he was a recipe for trouble.

On 19 January 1967 Frank was in his studio teaching a student when he felt giddy, complained of headaches and then just before he collapsed, was unable to speak. David Simon was called from a bridge game. He immediately had his father taken back to the Christian R. Holmes Hospital. They diagnosed a subdural hemetoma. It was a blood clot on his brain caused by the fall at home. He was operated upon, and this might have been enough if his arteries had not been so clogged. Nine days later, on 28 January, in room 315 of the Christian R. Holmes Hospital, he died. He was 77, precisely the age at which his father had died. The hospital report on his death mentioned a 'sudden onset of hypertension, confusion and melena'. He had a temperature of 103 degrees when he died at 2 o'clock, 'well nourished and obese'. The music man had played his last note, had conducted his last band.

20 · *Taps*

The *Middletown Journal*, which had covered so many of Frank Simon's triumphs, carried the story of his death at the top of page one, just below its masthead: 'Conducted Famed Armco Band. Middletown's Maestro Dr Frank Simon Dead.' Beneath it was a photograph of Simon and an obituary.

'Death Can't Mute Sound of Music', declared Paul Mason in the *Cincinnati Enquirer* two days after Frank Simon's death. It was the right thing to write when a leading citizen of a town died. It sounded an appropriate sort of tribute and took account of the long-running Broadway show which had made the phrase 'The Sound of Music' part of the language. Frank's picture and the notice of his death appeared on the front page of the *Enquirer*. What Mr Mason might not have realized all those years ago was that a quarter of a century later, the name Frank Simon continued to stand for the kind of sound of music that was still being played all over America.

No one could have been sure of that at his funeral at the Riverview Cemetery, Oakwood, conducted by his friend Rabbi Albert A. Goldman. A memorial service was going to be held two weeks later at the Cincinnati Conservatory, at which his musical genius was going to be the theme. 'I have come,' said Rabbi Goldman, 'rather to speak of him as the friend and the man, as father and husband, as neighbor and teacher . . . He was a complex man, yet simple, but not ordinary. He was highly sophisticated and yet could be completely at ease with anyone and everyone. He was driving and dynamic, yet tender and soft. He was highly pragmatic and profoundly spiritual. He could be demanding of his co-workers, yet easily moved to tears.'

All the former Armco men present could relate to the demands of a man who would apologize in advance just in case he lost his temper. Virtually everyone in the congregation had seen those tears. They knew how genuine they were and as they thought about it, they shed more than a few of their own. This was no Louis B. Mayer, who used weeping as a weapon. The Simon tears were always real expressions of emotion, just as were theirs as they heard the rabbi's valediction.

The Director Emeritus of the US Marines Band, Colonel William F. Santlemann, Dr Jack Watson and Ernest Glover were among the pallbearers. They were indicating how important Frank was for them and how vital band music had been to America. George Crout wrote in the *Middletown Journal*, 'The echoes of his golden cornet continue to haunt the memories of thousands of local citizens who listened to his music through a lifetime.' In a letter to Crout six years earlier, Frank had written: 'Having lived in my old home town for sixty-five years, I still love it, though many of the old friends and pioneers have passed on, it is a source of great pride to have had a small part in the cultural life of our city.'

Middletown had remained an essential part of Frank Simon's life. Now it was playing an equally essential part in his death. Not only was it the site of the services at the Baker Funeral Home before the Riverview interment, but the townspeople turned up in their hundreds to pay their respects.

Frank's music was not the popular force it had been in the Sousa days. It was not the almost addictive influence on entertainment it had been in the Armco years. But it was no less important in the schools and colleges to which Frank Simon had devoted his time and energy before his death. There were still youngsters in cheese-box hats with gold braid on their red tunics who turned out week after week for parades and concerts just as there had been a generation before. When they had their rehearsals, the name Frank Simon was still being invoked. The man who had given new meaning to 'clinic' but who had added a gold-plated gloss to that more familiar word in his circles, 'Band', had earned his place in his kind of history.

He could say with total justification just a few days before his death that he had never been out of work in that most precarious of professions. A friend who looked into his financial position was amazed at the quality of his stock holdings. His sons were not so surprised at the checkstubs they found had been hidden away – indicating money paid out to hard-up friends and acquaintances which his wife knew nothing about. But then he had never talked about them, never discussed his money with any sense of excitement, certainly never with the enthusiasm with which he discussed his music.

'The Closing Chord' was how *The International Musician*, journal of the American Federation of Musicians of the United States and Canada, headed their obituary of the man who had joined their organization to get a few cents raise out of the management of Sorg's Opera House. But in a way that chord still reverberates.

There remain a few of his records, transcriptions of his radio shows – none of which do justice to that electrifying Simon sound. There were also his marches: 'Here Comes The Band', 'Cincinnati Post', 'The Statesman', 'March of the Majorettes', 'The Man John Philip Sousa', 'The Little Giant' and 'Four Square'. But they did not play a huge part in his life. Certainly, they were never as important as was his conducting – or, above all, his playing. He never claimed any of them were up to the Sousa standard and was happy to accept that others wrote just as well as he did. But once Herbert Clarke had retired, only Frank Simon could play the cornet the way he played it. And when Sousa died, only Frank Simon could conduct a Sousa band.

There was, of course, one other vitally important memorial: 'Willow Echoes'. Only Frank Simon could have written that, too. And if the people at the funeral services heard any music that day, it was the chords of 'Willow Echoes' echoing through their minds.

There were plenty of ghosts around the day that Frank was laid to rest. The old Sorg, the Manchester Motor Inn, Carnegie Hall and Willow Grove Park and the office building where the Simons' store had once been and where Frank and Leo had made a noise they thought was music, all of them might have seemed to have a presence at that moment. The Armco plant certainly did, even if the chimneys continued to belch their smoke and the molten metal drained down the chutes without anyone initiating any particular ceremony. On Broadway when a big star dies they turn out all the lights. You cannot run down a steel mill that easily. Frank Simon and a lot of other people might have wished that the same applied to its band.

But the country was not allowed to forget their music man. As the National Association of College Band Directors declared at their silver anniversary celebrations soon after Frank's death: 'Throughout the years, his contribution as a cornet soloist, composer, teacher, a clinician and conductor of both professional and college bands will long be an inspiration to his fellow professionals.'

Frank Simon was now, in death, joining his great influences in life. His parents had gone long before. His musical 'fathers', Herman Bellstedt, Herbert Clarke and, of course, John Philip Sousa had also become just hazy memories for most people, even those in the band world, when Frank was buried on 31 January 1967. Nobody at all could remember Q. C. Buckles, but because he was Frank Simon's first teacher, he, too, had been given a place in band history.

Ernie Glover followed him before long. George Verity was dead and so was 'Witchie' Dowling. Bill McFee – who had written 'if there ever was a musician's musician and friend and benefactor, it was this man' – was soon to die, too. So was Meredith Willson. And then, after six desperately unhappy years living alone in her beautiful apartment, Mary, the beloved Maryla, was dead as well.

But although, like Irving Berlin's melody, Frank Simon's life may have ended, the sound of his cornet lingers on – along with his memory. There are still the concerts held by the Goldman Band in New York, the meetings of the American Bandmasters' Association. Today, William Revelli says: 'It was his sincerity that made Frank Simon's name live. He did more to establish the band's rightful status in the world of music than anyone I know. I idolized him.'

Even in the 1990s, a decade which to Frank Simon in death was as far away in the future as that of his heyday 1930s was in the past, Middletown still recalls one of its favorite sons. Whenever he has the opportunity, George Crout brings Frank into one of his 'Middletown Diary' columns in the *Journal*. In September 1989 there was a tribute to Frank and the Armco Band – appropriately, at Sorg's Opera House. The name was also perpetuated in the formation of a professional concert band led by his old pupil Dr Robert Hornyak – called the Simon Winds.

You will see Frank's name engraved on a brick laid into the sidewalk overlooking the flowing waters of the Great Miami River along with those of other distinguished citizens of Middletown, a place that still acknowledges it would have been a lot poorer without him. The people there do not look as if they had stepped out of an old Hollywood film any more. The traffic rushes through town just as it does anywhere else, but Frank Simon's memory is there to convince the locals that once it had been rather special.

During the city's Bicentennial in 1991 a committee selected the name of Frank Simon as one of the 91 outstanding citizens of its first 200 years. His citation read 'Cornet player who led the Armco Band, was Sousa's assistant director and nationally known musician'. On Middletown's Remembrance Rock, which stands on the banks of the old Miami–Erie Canal, along which a young Frank walked as a boy, near the hoist bridge whose deck served as his first bandstand, his name is inscribed. All it says and all it needs to say is 'Frank Simon – Musician – 1889–1967'. In Middletown's Historical Society Museum there is a portrait of him, holding, of course, that famous cornet.

Get a few of the old-timers together over a glass of beer and it will not be long before they talk about their old teacher – there are not many who played with him in bands who are still alive now. But Gene Young conducting that Goldman Band will take time off during intermission to explain just who it was who wrote 'Willow Echoes' and why it remains the best solo ever written for a cornet player. Take Al Wright or William Revelli aside and it will be Frank Simon who is still at the center of their conversation. And then there's Al Hirt talking on a TV show. The veteran on the verge of his own 70th birthday finds it difficult not to mention the man who discovered him playing in a little school band in New Orleans.

Simon was an endearing personality – with an equally endearing philosophy. Once, walking with his father, David Simon asked him how he had been able to achieve so much in his lifetime. 'Well, David,' he replied, 'the Lord blessed me with a little talent and I worked very hard.' The hard work – and the not-inconsiderable talent – showed.

Other people certainly thought so. Like Colonel Dale Harpham, who had been conductor of the US Marine Band. 'Frank Simon blew a sweet song,' he said. That was something everyone knew. What Harpham contributed to the knowledge of this man was to put on record the appreciation of a colleague who had watched him at close quarters:

> Sweeter was the song in his heart. And that song was love. And he lavished it on all of us who came his way – unstintingly, unselfishly. He was the only man I have ever known who had a thousand personal friends and no enemies. There have been beautiful men and there have been great musicians – but Frank Simon was both.

All that may have been true, but Frank Simon was not a man without faults. His younger son Joe knew that all was not perfect. 'He had a very serious fault,' he told me. 'He didn't live long enough.'

Index

Numerals in **bold** face indicate a main chapter/section.
Frank Simon is referred to as F.S. throughout the main index.